TODAY

THE JOY FIT CLUB

TODAY

THE JOY FIT CLUB

Cookbook, Diet Plan & Inspiration

Joy Bauer, MS, RD

Photography by Lucy Schaeffer

WILEY

JOHN WILEY & SONS, INC.

Food and author photography copyright © 2012 by Lucy Schaeffer

Food styling by Jamie Kimm

Prop styling by Megan Hedgpeth

Book design by Waterbury Publications, Inc., Des Moines, Iowa

Published by John Wiley & Sons, Inc., Hoboken, New Jersey

Published simultaneously in Canada

Library of Congress Cataloging-in-Publication Data

Bauer, Joy.
  The joy fit club : cookbook, diet plan & inspiration / Joy Bauer; photography by Lucy Schaeffer.
    Includes index.
  ISBN 978-1-118-18139-3 (cloth); 978-1-118-28065-2 (ebk.); 978-1-118-28066-9 (ebk.); ISBN 978-1-118-28067-6 (ebk.)
1. Reducing diets. 2. Weight loss--Psychological aspects. I. Title.
  RM222.2.B38587 2012
  613.2'5--dc23
                              2011049794

Printed in the United States of America

10 9 8 7 6 5 4 3 2 1

To my Joy Fit Club members for sharing your triumphant success stories and for reminding me how much I love what I do.

CONTENTS

ACKNOWLEDGMENTS

Nearly 25,000 pounds lost . . . and a group of dedicated professionals made this book possible.

Special thanks to my editorial director, Johannah Sakimura. Your enthusiasm and ability to articulate, organize, fact check, and keep me on a tight schedule is of immeasurable value. To Catherine Whitney for shaping each and every feature into a compelling read with compassion and grace. To my literary agents, Jane Dystel and Miriam Goderich, for your reliable advice and enduring support.

To Jim Bell, *Today's* EP extraordinaire, who gave me my dream job and the opportunity to grow it into something truly special. To my Joy Fit Club on-air powerhouse team: Hoda Kotb, Kathie Lee Gifford, Tammy Filler, Christine Cataldi, Jayme Baron, Melanie Jackson, Emily Goldberg, Liz Neumann, Ed Helbig, April Bartlett, and Bianca Henry (Lish and Alli too). I'm very lucky to be backed up by so much enthusiasm and talent. You make everything possible.

My deepest gratitude to Jaclyn Levin at *Today* who believed in this book from the beginning and helped it become a reality. I am also thankful to the team at NBC, including Kim Niemi, Amy Nichols, Ed Prince, Chris Lucero, Steve Coulter, Neysa Siefert, Joni Camacho, Joseph Ford, Stan Pottinger, Richard Greenberg, and Steve Chung, for their professionalism and support. And to Amy Rosenblum for creating the on-air series.

I am grateful to all my friends at *Today* for continuously supporting my health efforts: Steve Capus, Phil Griffin, Don Nash, Elena Nachmanoff, Noah Kotch, Debbie Kosofsky, Marc Victor, Rainy Farrell, and the countless producers and assistants who help me each week. The wonderful *Today* hosts make my job easier and are a real pleasure: Matt Lauer, Ann Curry, Al Roker, Natalie Morales, Savannah Guthrie, Lester Holt, Tamron Hall, Jenna Wolfe, Amy Robach, and medical guru, Dr. Nancy Snyderman. Also, I am indebted to the hardworking stage crew, prop department, wardrobe, hair and makeup staffs, as well as the exceptional staff at TODAY.com.

Thanks to everyone at Wiley who produced such a stunning product. In particular, my unflappable and talented editor, Justin Schwartz, deserves my admiration and gratitude. Justin, I loved working with you. Many thanks to the fabulous Lisa Kingsley, Ken Carlson, and their entire production team, including Laura Marzen, and to our topnotch photographer Lucy Schaeffer.

The 30 Joy Fit Club members profiled in this book, along with every other amazing Fit Club member who has appeared on *Today*, have earned my love and respect for their remarkable courage and determination. I am thrilled to be able to introduce them to readers as proof that people can lose weight and keep it off for good. My Joy Fit Club members always tell me how motivated they are to help others, and by sharing their stories with the world they are doing just that.

Special thanks to my agents at CAA: Olivia Metzger, Katie Maloney, Stephanie Paciullo, Ashley Davis, Gary Krakower, Will Hobbs, Carla Laur, and Lisa Shotland. And to Theresa Brown, Bethany Dick, and Jeff Lesh at WME.

Finally, hugs to everyone in my wonderful family (all 30 of you!), especially my mom and dad (Ellen and Artie Schloss); my other mom and dad (Carol and Victor Bauer), and my personal "Fit Club" members who regularly play double duty as recipe guinea pigs—my husband Ian and three kids, Jesse, Cole and Ayden.

INTRODUCTION

WELCOME TO THE JOY FIT CLUB

This is the story of aha! moments that led to lasting transformations. It's about courage, persistence, humility, and grit in the lives of ordinary people from all parts of the country who broke free of the bondage of obesity—and did it their own way. Any one of the 30 men and women featured inside these pages would walk up to you in a heartbeat and say, "If I can do it, anybody can." And they'd be totally believable because of the methods they used to achieve lasting weight loss without pills, potions, or surgery.

The idea for this book grew out of the phenomenal success of The Joy Fit Club, my series on *Today*, which has been running for four years. I feature an individual who has lost 100 pounds or more using his or her own strategies. We picked the number 100 because it was a barrier-breaking change, but many of our members—including some featured here—have lost 200 and even 300 pounds. We never imagined just how amazing the shows would be—and how much our viewers would love them. They're especially thrilled by the big reveal—seeing the before and after transformation on the split screen and hearing the happiness firsthand from the losers.

One of the most surprising aspects of my Joy Fit Club segments is how meaningful they've become for viewers who want to lose only 20 to 40 pounds. People with ordinary weight struggles watch the 100-pound-plus losers and they think, "If they can drop such a huge amount of weight, what's stopping me from losing 20 pounds?" These stories are pure inspiration. I've also discovered that the strategies used are much the same as those anyone would employ—just on a larger scale. In the segments I always go out of my way to make sure there are strong takeaway lessons that work for everyone. There are also emotional, psychological, and physical commonalities among overweight people, so even if viewers have only a fraction of the weight to lose as The Joy Fit Club member, they will almost always relate to some elements of the story.

The Joy Fit Club represents a transformation in the way people view losing weight. The dieters I work with are turned off by the idea of potentially risky surgery, and they've usually tried every quick fix in the book and don't want to fail again. They actually summon up the nerve to stare down the $60 billion weight loss industry, with its potions, pills and surgery, and say, "Thanks, but no thanks. I'll do it my way." The good news is that realistic and balanced eating and exercise plans work (now and for the long haul) if you have the right strategies and the core motivation.

Every time we do a Joy Fit Club segment, our mailboxes are crammed with responses and the phones ring off the hook.

Because television segments are relatively short, our viewers are always clamoring for more details. They want to know more about the individuals we feature—how they really coped on a day-to-day basis, how they overcame the obstacles on their long journeys, what they ate, where they found support, how they got back on track when they slipped up—questions literally pour in with each feature. Once we bring a Joy Fit Club member into the viewers' homes in such an intimate way, they feel as if they know the person and want to continue to draw inspiration. In the following pages, I will take this winning concept a step further by expanding on the stories and strategies and providing a level of content that simply isn't possible on television.

While you're reading, I hope you find points of commonality, areas you want to pursue, and individual strategies you want to follow. I think you will. You can use this book as your personal inspirational blueprint, knowing that every time you start to falter you can draw strength from Cari or Jodi or Rosie or Gregg or Tamara or Howard or Lynn—or one of the other terrific people you'll come to know from the inside out.

TODAY

JOY'S WINNING
WEIGHT LOSS RULES

What are the strategies that make our losers winners every time? As I reviewed the experiences of my Joy Fit Club members, I repeatedly found them abiding by the strategies I've identified as common to successful dieters. I know these are the very same strategies that work for people who have less than 100 pounds to lose because they're the methods I've taught to my personal clients over the past two decades—tens of thousands of people from all walks of life with varying amounts of weight to lose, from A-list celebrities to soccer moms, as well as CEOs, young children, elite athletes, and couch potatoes.

I call them Joy's Rules. Keep them at the front of your mind as you read the stories.

RULE 1: GET YOUR HEAD IN THE GAME

People always ask how Joy Fit Club members are able to finally lose so much weight after many years of diet failure. The primary reason is not what they do but what they think. If you're not truly ready to make a full-time commitment, chances of long-term success are pretty slim. That's because when efforts are half-hearted from the get-go, people typically lose interest in their diets soon after they start. The sad truth: It's not really worth starting a weight loss program if you're not mentally, emotionally, and psychologically committed. Cari, who was obese her entire life, was admitted to an eating disorder treatment center when she was 18. She lost 80 pounds and learned all about eating healthfully. However, within a year she had gained the weight back, and she continued to gain more for another 13 years. Why didn't the experience stick? The answer is

obvious to me: Her head wasn't in it. Sure, she desperately wanted to lose weight, but that was her only goal. She didn't identify a meaningful and long-lasting source of personal motivation that would enable her weight loss plan to stick. She didn't take advantage of the psychological help offered at the treatment center—only the menus and diet plan. Having your head in the game means understanding your personal goals, being willing to go the distance, and seeing the journey as a lifelong approach to health. When you have your head in the game from the start, you are much more likely not only to lose the weight but also to keep it off for the long term.

RULE 2: TRACK YOUR PROGRESS

All of these successful losers are diligent about keeping records—of what they ate, how they exercised, and how they felt. They also use weekly weigh-ins and self-measurement to record their progress. There's nothing like watching the numbers on the scale change. It's a tangible sign that progress is being made. Plus, a simple gesture like recording each food item with calories, fat grams, sodium, and other nutritional information serves two purposes. First, writing it down is an effective way of recommitting. Second, people who track their progress are more likely to stick with their goals, to control portion sizes, and to feel better about themselves as they watch their success.

Most Joy Fit Club members spend a lot of effort keeping track of their daily eating and exercise. Kim, who was an accountant, found that she thrived with an organized plan and loved making her computer spreadsheets. Gina, a teenager, did well using an online diet tracker. Whatever your method, keeping track is a necessity if you want to stay on track. I'm not suggesting you drive yourself crazy by writing down every incremental gram of fat or sugar or every half-calorie in a stick of gum. It's important to know your personality and to craft a tracking program that is beneficial and manageable—one that doesn't become an obsessive hindrance.

RULE 3: EXERCISE DAILY

One of the most rewarding aspects of The Joy Fit Club has been watching formerly sedentary couch potatoes blossom into active people who love to walk, dance, hike, and even run marathons. Many of these people could hardly walk up a flight of stairs without panting and breaking out in a sweat. Now they love to exercise. Believe me, it didn't happen overnight, but they steadily achieved mastery of the simplest thing in the world—moving.

When you're just starting out, it may be hard to do much. Most of my losers kept it simple. For example, Jon, who lost more than 200 pounds, started out walking about 500 feet and very gradually built it up until he reached his current average of 3 to 5 miles a day. Most Joy Fit Club members worked at a similar pace, realizing that as long as they kept moving, even in baby steps, they were reaching toward their goals.

The exercise component is important to maintaining energy, boosting metabolism, and helping you feel better every day of the diet. The point is, the smallest amount of physical activity, if done regularly, can reap big rewards. Many Joy Fit Club members, who were quite obese at the start, found it hard to even walk around the block. But they took their time and gradually improved. Rosemarie, who had been obese all her life and had never exercised, is now a medal-winning marathon runner, as are many Joy Fit Club members who fell in love with walking, running, and just being fit.

RULE 4: ELIMINATE THE EXTRAS

Think about all the extras you potentially consume during the day—a few chocolates from the office candy bowl, a bite of your kids' leftovers at lunch, extra tastes while you're cooking dinner; the list goes on and on. If you cut out the extracurricular nibbles and follow a structured meal and snack schedule, you can easily trim 1,000 calories from your week's total.

A lot of people have the idea that nibbles don't count. Stacy, a teacher who kept candy and cookies in her desk drawer, was a regular nibbler throughout the day. Often her students' parents would drop by to show their appreciation with cakes and pastries, and she'd dip right in. (Nobody seemed to have heard of bringing an apple for the teacher!) Carolyn found it impossible to watch her favorite TV shows without a bag of chips at her side. Most Joy Fit Club members couldn't resist snacking when the opportunity presented itself, whether it was a plate of cookies in the office lunchroom or leftover food on a child's plate. By changing mindless eating to mindful eating, they could create a meal plan that wasn't open to sabotage by the extras.

RULE 5: FIND A SUPPORT NETWORK

Having a solid support network in place is really critical to success. That could be a supportive family, a therapist who helps you probe your relationship with food, or a coworker or friend you can buddy up with at the gym. Some weight loss programs offer group counseling, which is another terrific source of support. Or find an online community to share your ups and downs

with—especially if you don't feel comfortable discussing your diet or your weight with your closest friends and family members. Having the support of individuals or a group of people to help keep you motivated, celebrate your milestones, reinforce good habits, and troubleshoot challenges can dramatically increase your chances of success. In fact, a study from Indiana University showed that the 12-month dropout rate for couples participating in a fitness program was just 6 percent, compared to 43 percent among individuals who joined the program alone. Nearly every Joy Fit Club member had a support network. One of the most effective I saw was Ben's. He did two things that were crucial to his success. First, he started a blog the first day of his lifestyle change and posted commentary and photos on a daily basis, letting friends and strangers hold him accountable. Second, he enlisted his brother Jed, who needed to lose some weight himself, to join him. The brothers ran on a track together, did supermarket shopping, and prepared healthy meals together. Together, they were an unbeatable team.

RULE 6: ELIMINATE LIQUID CALORIES

As you'll see, most of the people in this book had huge soda habits. Several of them drank two to three liters a day of regular soda and filled up multiple times at the drinks bar at the fast-food restaurant. This infusion of calories and pure sugar was among the worst things they could do to their health, yet on some level people manage to convince themselves that drinkable calories don't count. But if you cut out just one 20-ounce soda each day for a year, you'll save 91,000 calories, prevent 108 cups of sugar (See? It's seriously liquid candy) from entering your body, and potentially lose 26 pounds!

It's also common for people to drink an elaborate coffee concoction at a cafe and think, "I only had a coffee," when the reality is their drink includes whipped cream, chocolate, and sugary syrups. Lynn, who lost 156 pounds, found out that by switching her daily coffee habit from two lattes with

cream to calorie-free tea she saved 116,000 calories in one year. That's the equivalent of losing 33 pounds from this one simple swap. Cutting out the liquid calories is often one of the first and most effective steps to losing weight.

RULE 7: GET COMFORTABLE IN THE KITCHEN

Eating excessive amounts of prepared, packaged foods—and that includes fast-food and restaurant meals—is a common enemy of effective weight loss. I'm not saying you can't splurge sometimes or go out to eat. But the majority of time should be spent in your own kitchen. This idea can seem overwhelming to people who are not natural cooks or whose busy lifestyles squeeze them for time. But by planning ahead and stocking a few easy staples, it's a habit that can be learned. In almost every case, the people featured in this book ate out at least a few times a week—some every single day for multiple meals. Now they've learned to become comfortable in their own kitchens, as their delicious recipes will show you.

I advise people to follow these basic rules:
1. Eat breakfast at home.
2. Pack snacks for work or school.
3. Brown-bag lunches.
4. Add your own low-calorie condiments at meals.

Not only will you shave off hundreds of calories a day, you'll also save money in the bargain. Many Joy Fit Club members who admitted they rarely prepared meals before the diet now tell me how much pleasure they get from spending time in their kitchens. For example, Doree learned to prepare most of her meals and snacks at home and tote them to work. She started taking her lunch to work at the dental office every day instead of ordering out, which mostly meant fast-food sandwiches, heavy Chinese food, or other high-fat takeout. She packed healthy, satisfying snacks like fresh fruit, yogurt, and portion-controlled bags of nuts. She also learned to prep food ahead on the weekends so she would have nutritious meals ready to go for busy weekdays. For example, she'd make a big pot of homemade veggie chili, take a serving to the office for lunch, and freeze leftovers in single-serve containers for extra meals. She'd grill or bake a bunch of skinless chicken breasts on weekends and package them in the fridge so she could use them for salads, sandwiches, and pasta dishes throughout the week. She'd also hard-cook a dozen eggs on the weekends to use for convenient breakfasts and snacks throughout the week.

RULE 8: AVOID TRIGGER FOODS

Everybody has them—those irresistible foods that elicit the "I'll bet you can't eat just one" response. Pizza, corn chips, brownies, fried chicken, chocolate chip cookies, Chinese food—even something as innocent as a finger dip in the peanut butter jar or a handful of dry sugary cereal

out of the box is enough to send some people off and running into binge mode. Recognizing and avoiding trigger foods is a great place to start, whether your goal is to lose 20 pounds or 100. Carolyn knew she had an irrational weakness for french fries, and she cut them out of her diet. She won't even walk past a plate of french fries. Kim's trigger was pasta. She could literally swoon thinking about it, but she hasn't eaten it in seven years. Most Joy Fit Club members can name their triggers, and they find that knowledge is power. For many people, it's easier to completely cut out their trigger foods and avoid the painful temptation altogether than to try to satisfy a craving with a small portion. The biggest surprise comes when people discover that their old triggers aren't that appealing anymore. Soda tastes too sweet, fries are too salty, creamy sauces are too rich. By eating healthfully they've changed their taste buds and many of the old cravings are gone.

RULE 9: FORGIVE SLIP-UPS

Everyone slips up. But often, when people give in to temptation and subsequently fall off the wagon for one meal or one day, they tell themselves they've blown their diet and throw in the towel for good. This is an incredibly common reaction that I see time and again. To be successful, you have to learn to overcome these temporary setbacks. You can't let one binge or one off day turn into a full week, or month, of splurging.

Don't dwell on your mistakes. Instead, shake them off and get right back on track at your very next meal—or the very next day. And always remember, nobody gains weight from one rich meal or a single slice of cake. The real trouble starts when you allow that isolated splurge to snowball into an all-out eating frenzy. So take it one meal at a time and learn to forgive yourself; every dieter has slip-ups, but the successful ones know how to keep those occasional lapses contained.

Gregg was a lifetime yo-yo dieter who would start each week with a new resolve. But if he made even one slip, "That was it." For example, if Gregg gave in to temptation and had a few chocolate chip cookies, the "I've blown it" mentality kicked in and he'd polish off the rest of the cookies, plus leftover Chinese food, some ice cream in the freezer—even drive through a fast-food chain and order a few cheeseburgers with the works. He would then vow to start his diet fresh on

---

FITNESS TIP

JOY'S WINNING WEIGHT LOSS RULES

1. Get your head in the game.
2. Track your progress.
3. Exercise daily.
4. Eliminate the extras.
5. Find a support network.

6. Eliminate liquid calories.
7. Get comfortable in the kitchen.
8. Avoid trigger foods.
9. Forgive slip-ups.
10. Set short- and long-term goals.

Monday—even if it were only Tuesday. He was finally successful when he realized that he'd just been using his slips as an excuse to stop. Whenever she hit a block, Kim always told herself, "You can go forward or backward," and then she chose to go forward.

RULE 10: SET SHORT- AND LONG-TERM GOALS

At nearly 300 pounds, Lynn was completely overwhelmed by the idea of all the weight she had to lose. She thought getting healthy was hopeless—a lost cause. But when she was finally ready to commit, she broke up her weight loss into short-term goals. Losing 150 pounds seemed a distant goal, but losing 10 pounds was doable. She focused on losing 10 pounds at a time. Every few weeks, she hit another 10-pound goal and celebrated her victory by giving herself a nonfood reward—a new book, new walking shoes, a trip to the movies, and so on. This helped her stay motivated and avoid getting depressed at how long it would take to reach her ultimate ideal weight.

I think long-term goals are terrific, but short-term goals can be even more powerful because they reinforce success every step of the way. I found Kim's perspective on this quite touching. She took the view that the journey itself was the success. Kim reports that she was happy and motivated every day of the two years it took her to lose more than 200 pounds.

The point is, keep your goals in perspective. You have an idea of where you want to be, and that long-term goal may change over time. But in the day-to-day process, it's the short-term goals that keep you going.

Every Joy Fit Club member created his or her own unique path to weight loss. But they all had commonalities. Joy's Rules are a good first step to plotting your own plan.

TODAY

JOY FIT
SUPERSTARS

CARI HARTMAN

FROM Muskegon, Michigan
AGE 37 | HEIGHT 5' 9"
BEFORE WEIGHT 307 | AFTER WEIGHT 172 | POUNDS LOST 135

For many people, the suffering that leads to overeating and morbid obesity begins with emotional wounds suffered in childhood. Children are innocent. They don't have the skills to handle family upheavals or the tools to figure out how to negotiate their own way in life. Yet overweight children are often made to feel as if it is their fault that they can't get control of their eating or lose weight. This was true of Cari. A child of divorce, she was shuttled back and forth to her father's home every other weekend. Her dad and brother were slender and physically fit, and Cari longed to be like them instead of being heavy like her mom. Sometimes her father would say to her, "Do you really need to eat that?" She would look at him and not know how to answer. She thought she did need to eat it, but the disapproval in his voice told her otherwise. His words made her feel ashamed. She didn't know how to control her food intake or how to make the right choices, and she felt guilty about that even though she was just a kid.

AFTER

BEFORE

As a single parent, Cari's mother worked a lot. So starting in elementary school, Cari did much of the cooking, serving up mac 'n' cheese, fish sticks, tater tots, and other easy but unhealthful fare. Sometimes the family would order pizza or get fast-food takeout. Like many people, their lives were too busy for nutrition. Cari was always the biggest one in the class. For clothes, her mother took her to the Pretty Plus Department at Sears, but the clothes were anything but pretty. She still remembers one outfit she had in the fourth grade. It looked like something a grandmother would wear—an ugly dark dress with a matronly, below-the-knee cut and frills in all the wrong places. Meanwhile, the other girls were wearing cute blouses, flouncy skirts, and stylish jeans. They looked great, and Cari thought she looked ugly and fat. It was bad enough that she was overweight, but being dowdy made it worse. She never had the experience of having people tell her she was cute, and later she would feel very sad for that awkward little girl.

In spite of her struggle with weight, Cari was extremely outgoing and had many friends. However, she couldn't help noticing that there were always one or two kids from every group who were mean to her. In the eighth grade some of them started calling her "Shamu," which was very hurtful. The kids thought they were just being lighthearted, and because Cari laughed—to cover her embarrassment—they thought it was okay to continue. She dealt with the embarrassment by becoming the class clown, making people laugh so they'd be laughing with her, not at her. But as she got to the end of high school, weighing 279 pounds, she was aching inside. She dreaded the future. She was completely defined by her weight, and she couldn't envision having a successful profession, much less romance.

While Cari's friends were excitedly planning for college and careers, Cari felt she was different. It was as if she didn't have the same right as other girls to pursue her dream because she was fat. Cari had always longed to be a sportscaster. She often closed her eyes and imagined herself reporting on the big games. Alone in her room she practiced the scripts, and sometimes she thought, "Hey, I'm good." She had a perfect command of her subject. But then she would look in the mirror and her heart would sink in despair. She had never seen a sportscaster on TV who looked like her. So she put aside her dream and once again settled for something less wonderful but more realistic—studying business management at the community college.

It's not that Cari didn't try to get her weight under control, but it always seemed like such an insurmountable task that required drastic measures. On several occasions she and her mother joined weight loss programs together, but they were never successful. At 18, Cari was admitted to an eating disorders treatment center. It was a giant step for her—a formal admission that she was out of control. She put tremendous effort into rigorously following the program and lost 80 pounds. But her head wasn't in the game. The clinic diagnosed her as a compulsive overeater, but she didn't understand what that really meant or how to change it. She didn't make the internal adjustment that would help her continue to be successful. The weight came back on, and Cari was heartbroken. Imagine the sense of defeat to go to such great lengths and then fail. I hear this story all the time. In Cari's case, the clinic gave her good information, but she didn't make it part of her life. It was a "diet" mentality, and once she lost weight she quickly slid back into her prior habits.

CARI'S STRATEGIES FOR SUCCESS

- Make small changes at first instead of drastic changes. For example, if you drink five sodas per day, cut it down to two.
- Make moderation your goal. If you're going to eat pizza, get good pizza (not fast food) and eat a slice or two.
- Allow yourself special treats once in a while, but be sure it's an occasional thing.
- Prepare a week's worth of favorite meals in advance.
- Never listen to the negative voices. Surround yourself with encouragement.

Although she was a young woman, Cari had the kind of physical problems suffered by many older people. She suffered terrible back pain, achy joints, and sore feet. Everything always hurt. Each winter she came down with colds and the flu and spent a lot of time at the doctor and chiropractor. When she visited her family doctor, he would mention her weight every time, but she always refused to get on a scale. It wasn't that she was in denial. She knew her weight was very high. She just didn't want to face it in a room with the nurse. She didn't want to hear the weight lecture one more time. Often when people lecture their overweight friends and family members, they think they're blindly refusing to accept the truth and need to be confronted with their weight problem, but that's not usually true. Fat people *know* they're fat. They know they're unhealthy. But the leap from knowing you have a problem to deciding to do something can be very difficult, and the motivation has to come from inside.

When Cari was a young adult, she was urged by many people to have gastric bypass surgery. They said it was the only solution. Her mother had some success with the procedure, and Cari was proud of her. But Cari always felt that surgery was out of the question. She was a young woman and she wanted to have a child one day. She wasn't sure that surgery was good for her health, and she was scared to death of taking the risk. But she didn't know what the alternative could be.

Then, in 2005 Cari got the wake-up call that made the difference. She had gone to the doctor the day after her birthday. This time when she declined to get on the scale, the nurse said, "No, we really need to get your weight today." When Cari stepped on the scale, it said 307 pounds. She was shocked and mortified. She had always told herself that if she got over 300 pounds she'd kill herself. Now, however, the terrible number on the scale spurred her to change her life. She had few illusions after a lifetime of failure. But the number 307 was a literal shock to her system.

Four days later Cari joined a gym. It was the fourth time she had tried the gym, and the salesperson said in a critical way, "I see you have been a member here a few times before. Why do you think this time is going to be any different?" Cari sat there and thought angrily to herself, "Well, you little jerk, it's because I have never been this fat before!" Cari stayed angry at the salesperson for almost two years before she let it go, but she now believes the incident helped her push herself that much harder. She wanted to prove to that person that she could do it.

SMALL, MANAGEABLE GOALS

Initially Cari decided that she'd start making a few simple changes so as not to feel too overwhelmed. She rode a bike at the gym for 10 minutes. She started slowly cutting back on her huge daily consumption of diet soda, eventually allowing herself to drink it only on Saturdays.

Another simple change Cari made was to pack her own lunch instead of going out to eat at a fast-food restaurant every day. Usually she hopped in her car and hit a greasy drive-through. Now she made a healthy sandwich or salad and brown-bagged it. Cari was a big sweets lover, and while she didn't eliminate candy altogether, she cut her consumption to three days a week. All of these changes added up, but for Cari they felt manageable. Just by making the adjustments, Cari reduced her intake by thousands of calories a week.

Cari set small weight loss goals, wanting to be realistic and to not get ahead of herself. That way she could always feel successful as she realized incremental achievements. Her mantra was "Never set a goal that's too hard to achieve." She set her goal in 10-pound increments, and she was thrilled when she lost 10 pounds in the first month. Suddenly she thought, "I can really do this." She kept reminding herself that the weight didn't come on overnight, and it wouldn't come off overnight either. This is an extremely important realization. Most people who have tried and failed at diets, as Cari had, are used to seeing the process as something that should happen quickly. To make her new approach work, Cari had to let go of the idea of overnight success.

Within three months Cari was seeing noticeable results and she was excited. Progress kept her motivated. She kept making adjustments to her diet, experimenting with ways to satisfy her hunger in a healthy way. She invented her own version of a popular fast-food egg sandwich, one of her favorite breakfasts. Hers involved a high-fiber English muffin, two egg whites, and a slice of turkey bacon. It was delicious and got her day off to a high-protein start. Before, she would have snacked on a bag of chips and a whole tub of dip; now she found herself being satisfied by fruit or a nutrition bar. Her exercise routine expanded as the months went by from 10 minutes on an exercise bike to 30 minutes a day plus light weights. Even when she hurt her knee at the gym, she didn't give up. Instead she started physical therapy and wore a "hideous" brace when she exercised.

When she'd lost 70 pounds, Cari went out to dinner with a friend. "I distinctly remember her looking at me and saying, 'I just don't see it,'" Cari recalls. She couldn't believe it. What a bummer. Was she so big that a 70-pound weight loss wasn't visible? Needless to say, the friend was incredibly insensitive. But what's interesting is Cari's response. In the past she might have been derailed by such a comment. But by then her self-esteem was high enough that she didn't take the harsh critique to heart. She knew she was succeeding, and one day—if not that day—the world would see too.

In all, it took Cari three years to lose most of her weight and a fourth year to lose the final pounds. By then she was going to the gym for an hour and a half to two hours six days a week. She'd never imagined how much fun working out could be—and she was thrilled by how much energy she had. Her life was transformed along with her size. "What a great feeling it was to say goodbye to Lane Bryant," she says.

As she got thinner, Cari didn't lose the memory of her shame and struggle, and she made it a point to reach out to others at the gym. If she saw a new heavy person, she would say, "Good for you" and "You can do it," knowing how much that encouragement would have once meant to her. She feels you can never underestimate the power of positive reinforcement and support. "I have a great deal of compassion," she says. "I know that people are repulsed by obesity. It's like the last acceptable form of prejudice. If I can do something to ease another person's burden and offer encouragement, I want to do that."

ONE LAST BREAKTHROUGH

Losing 135 pounds over the course of four years was an accomplishment Cari could not have imagined. She was proud of herself and, most important, was learning to love herself for the first time. But one thing was still weighing on her—the substantial loose skin that was hanging, especially on her arms and lower body. This extra skin is one of the consequences of losing a great deal of weight, and for the most part it cannot be eliminated through exercise or toning. It must be removed surgically. For Cari this was an important step. In January 2008, Dr. John Renucci removed more than 4½ inches of skin from each of her arms. Having this done allowed her to look in the mirror and start to see the person she was becoming, rather than the person she had been. She was happy to no longer have to look at her old arms. But she still had far to go. In Cari's mind, the heavy, loose skin was a taunt from her previous self to her new self that was preventing her from fully embracing her life.

   In June 2009 she returned to see Dr. Renucci and talked to him about what else she could do. They settled on a lower-body lift. Cari recalls Dr. Renucci's description of the procedure. "He said he would basically pull the skin on my legs up like a pair of pants. And then he'd take the skin on my torso and pull it down like a shirt—and then cut everything out in the middle." Cari was beyond excited to think that she would be free of the past. She said, "I couldn't wait to look in the mirror and finally see the person who I had fallen in love with over the past four and a half years rather than the person who I didn't love for 31 years."

   Her lower-body lift was done on October 2, 2009. It was a great success. Afterward Cari wrote a

JOY'S WORDS OF ADVICE

THE PROBLEM WITH DIET SODA

Cari had a huge diet soda habit. While many people think they're helping their weight loss efforts by drinking diet sodas because they don't add any calories (which seems logical), in my experience constantly sipping diet beverages can make it harder to stick with your healthful eating plan. For some people, the artificial sweeteners in diet soda—and other diet beverages such as diet iced tea and fruit drinks—can actually intensify sweet cravings. Although diet soda does not have the calories of sugar-sweetened beverages, it keeps the taste of "sweet" in your mouth and on your mind, which can make conquering sugar cravings difficult. Zero-calorie, naturally flavored seltzers or sparkling waters have the same fizzy pop as soda but are free of sugar and artificial sweeteners, so they're a terrific alternative.

letter to her friends and family, telling them about her sense of renewal following the removal of her excess skin. "I think that I may celebrate this day every year now as kind of a re-birthday," she wrote. "I am finally free from the Cari of the past. I am now me, the one that I love. I love me more than anything or anyone in the world, and to finally be able to say that after almost 36 years is the best feeling one can ever have. Much love to all and many, many thanks to everyone who has always loved me even when I didn't love myself. You are the ones who have helped me get to this place in my life where I can say I DO LOVE ME!!!"

CARI'S DAILY DIET COMPARISONS

BEFORE	AFTER
Breakfast	**Breakfast**
32-ounce diet soda	Healthy egg sandwich:
Breakfast toaster pastries	High-fiber English muffin
Large donut	2 egg whites
	Piece of turkey bacon
Lunch	**Lunch**
Supersize fast-food chicken tender meal	Big salad with shredded chicken
Large fries	Pita chips and hummus
60 ounces diet soda	
Dinner	**Dinner**
Fast food: Beef & cheddar melt, cheese sticks	Garlic chicken
Bacon cheeseburger	Oven-roasted zucchini
Pizza	Low-calorie dessert—personal creation
4-5 cans of diet soda	
Snacks	**Snacks**
Cookies, candy	Protein bar
Ice cream	Banana with peanut butter
Chips with French onion dip	

CARI'S PANTRY

BEFORE	AFTER
Box of mac 'n' cheese	Olive oil
Seasoned rice mixes	Balsamic vinegar
Canned soup	Flavored oil
Bags of chips	Herbs and spices
Boxes of sugary cereal	Oil spray
Cookies	Salsa
Sloppy joe mix	Whole grain couscous
Processed meal kits	Brown rice
Bottled spaghetti sauce	Sugar substitute
	Whole wheat flour
	Oatmeal

Almond-Crusted Chicken

BY Cari Hartman
MAKES 4 servings
SERVING SIZE 1 chicken breast

    Oil spray
¼ cup smoked almonds
¼ cup bran flakes or high-fiber bran cereal
1 tablespoon Parmesan cheese
1 teaspoon herbes de Provence
    Black pepper
4 boneless, skinless chicken breasts, pounded thin

1 Preheat oven to 400°F. Line a baking sheet with aluminum foil and liberally coat with oil spray.

2 In a food processor combine the almonds and cereal; grind until almost fine. Add the cheese, herbes de Provence, and pepper to taste; pulse the mixture a few times to combine.

3 Moisten the chicken breasts with water and coat with the breading mixture on all sides. Place the breaded chicken on the prepared baking sheet. Bake for 18 to 20 minutes or until juices run clear.

NUTRITION INFORMATION Calories: 246, Protein: 41 g, Total Fat: 7 g, Saturated Fat: 1 g, Cholesterol: 100 mg, Sodium: 160 mg, Carbohydrate: 4 g, Fiber: 1 g

Whole Wheat Pumpkin Pancakes

BY Cari Hartman
MAKES 4 servings (12 pancakes total)
SERVING SIZE 3 pancakes

1¼ cups whole wheat flour
¼ cup oat flour (see Note, below)
2 teaspoons baking powder
1 teaspoon pumpkin pie spice
½ teaspoon kosher salt
1½ cups skim milk
½ cup canned 100% pumpkin puree

1 large egg
1 tablespoon granulated sugar
1 teaspoon vanilla extract
Oil spray
Optional toppings: dollop of pumpkin
 puree, dash ground cinnamon,
 1 teaspoon pure maple syrup

1 In a medium bowl whisk together the flours, baking powder, pumpkin pie spice, and salt.

2 In a large bowl beat together the milk, pumpkin, egg, sugar, and vanilla. Sprinkle the dry mixture over the wet ingredients and fold until just moistened.

3 Liberally coat a griddle or large skillet with oil spray and heat over medium heat. Ladle about ¼ cup batter per pancake onto the surface. Cook until the batter starts to bubble, 1 to 1½ minutes. Flip the pancakes and cook 1 minute or until golden brown on the second side. Recoat the griddle or skillet with oil spray between batches to prevent the pancakes from sticking. If desired, top pancakes with pumpkin puree, ground cinnamon, and maple syrup.

NOTE Oat flour can be purchased at most supermarkets, but it's also very easy to make at home. Simply put plain, dry rolled oats (old-fashioned, quick-cooking, or instant) in a food processor and process until they reach a fine flour consistency.

NUTRITION INFORMATION Calories: 226, Protein: 11 g, Total Fat: 3 g, Saturated Fat: 0.5 g, Cholesterol: 55 mg, Sodium: 320 mg, Carbohydrate: 42 g, Fiber: 6 g

KIM EVANS DOERING

| FROM Lake in the Hills, Illinois
| AGE 44 | HEIGHT 5'5"
| BEFORE WEIGHT 347 | AFTER WEIGHT 128 | POUNDS LOST 219

After Kim lost more than 200 pounds, a person she'd just met saw her "before" picture and asked, "How long were you overweight?" Kim replied, "Just since birth!" She was the cute, fat baby, the butterball with the chubby cheeks people loved to pinch. When she cried, she would get fed, and it did the trick. She loved visiting her paternal grandmother, who had a table in the basement filled with all sorts of candy. Kim would run downstairs to the candy table and gorge. Before she could say very many words, she learned to ask for "candy."

AFTER

BEFORE

As she got older and started school, Kim found that being overweight wasn't so cute anymore. It was immensely hurtful to be the fat kid at school, involving experiences that would wound Kim for life. She still remembers Valentine's Day in the second grade, when the kids made cards for every person in the class. When she got home from school, clutching her cards, she was filled with excitement as she started to open them. She immediately noticed that every single card had an elephant on the front. Her classmates had gotten together and decided to give her elephant cards. She burned with shame and couldn't stop sobbing for the rest of the night. She didn't want to go back to school ever again. Even today, so many decades later, Kim says, "That day will never leave me."

Riding the school bus was torture. Kids made fun of her every single day. She even got teased at home. Although Kim's parents didn't admonish her for being overweight, her dad kidded her. His nickname for Kim was "440." She laughed it off and never let him see how much it hurt her.

Kim now realizes that the "fat suit of armor" she created and wore had a deeper psychological meaning that went beyond food itself. It was a way to protect herself from men. Her childhood relationship with her father wasn't good. He let Kim know at a very young age that men had the power and you'd better watch yourself around them. She became terrified of men, and she promised herself that she was never going to be hurt by them. The best way to avoid hurt was to avoid men, and the best way to avoid men was with her fat suit of armor.

Kim threw herself into her studies, believing that if she could do well it wouldn't matter that she was fat. But there was no avoiding gym, a virtual torture chamber that required a ghastly looking exercise uniform that accentuated her weight. Kim was horrible at sports, and she knew she was funny looking when she tried to do any kind of physical activity. The most dreaded activity—which she would gladly have banned from gym classes nationwide—was square dancing. They'd line the boys up on one side and the girls on the other and say, "Pick your partner." She was never picked, and then she had to watch the face of the last boy not to have a partner as the realization dawned on him that it would be Kim. That boy would be subjected to vicious teasing by his friends for having to dance with her.

She looked forward to being an adult, thinking it would be easier and the cruelty would end. When she was 20, she found a job at a printing company (where she still works today) and worked extra hard to prove that despite her weight she could be a competent, valued employee. She loved her job, but life itself was a constant struggle. The day-to-day humiliations chipped away at her self-esteem. She was always worrying: Would she be able to fit into the restaurant seat? Once a waitress asked her in front of everybody at a business luncheon, "Would you like me to find you a bigger chair?" Could she go to a movie? Ride in a plane? She would worry for days before a flight about who would sit next to her. She dreaded approaching her assigned seat and seeing the look of disgust and hostility on the face of her seatmate. She couldn't blame those unlucky people. The flight would be just as uncomfortable for them as for her, with her body spilling into their space. Once she took her young niece to an amusement park. When they walked up to a cable car ride, the man said, "There is a 250-pound limit on this ride." She assured him she was under the limit, although she wasn't sure that was true. The ride was agonizing as she fretted that she was putting her niece's life in danger and the cable would break. Later she just couldn't forgive herself for her recklessness, but she also felt very depressed that her weight should have interfered in the first place.

Buying clothes was a nightmare. Her size, 5X, was even too large for the larger-women's clothing stores, so she ordered most of her clothes from catalogs. Shoes were especially difficult. They had to be flat because no heels would hold her up, and it was almost impossible to find comfortable shoes. When the clothes arrived, Kim would try them on and then get upset because nothing looked good on her or fit right—nothing made her look normal. She would end up shipping most of the clothes back, and in her misery she would eat and eat.

She couldn't stop eating. Food was her friend, her blanket, her comfort, her lover, and her soul mate. It was her drug, and she walked around in a food coma. Little did she realize that her "friend" was slowly killing her.

Once Kim entered the work world, she made an amazing discovery: All men were not like her father had portrayed them to her. She began to see men behaving as loving boyfriends, husbands, fathers, and friends. She saw that her home life growing up was not the model for most people. Maybe there was a chance for her after all. Kim was a romantic, and when she was young she believed she'd find true love and also that she wouldn't be fat forever. But she slowly began to lose hope that it would ever happen. She had never been on a date, never been kissed, didn't even know how to act in a romantic situation. Often her heart ached with loneliness. At 350 pounds, she felt like an outcast, and her health was deteriorating. She had terrible stomach cramps several times a day and could not catch her breath after the slightest exertion. She never had normal menstrual cycles. It seemed as if her body was shutting down, but she felt helpless to stop it. She believed it was too late.

One night, working late, she was feeling lower than she'd ever felt. The pain and loneliness were getting to be too much. Sitting at her desk, with tears streaming down her cheeks, Kim wrote a goodbye letter to the people who loved her. Then, when she'd vented her sorrow, she tore the letter up, left the office, and picked up a large fast-food meal. Food, as always, lifted her spirits. But it was getting harder to survive.

THE MOVIE THAT CHANGED KIM'S LIFE

Life is mysterious, and to this day Kim can't fully explain the transformation that occurred on Sunday, January 29, 2006, shortly after she celebrated her 39th birthday. She was home eating breakfast and channel surfing, and one of the premium channels was showing *The Phantom of the Opera*. She began to watch it, and the portrayal of the Phantom by the actor Gerard Butler penetrated her heart. His soulful performance woke her up from her food coma and made her feel a strong sense of being alive that had been deadened in her for as long as she could remember.

PEP TALK

KIM'S STRATEGIES FOR SUCCESS

1. Stopped eating all fast foods.
2. Researched websites for fat and calorie content in foods.
3. Stayed away from fried foods.
4. Started to walk.
5. Started to ride stationary bike.
6. Started to ride real bike and lift weights.

There is no rational explanation for such an event. To this day Kim can't explain what happened to her, except to say that she was touched in a new way that could be called miraculous. I have never heard a story quite like Kim's before, and yet it rings so absolutely true. That very day she started to change her life.

DOING THE MATH

Kim didn't broadcast her decision to lose weight. She didn't want to deal with people judging her. She just started an action plan. It took a lot of consideration. Kim was a rarity in that she had never been on a diet before. The good news is that her mind wasn't filled with the wrong ideas about weight loss. So she figured it out on her own. As an accountant, Kim was used to crunching numbers, and she found that she could control her diet by counting calories. She read everything she could about calorie counting and located an online site to help her keep track.

EMOTIONAL EATING

Kim was an extremely emotional eater. As she herself put it, food was her lover and best friend. Her eating habits had little to do with actual hunger—she didn't even know what that felt like anymore. Instead she ate when she was feeling stress, anxiety, sadness, boredom, anger, loneliness, and poor self-esteem. Emotional eating is common for many if not most overweight people. I suggest using the following strategies to help break the emotional ties.

KEEP A FOOD/MOOD JOURNAL. Write down your food choices and portions, where you eat, why you eat, how you feel, and anything else that allows you to see your eating patterns. This will allow you to identify when eating has an emotional component.

FIND A DIET BUDDY. Some people do better if they have a friend, spouse, online community, therapist, or other confidant they can talk to about successes or setbacks. Ideally this person is nonjudgmental and unconditionally supportive. If you thrive with a little help from your friends, go ahead and ask for their help and guidance.

START A NEW HOBBY. Spend less time obsessing over food by redirecting your focus and energy. Pick up quilting or sewing, play tennis, learn a new language, volunteer for a favorite charity—anything goes.

HAVE A BACKUP PLAN. Prepare a list of activities that are personally appealing and handy for those times when you are tempted to overeat. Go for a walk, call a friend, listen to nostalgic music, take a hot bath, clean your house, polish your nails, surf the Internet, watch something on TiVo, organize your purse or closet, look through a photo album, and so on.

The first thing she did was stop eating all fast food—except sandwiches from the sub shop near her office, where she could have a satisfying lunch within her calorie framework. She started exercising by walking a block or two and back, and at first her back hurt so much she could barely move, but she kept at it. She also started a journal to follow her progress. She was so big to begin with that she saw results immediately, and they spurred her on.

But it wasn't an easy process. Some weeks she'd lose a couple pounds, and other weeks she wouldn't lose anything. She decided to trust the process and accept the fact there wouldn't be a weight loss every week.

BEFORE

As Kim progressed, she began to get tremendous support from her family and friends. Her mother was her greatest fan, experimenting with different ways to prepare chicken and fish that were flavorful and healthy. Kim's little brother DJ was her cheerleader. He promised to buy her a whole new wardrobe when she lost her weight. Her dear friend Mark invited her to dinner often and prepared wonderful low-calorie, low-fat feasts. Her friend Linda baked healthy muffins. Kim was gratified to have such a terrific team of people who believed in her and wanted her to succeed. She knows that they were the difference between success and failure.

People have often asked Kim how she did it, and in particular they want to know about her struggles. But Kim just smiles and tells them, "I was happy every single day doing this. I didn't wait for two years to be happy. I was so excited all along." This perspective is quite remarkable. It's very difficult for people who have a lot of weight to lose—or any weight, for that matter—to avoid the sense that the final number on the scale is the light at the end of the tunnel. Kim, however, was so completely engaged in the transformative process that she came to love it as much as the result. She knew it would take a long time to lose the weight, and she just wasn't willing to put off her joy. A truly remarkable lady.

Kim has a deeper understanding now about her use of weight to make herself unavailable to men. She was terrified of intimacy and of being hurt, and she hid behind her weight. But she came to see that it wasn't just the weight that was sending out the "do not touch" signals. She noticed large girls dating and getting married. She had to face the fact that the key was her attitude. It's an important message. Kim's early life provided her with a twisted truth—that overweight people don't deserve and can't have love. The real message is that obesity is a health crisis and often a psychological crisis. When an individual is ready to make a change, she will know it.

When Kim had lost the weight, her mother started pushing her to go out. She was nervous about that because she had never dated in her life. "I was the 40-year-old virgin who had never been kissed," she said. One night a friend took her to a bar and she met Jimmy. They played pool and Kim was terrible, but she had a great time. When Jimmy said he wanted to take her out, she was amazed. This was it—the normal life she'd never had a chance to live. But she felt so at ease with him. On their second date she experienced her first kiss. When she got up the nerve to tell Jimmy that she had never been kissed before, he grinned and said he wished he'd known, he would have made it even more special. But it felt plenty special to Kim.

After several dates Kim told Jimmy her story, and she found that she didn't feel ashamed. He was blown away by her achievement, and instead of running for the hills he stuck around. They were married in February 2010.

With Kim's suit of armor gone, life changed for the better in every way. "People say all the time that I'm a different person," Kim says. "I am the same person. I was just hiding. And now I've come out." She has a great deal of empathy for people who are struggling with their weight. "I know they're sitting there thinking it's too late," she says. "I want them to know it's not too late."

KIM'S DAILY DIET COMPARISONS

BEFORE	AFTER
Breakfast	**Breakfast**
Breakfast burrito	Whole grain cereal
Egg sandwich	Skim milk
Hash browns	Blueberries
Lunch	**Lunch**
Cheeseburger	6-inch turkey sub, no mayo, with veggies, tomato, onion
Fries	1 snack bag light potato chips
Soda	Diet soda
Dinner	**Dinner**
Fried chicken (2-3 pieces)	Baked chicken or fish
Mashed potatoes with gravy	Steamed vegetables
Bread	Green salad
6 glazed donuts	Fat-free pudding cup with fat-free whipped cream
Snacks	**Snacks**
Candy	Fruit
1-2 king-size candy bars	Sugar-free frozen pops or gelatin cups

GREGG MCBRIDE

| FROM North Hollywood, California
AGE 38 | HEIGHT 6' 0"
BEFORE WEIGHT 450 | AFTER WEIGHT 175 | POUNDS LOST 275

AFTER

BEFORE

Gregg is an amazing, smart, funny, talented guy with a great sense of self and a kind manner. You'd never guess what an extraordinarily difficult childhood he lived. Gregg's father was in the Air Force, and he spent many of his childhood years living in military housing in Germany. While trying to put on the façade of a normal family—because that was highly valued in the military—Gregg's parents barely lived together, his father coming home only once a week. Gregg's mother resented being burdened with children; she wanted to party and have fun, so she was often away. Gregg remembers feeling alone and panicked, even wondering how he and his sister would eat if his parents left and didn't return. Nobody noticed Gregg's plight, and he was too intimidated by his parents to reveal their secrets.

Gregg's mother prided herself on being "the beautiful blonde," and the appearance of youth and perfection was extremely important to her. She lied about her age to make herself attractive to men, and—realizing that Gregg's age contradicted her lie—she began to tell people he was adopted. She had no feelings for what that lie did to his psyche. Once he asked her, "What were my first words as a baby?" She snapped at him, "How would I know?" It was as if she herself believed the lie about his adoption. She carried the lie to her grave. Her 2004 obituary read that both of her children were adopted.

Sometimes when Gregg's mother had a man staying over, she'd make Gregg sleep in their basement storage unit. In the morning Gregg would trudge up the stairs and knock on the door, pretending to be the neighbor kid coming to walk the dog. His whole life felt like an endless string of lies and abandonment, and he had nowhere to turn—except food.

Gregg's room was his sanctuary, and his closet was like an altar—crammed with food that he would gorge on to soothe his constant anxiety. He'd put on headphones, crank up the stereo, and eat. Sometimes he'd sneak into his dad's wallet and steal money. He'd go to the grocery store, buy as much junk food as he could afford, then hide in his room and stuff it down quickly before he got caught. He continued to push the world away with his growing size, insulating himself from his troubles. He was carrying both physical and emotional weight. Food was his life preserver.

As he put on weight, Gregg's mother and father expressed disgust. Gregg's mother started telling people another lie—that Gregg was overweight because of a medical condition. Gregg remembers friends saying he shouldn't feel bad about his weight—"We know you can't help it. It's a medical condition." But he knew the truth, and the lie just made him feel worse about himself. Meanwhile, the more his parents cracked down, the more he wanted to eat. "As a young kid, being put on a diet taught me how to binge and actually did more harm than good," he says. Without a sense of balance, the tools for healthy eating, or parents who cared enough to make the home a welcome environment, any weight loss efforts were doomed.

He tried to diet. In high school he went on a liquid fast during which he didn't consume solid food for months. But one day when he saw a half-eaten bag of potato chips in the trash, he stared at it for an hour before pulling the bag out and devouring the stale chips. Food controlled him.

Gregg dealt with the social issues by becoming the ham, the funny guy, the one who would make jokes. He developed a caustic wit. He had friends in high school, but never let relationships reach any point of intimacy. He dreaded having people hug him, for fear of seeing their shock when they wrapped their arms around his body and realized how large he was. He felt that his weight was like wearing a neon sign that blared: You're a failure.

Gregg was relieved to escape his mother's grip and go to college in Florida, but it was a very alienating environment. He didn't know anybody, but he didn't dare eat in the cafeteria, where people would watch and judge him. He was on the sidelines during college, a time when people make lifelong bonds. His gorging escalated, and when Gregg graduated he weighed 450 pounds. On job interviews he could see the horror in people's eyes. He was used to them not making eye contact with him. He found that often his interviews were cut short once the interviewer laid eyes on him. His only job offers came from women- or black-owned companies—he thought because they were used to being judged on appearance and were less prejudiced toward him. One of his first jobs was as a copywriter for Macy's, writing fashion copy for ads featuring size-zero models. He continued to live life from the sidelines, not brave enough to make friends, much less attempt romance.

Food was everything. While he was eating breakfast he was thinking about lunch, and while he was eating lunch he was thinking about dinner. Whenever he started a diet, he would get depressed, believing he'd never have his favorite foods again. His "last supper" binges were so

IT'S NOT JUST CALORIES

Like most of the people in this book, Gregg had a pretty big fast-food habit when he was obese. Americans are in love with fast-food restaurants, and every once in a while someone asks me if he or she could lose weight on a diet of, say, two double cheeseburgers a day, totaling 1,500 to 1,600 calories. The fact is, that person might lose weight because calories are calories. However, this diet wouldn't be sustainable or healthy. Even as you were losing weight, you'd be clogging your arteries, firing up inflammation throughout your body, depriving yourself of vital vitamins and minerals, and making yourself sick (and tired, cranky, and bloated from all of the fat, white starch, and salt). Even without the health considerations, as yummy as your plan might seem, it would probably only take a few weeks before you couldn't stand the sight of a cheeseburger. In order for a weight loss plan to be effective, it shouldn't be too different from "normal" eating. If your weight loss plan is too monotonous or restrictive, it perpetuates an on/off mentality that inevitably leads to weight cycling.

extreme, he'd be in pain from stuffing himself. After starting a diet, if he made one slip, that was it.

Gregg hated eating in the company of other people. He would usually order a salad or some other healthy meal. After growing up with a mother who always pretended to be someone she wasn't, Gregg was horrified to find himself falling into a similar pattern. When he went to a drive-through, he carried a list and pretended he was ordering for a group of people, saying, "Mike wants a double cheeseburger, extra fries for Sally." He even included several drinks so the order taker wouldn't be suspicious. At home he would order a large pizza, and when the delivery guy rang the doorbell, he'd call out, "I'll get it," pretending he was in the house with a group of people.

At 450 pounds Gregg mostly wore sweatpants and an oversize T-shirt. "My fashion options had become virtually nonexistent," he says. "But damn it, I could control my head of hair. And I was going to do so by getting a perm, which I guess was in style at the time. So even though I wanted to hide in my apartment for fear of being judged, I went to my salon of choice and ordered up some tightly wound curls." Today Gregg is a bit embarrassed by that perm, but it did show that he had a desire to look good—a definite clue that there was a motivated guy beneath all the fat.

GREGG FINDS HIS TRUTH

For years Gregg had been trying to figure out the psychology behind his food obsession while he tried every diet imaginable without success. Too often, he got the wrong kind of support. Once he gained seven pounds in a week and a friend said, "That's okay. You'll do better next week."

He says now, "It wasn't okay." But what to do? He has a vivid memory of seeing a well-known actor, who was heavy, on TV. Even though he was just standing there talking, Gregg saw that he was sweating profusely and laboring for breath. Gregg felt as if he were seeing a mirror reflection of himself. He knew he had to lose the weight, but the task felt overwhelming. One day someone at work advised flippantly, "Just stop eating so much." Gregg was initially offended, but the words stayed with him. Something in his brain clicked. He decided to stop the tricks, the gimmicks, and the analysis and do just that. "No tomfoolery," as he puts it.

Gregg was a smart guy. He realized he'd never been in touch with what healthy foods tasted like or what comprised a reasonable portion. He found that certain diet guidelines helped him establish that baseline. Most diet principles were basically the same: Eat less. Move more. Nothing fancy about that. Gradually he also started limiting processed foods and found that his taste buds actually craved natural foods and, for the first time, fruits and vegetables.

It wasn't all fun and games. When he initially cut his 9,000 calories a day down to around 1,700, there was a period of six weeks to three months when he suffered. He had to relearn how to recognize hunger signals. He kept a scrapbook, cutting out pictures from magazines as aspirational tools. He also took a picture of himself every week to track his progress. He knew his friends had doubts. Everyone was so used to Gregg going on a diet that sometimes his friends didn't know how to respond. "I'd always been known as the funny fat guy," he says. "Suddenly all my talk of getting healthy—which they'd been hearing for years—was being followed up with real success. I think this freaked some of them out." There were occasional flurries of resistance, such as when Gregg

GREGG'S DAILY DIET COMPARISONS

BEFORE	AFTER
Breakfast	**Breakfast**
2 diet sodas (Gregg would wake up with such a food hangover from the previous night's binge that he usually skipped breakfast.)	½ grapefruit 2 slices all-natural cinnamon raisin toast Black coffee
Lunch	Lunch
Several cartons of Chinese food Several diet sodas Ice cream	Fruit salad with cottage cheese, lowfat sour cream, and walnuts—his special recipe
Dinner	Dinner
Fast-food takeout meal, usually enough for 2-4 people Ice cream Bag of cookies	6-ounce salmon steak, broiled 1 cup cherry tomatoes 1 cup steamed green beans
Snacks	Snacks
Candy bars Milk shakes	Banana with cinnamon

declined to go to a party or out to dinner because he didn't trust his willpower. But within four months he was buying new clothes and showing everyone how serious he was.

Gregg signed up for an aerobics class with a group of women who became some of his biggest fans. He was amazed to have this instant support system of former strangers. There were moments of pure pride. One day at the gym a stranger came up to Gregg and said, "I don't know you, but I saw you six months ago. You're half the person you were." Gregg felt great. Yes, he was.

As he lost weight Gregg began thinking about relationships for the first time in his life. Suddenly people wanted to go out with him, and intimacy was the scariest thing in the world. He didn't even know how to go on a date, much less be a partner. But he saw himself at last coming out of his shell. His wit was less harsh, and others commented that he was a nicer person. A big part of his transformation has been letting go of anger. He believes his experiences have shaped him, both good and bad, and that if he carries the pain from his childhood in his heart, it will be the fastest route to a relapse.

Gregg "just stopped eating so much" and took off more than 275 pounds in less than a year. He has kept the weight off for more than 10 years. Because he was overweight for a large part of his life, Gregg knows that eating healthy foods in healthy portions is something he must be vigilant about. He likens it to riding a bicycle. "The minute I stop peddling, I fall down, skin my knees, and potentially gain 250 pounds."

Gregg had always longed to be a screenwriter, and after he lost the weight he made the most daring move of his life—to Los Angeles, home of the youth-and-body-obsessed. He jokes that he could never have done it when he weighed 450 pounds. "They wouldn't have let me in."

Like many others, he was plagued by the sight of flabs of skin hanging on his body. Someone he dated once commented that he looked like a sherpa dog with his clothes off, and that comment really stung. The mythical Hollywood body was eluding him. He once stood in a dressing room trying on pants that would have looked sensational, were it not for the bulge created by loose skin at his pelvis. Eventually he found a doctor in San Francisco and had skin removal surgery.

Today, weighing 175 and being perceived as "normal," Gregg is very conscious that being thin and attractive is highly valued in Hollywood—even for a writer who works behind the scenes. Sometimes he feels a twinge when he walks into a meeting and people greet him with smiles. He can't forget how they once looked away in barely concealed horror. "It's fascinating to have lived life on both sides of the spectrum," he says. But his motivation comes from the notion that in the end, it's not about image or presentation. It's about choosing life and health.

Corn, Avocado, and Tomato Salad

BY Gregg McBride
MAKES 8 servings
SERVING SIZE ¾ cup

Gregg says: "I make this salad at least once a week, all year long, assuming I can find the fresh ingredients at my local grocery store or—even better—farmers' market. The trick is to make the salad while ingredients are at their freshest. And make plenty of it because it's sure to be a hit with anyone you serve it to (including yourself)! This also makes a great dish to bring to any party. I promise, it will be a big hit. Double the recipe and make it shortly before you leave. Do not add olive oil, balsamic vinegar, or pepper until just before serving."

4 ears of fresh corn (may substitute 4 cups frozen, thawed corn kernels)
1 large, ripe avocado, cut into ½-inch chunks

2 pints grape tomatoes, halved lengthwise
4 tablespoons olive oil
2 tablespoons balsamic vinegar
   Black pepper

1 Remove the corn kernels from the cobs with a sharp knife and transfer the kernels to a large bowl. Add the avocado, tomatoes, oil, and vinegar and toss all the ingredients together. Season with pepper to taste and serve immediately.

NUTRITION INFORMATION Calories: 144, Protein: 2 g, Total Fat: 10 g, Saturated Fat: 1.5 g, Cholesterol: 0 mg, Sodium: 15 mg, Carbohydrate: 14 g, Fiber: 3 g

STACY ALLENDORF

FROM Columbia, South Carolina
AGE 52 | HEIGHT 5' 7"
BEFORE WEIGHT 288 | AFTER WEIGHT 168 | POUNDS LOST 120

AFTER

BEFORE

When Stacy walked into the cafeteria of the elementary school where she taught second grade, she was always greeted with a big smile by the cook. "Ms. Allendorf, we've got your plate ready for you," she'd say, handing Stacy a heaping serving of Southern home cooking. Stacy would eat every last bite, rushing to finish before the bell rang.

She was a busy and dedicated teacher, who regularly worked 10- to 12-hour days, and the last thing she thought about was her weight or health. Stacy was selfless, and what mattered most was being a good teacher and a good single mom to her growing son. For years she worked for a particularly demanding principal. She loved the challenge and felt that she truly became a great teacher during that period. But she definitely put her own needs on the back burner. The weight crept up, eventually reaching 288 pounds. Stacy ignored it. I think many readers can identify with Stacy. She was so devoted to her child and her work that she literally didn't come up for air for years. People always wonder how the weight gain happens. Well, it was a slow and steady creep, and it happened over the years through inattention and the stresses of life.

As a child Stacy had always been fit and active, and she continued that lifestyle into her twenties, playing softball and going to the gym with her girlfriends two or three times a week. She loved food—unhealthy, fattening food—but because she burned so many calories through exercise, she never had to worry about a weight issue. But that changed after she gave birth to her son. In addition to the normal stresses of caring for a new infant, Stacy experienced a huge emotional blow only three weeks after the baby was born when her husband walked out on her. Stacy deserves a lot of credit for having the courage to pick up and go forward on her own, but one thing she sacrificed was time for exercise. In a sense Stacy felt that her only role in life was to be a caretaker—of her son and her students. She didn't feel as if she had the right to give time and attention to herself, even for her health. She spent the next 21 years ignoring her health and weight in a big cycle of "denial, denial, denial."

Stacy would later realize that being a teacher contributed to her bad habits. "Teachers typically don't eat well," she said. "They don't have time to. They never sit down, so they're always grabbing food on the go. And kids show their love not with apples but with home-baked cookies, pies, and cakes. My students' parents spoiled me rotten—with food." Between classes Stacy would grab candy and cookies from the stash she kept in her desk drawer. At the end of the day, exhausted, she would go home and crash on the couch. She kept gaining weight and put the embarrassment and the emerging medical problems out of her mind.

Stacy's long journey of change began when her beloved father died in 2001 from complications following heart surgery. He had lived with heart disease and type 2 diabetes for years. Although Stacy was more than 200 pounds at the time, it didn't register that she was headed for the same fate. She was overwhelmed with grief over the loss of her father, and she sank into a deep depression. She couldn't get through a day without breaking down weeping.

Stacy and her son were seeing a counselor during that period, and at one appointment she asked her son to wait outside. "For the past two months all I've done is weep," she told the counselor, tearing up as she spoke. She knew she needed help. She was scared, and when the counselor gently asked her to think about her own life and happiness, it was something she was not used to doing.

PEP TALK

STACY'S STRATEGIES FOR SUCCESS

IT'S OKAY TO BE SELFISH. Find time for yourself and make your health a priority.

BE YOUR OWN ADVOCATE. Convince your friends to choose restaurants where you can eat healthfully.

KEEP MOVING. Even if you can only walk a short distance and back, not only will you burn calories, but you'll also get a great psychological boost.

START SLOWLY. Choose one unhealthy food you can live without, and then another.

FIND MOTIVATION IN YOURSELF. Make a private pledge to change your life, even if no one else knows about it.

AFTER

BEFORE

She didn't even know where to start. At the end of their conversation the counselor put a name to her problem, saying, "You have depression." What did that mean? Stacy didn't want to be diagnosed as depressed. She had always been a go-getter, a person who handled things. She didn't know how to look inward, and she was very nervous about what she'd find if she did.

For a long time after she was diagnosed with depression, Stacy didn't change her life. She didn't see how she could. She was too busy, and she continued to put on weight. In 2003 she was diagnosed with type 2 diabetes. She refused to accept it. And she also failed to make any changes to address her growing medical problems.

A MOTHER'S MOMENT OF TRUTH

In 2004 Stacy's son graduated high school and started his first year of college. One day she looked at him and realized that he'd put on a lot of weight during that period. She knew the road he was going down—it was her road. She gave him the "do as I say, not as I do" lecture. But it didn't have an effect. In January she went to a conference on the West Coast with colleagues, and it was pure torture trying to fit into an airplane seat. On the way home she had to ask for a seat belt extender, and she practically whispered her request, hoping people wouldn't hear. Other day-to-day issues mounted. Buying clothes in the double-Xs was deeply humiliating. She couldn't get down on the floor and get back up again without help. More and more she stayed at home when she wasn't working because it was too much effort to be active and social.

Lonely and miserable and feeling much older than her 45 years, Stacy finally saw her future. Retirement was going to be her lying around slowly dying, unable to enjoy what could be the best time of her life. That summer she took a first step, ordering a glider exercise machine for her forty-sixth birthday. It didn't seem like much, but at least it was something.

Stacy didn't immediately make any change to her diet. She started with exercise, because she remembered it had been so effective when she was young. She began in secrecy and exercised away from other people. She got up at 4:00 every morning to exercise. She started with 5 minutes every other day, then 10 minutes, and after a month she was exercising 30 minutes every other day. That's when she began to pay attention to her diet.

Food was a much harder issue for Stacy. She had to figure out what was right for her. She began with a simple question, "What foods would be easiest for me to do without?" She decided to start eliminating some of the fried foods she ate every day and cut out the fat, such as mayonnaise on sandwiches, wherever she could. She started counting fat grams and settled on 30 per day, eventually dropping to 15 fat grams as she continued to lose weight. Once a week she would look forward to a healthful splurge in the form of a big baked sweet potato with cinnamon and sugar or a homemade bran muffin—a childhood favorite that she modified to be more nutritious.

Within six months Stacy had eliminated fried foods and calorie-loaded condiments from her menu and focused on fresh foods and lean meat and chicken. She also moved to a middle school with a less frantic pace and used the breathing room to "work smarter, not harder." Sundays were devoted to preparing meals for the week and storing them in portion-controlled containers for the fridge and freezer.

In the early months, even as she continued to lose two or three pounds a week, Stacy kept wearing larger clothing sizes and only told one close friend what she was doing. She was terrified of failing. When people had commented on her weight loss during past efforts, it had had the opposite effect of defeating her. She didn't want to jinx herself. Not until she had lost 70 pounds did she say to herself with full confidence, "I'm going to make it."

JOY'S WORDS OF ADVICE

GET YOUR KIDS MOVING

As a teacher, Stacy is deeply concerned about the epidemic of childhood obesity, which she has observed firsthand. Teachers can play a big role in encouraging parents to help their children lead active lifestyles. Here are a few suggestions:

BE A FITNESS ROLE MODEL. Studies show that parents' participation in a physical activity increases the likelihood that their kids will partake in similar activities. Get fit yourself—join a gym, practice yoga, or jog regularly. Teaching by example works.

INTRODUCE EXTRA ACTIVITY EVERY DAY. When you go to the store, park a little farther away. Skip the bus and walk the kids to and from school. Take an evening stroll, shoot some hoops in the driveway, or sign up for a fitness class with your teen. This isn't just a fitness benefit; it's also a great way to open up a new communication channel with your kids.

EXPLORE "ACTIVE" VIDEO GAMES. If your kids are technology junkies, all is not lost. Seek out the variety of video and electronic activities that get kids off the couch and moving.

PAY ATTENTION TO WHAT THE KIDS LIKE. Each child is different. Maybe yours like activities that aren't your typical after-school sports. Explore your community's bike paths or hiking trails. Enroll your child in yoga, swimming, hip-hop dance, or martial arts classes. Visit a rock-climbing gym or have some old-school fun at a roller rink. Whatever elicits a positive response is the way to go—and keep going!

BREAKING THE CHAINS

As Stacy continued to lose weight, she suddenly noticed that something was going on with her son. The sodas that he kept in the refrigerator weren't disappearing. And there were bottles of water there. Without telling her, he had decided to lose weight too. He eventually dropped 40 pounds. It was one of her most gratifying moments. At last she felt she was a good role model.

For the first time in years Stacy was socializing. "I'd forgotten how much fun it was to be active," she says. When she was down 80 pounds she started walking with a buddy, and she felt like she was 20 again. Gradually her attitude about food changed as well. Before, it was everything to her—her comfort and friend. If she had a hard day at school she would turn to macaroni and cheese or candy bars from the stash she kept in her desk. That changed with a more active lifestyle. Now when she got together with friends, it was not necessarily to eat but to walk in the park or go to the movies. Even restaurant meals changed. She was more likely to order an appetizer or share a main course.

There is no longer any sign of diabetes, and Stacy's cholesterol is perfectly normal. Her doctor hugs her when she comes into his office for her annual checkup.

It took Stacy two years to lose 120 pounds, but when she had done it, she felt a great sense of

STACY'S DAILY DIET COMPARISONS

BEFORE	AFTER
Breakfast	**Breakfast**
Scrambled eggs and toast	Low-fat pancake with fresh fruit
Pancakes	or
Toasted bagels with butter or cream cheese	Yogurt and granola bar
Lunch	**Lunch**
Ham sandwich with mayo	Salad with chicken or fish and sundried
Lots of diet soda	tomato dressing
Dinner	**Dinner**
Hot dogs	Broiled or grilled fish or chicken
Batter-fried chicken	Steamed vegetables
Mashed potatoes with butter and gravy	Low-fat fudge pop
Corn with butter and salt	or
Lots of bread and butter	Whole wheat thin-crust pizza with arti-
Comment: "In the South, we fry our vegetables.	chokes, spinach, and sundried tomatoes
If it can be fried, it's fried."	
Snacks	**Snacks**
Candy and cookies throughout the day	Apple, celery or carrot sticks

freedom. "I broke the chains I had put myself in," she reflects. "I was so trapped, and then I wasn't." One night her son looked at her across the dinner table and said, "Mom, you're so much happier now." That surprised her. She'd always thought she'd managed to put on a happy face for him, but he'd seen the truth.

When Stacy was selected to appear on *Today* and be inducted as a Joy Fit Club member, she told very few people, and she only mentioned it to her students the day before she left for New York. It was test week and she didn't want them to be distracted. However, when she returned to school after the show, she was mobbed in the hallways. She discovered that the administration had set up televisions throughout the school and 1,000 students watched her. Many of them, especially those who struggled with their weight, told her they had cried because her story was so inspiring. She was thrilled that her example could be an inspiration to young people struggling with their weight.

Now Stacy looks forward to her future with anticipation. "I'm learning that I can enjoy life. It doesn't have to be only about work. I'm not going to be dead in five years," she says joyfully. "I'm going to be the old lady on cruise ships who flirts with the young guys!"

Broiled Parmesan Vegetables

BY Stacy Allendorf
MAKES 4 servings
SERVING SIZE 1¼ cups

	Oil spray	1	pint grape tomatoes
1	sweet pepper (any color), cut into bite-size chunks	1	tablespoon salt-free garlic-pepper seasoning
1	red onion, cut into bite-size chunks	2	tablespoons grated Parmesan cheese
1	bunch asparagus, cut into 2-inch pieces		

1 Preheat the broiler. Liberally coat a baking sheet with oil spray.

2 Spread the vegetables on the baking sheet in a single layer. Liberally coat the vegetables with oil spray and sprinkle with the garlic-pepper seasoning.

3 Broil 4 inches from the heat until the vegetables begin to brown, about 7 minutes. Remove the baking sheet from the oven and sprinkle the vegetables with the Parmesan cheese. Return the baking sheet to the oven and broil until the cheese melts, 1 to 2 minutes.

NUTRITION INFORMATION Calories: 55, Protein: 4 g, Total Fat: 1 g, Saturated Fat: 0.5 g, Cholesterol: 0 mg, Sodium: 45 mg, Carbohydrate: 13 g, Fiber: 3 g

Banana Bran Muffins

BY Stacy Allendorf
MAKES 12 muffins
SERVING SIZE 1 muffin

This recipe was adapted from a childhood favorite bran muffin that Stacy didn't want to let go of—so she found a way to make it healthy.

Oil spray
1 cup high-fiber bran cereal or crushed bran flakes
¾ cup skim milk
1 large ripe banana, mashed
¼ cup unsweetened applesauce

1 large egg, lightly beaten
1 cup all-purpose flour
¼ cup granulated sugar
2½ teaspoons baking powder
¼ teaspoon kosher salt

1 Preheat the oven to 400°F. Coat a nonstick muffin pan with oil spray.

2 In a small bowl soak the cereal in the milk until soggy, about 10 minutes.

3 In a large bowl combine the cereal and milk mixture, mashed banana, applesauce, and egg until well blended.

4 In a medium bowl whisk together the flour, sugar, baking powder, and salt. Sprinkle the flour mixture over the wet ingredients and stir until just combined.

5 Divide the batter among the muffin cups, filling them about two-thirds full. Bake for 15 to 18 minutes or until a toothpick inserted in the center of a muffin comes out clean. Cool for 10 minutes in pan before removing.

NUTRITION INFORMATION Calories: 88, Protein: 3 g, Total Fat: 1 g, Saturated Fat: 0 g, Cholesterol: 20 mg, Sodium: 100 mg, Carbohydrate: 20 g, Fiber: 3 g, Total Sugar: 7 g

Variation Add ½ cup raisins and/or ½ cup chopped walnuts to the batter.

LYNN HARALDSON

FROM Clarion, Pennsylvania
AGE 48 | HEIGHT 5' 5"
BEFORE WEIGHT 296 | AFTER WEIGHT 140 | POUNDS LOST 156

AFTER

BEFORE

Lynn glows with health and energy. She has a vibrant personality and a dazzling smile, and to look at her is to see a total woman, living to the max. It's hard to believe that only a few short years ago, Lynn's weight ruled her life. It crushed her career dream, turned her into a recluse, and made her an unavailable mother. But the decline was a long time coming.

Lynn was 11 when she first noticed the way fat kids were treated by their classmates. She did everything she could to not stand out, but one incident stands out to this day—a public weigh-in when she was in the sixth grade. Everyone lined up in front of the nurse with her big scale, and one by one they had their weights recorded. "When I stepped on the scale," Lynn remembers, "the nurse moved the big metal weight from 50 to 100. It made a loud 'cachunk' sound when it settled in the groove, announcing to everyone in line, 'Lynn's gone over 100.'" After the weigh-in Lynn felt much more conspicuous. Although she was the same person she'd been before she stepped on the scale, she feared the other kids looked at her with new eyes. She could see them huddling in groups at recess, and she imagined they were whispering about her weight. Formerly friendly children would turn into taunting, rude monsters, and she couldn't understand it. It seemed as if the bullies felt personally insulted, as if they thought that fat kids were taking something away from them.

Somehow Lynn made it through school by focusing on her studies and her writing. She dreamed of being a journalist one day, but that dream was deferred when she married young and soon gave birth to a baby daughter. She and her husband Bruce lived on his family's farm, and although Lynn weighed 200 pounds, she felt content during that period. Then, when she was only 19 years old and still nursing her infant, Bruce died suddenly. Lynn was destroyed and felt as if her world had come crashing down. She moved in with her parents and tried to climb back out of her despair. Everyone assured her that life would go on, but she wasn't convinced. When a friend who was marrying her husband's best friend asked her to be in the wedding party, Lynn clung to the hope that the wedding would be the start of a new life. She decided that she was going to lose weight, and as an incentive she ordered her dress a size smaller. She joined a diet program that promised rapid weight loss on an 800-calorie-a-day diet. The diet made her feel lousy. She was dizzy, constipated, and hungry, but it didn't matter. The important thing was that in four weeks she lost 20 pounds, and her smaller-size bridesmaid dress fit perfectly.

Unfortunately the wedding wasn't for another few weeks, and Lynn couldn't keep it up. She started to eat normally again, and the weight came roaring back. A couple of weeks before the wedding she couldn't get the zipper of the dress past her waist. She was too ashamed to admit the dress didn't fit, so she told her friend she couldn't be in the wedding party because she was still grieving for Bruce. "As the bridesmaids walked down the aisle, I was crushed by jealousy," she

JOY'S WORDS OF ADVICE

KNOW YOUR PORTIONS

Lynn was shocked to find out how large her portion sizes were—often two to four times a normal serving. Here are some aids to retrain yourself to recognize appropriate portions:

1. Buy a small kitchen scale to weigh meats and other foods so you know you have it right. Eventually you'll be able to eyeball 4 to 6 ounces of meat.

2. Always use measuring cups and spoons when portioning out cereal, pasta, rice, salad dressing, nut butters, and other measurables. In the beginning you'll probably find that a cup or a tablespoon is much smaller than you think, but eventually you'll hone your portion awareness and the amount will look just right. (On a related note, make sure you note the difference between teaspoons and tablespoons. One tablespoon is equivalent to 3 teaspoons, so if you mix up the two when measuring high-cal ingredients like vegetable oils or nut butters, you can get three times as many calories as you bargained for.)

3. Before you eat a packaged item, read the "servings per container" line. Often items that might seem to be single servings are actually considered two or three servings. When that's the case, you need to multiply the calories, fat, and other nutritional stats by the number of servings per container to calculate the total amount consumed for the entire package.

recalls. "They were smiling, which I couldn't do, and wearing the dress I couldn't wear. Once everyone was safely up front, I did the only thing I knew to do. I left."

Lynn kept working on her weight and got it down to 165. Then she had a great breakthrough opportunity—a job as a journalist at a local newspaper. They even gave her a column, and she loved writing that column more than anything. The words flew as she wrote. For a while Lynn was content again. She had two daughters by now, the second from an ill-fated second marriage, and nothing meant more to her than her girls. She thought she was finally getting her life in order. But with the stress of her job and raising two children, she stopped being careful about what she ate. Gradually the weight started to pile back on, and as she got heavier, the job became more difficult, and she became increasingly ashamed. When her weight reached 260 pounds, Lynn was told that the paper wanted to publish her photo at the top of her popular column. She chose to stop writing it because she couldn't bear to have her photo published. "No way was I putting my face out there," she says. Eventually she quit her job altogether because she couldn't stand the public scrutiny. But as she would later realize, it wasn't the public she was running from; it was herself.

At that point her two beautiful daughters were teenagers. Lynn had always been determined to raise them with healthy body images, and neither one of them ever had food or weight issues. But Lynn was leading a double life. Even as she was encouraging her girls, she was avoiding activities and becoming a near recluse. She avoided school games and band practices, always making excuses for why she couldn't attend. She even stopped visiting family in other parts of the country because she didn't want them to see her so heavy.

In 2002 Lynn was diagnosed with an underactive thyroid, which explained part of her rapid weight gain. But it was two more years before she began to take responsibility for the greater part—the way she was eating. Her triglyceride and sugar levels were skyrocketing. She was approaching 300 pounds, with a whole host of medical conditions, and she finally realized that she would either have to accept her shrunken life or shrink her size.

The deciding moment came on a snowy night in December. It was her daughter Cassie's

---

PEP TALK

LYNN'S STRATEGIES FOR SUCCESS

CHOOSE A DIET THAT WORKS FOR YOU. Lynn became a vegetarian because it allowed her to eat a larger volume of food.

BITE IT, WRITE IT. Lynn has kept a food journal every day for the last five years. It keeps her accountable and on track.

NO DEPRIVATION, ONLY MODERATION. She doesn't deprive herself of her favorite treats, such as chocolate and an occasional glass of wine.

---

birthday, and Lynn was prepared to fix a celebratory meal at home. But her daughter insisted they all go out to eat, even though it was snowing. Lynn hated going out. She had little to wear anymore; she barely fit into her largest size 28 and didn't have the money to go up to a size 30/32. She forced herself into black stretchy pants and a red sweater, and when she walked into the restaurant she imagined—as she always did—that everyone's eyes went to her, thinking, "Oh my, she's big."

Lynn's daughters didn't seem to notice anything. They loved their mom at any size. They were happy and animated, and Cassie insisted on having her picture taken with Lynn. "That's a nice picture of us, Mom," Cassie said, showing her the camera image. Lynn agreed, but she didn't mean it. No picture of her was nice. But then she noticed something. "Cassie had placed her cheek next to mine and she was beaming. She was happy because she was with her mother on her birthday. Not her morbidly obese mother, her ill-dressed mother, her isolated, guarded, self-loathing mother—those were my descriptors. Cassie loved me just the way I was."

Something woke up inside of Lynn when she saw that photo and thought about the love of her daughters. She realized that she had allowed her weight to become her essence, but she was so much more than that. Suddenly she had an overwhelming desire to live and be there for her daughters. She decided to shrink her size, and this time vowed to make it last. She knew it would have to be because she didn't have room in her life for another failure. She couldn't make the round trip up and down the scale again.

Before she even began, Lynn turned to writing to help her decide how to proceed. She began a daily journal that would become an important touchstone for her journey. On paper she asked herself some probing questions: How do I feel about my body? How much do I love myself? Am I worth changing for? Her reflections on paper helped Lynn realize that she did value herself, and writing gave her a sense of control. The journal was like a friend with whom she could share her hopes, pain, and daily struggles.

THE "DECADES" PLAN

Lynn had experienced weight loss in the past. She'd repeatedly lost and regained the same 20 or 50 pounds. In 1986, after her second daughter was born, she dropped 100 pounds "basically by starving myself." Before long she had gained it all back, and more. The experience drove her into a deep depression, which she turned to food to ease. She felt that she was the same person inside, but her body had become unrecognizable.

This time she knew she had to do things differently. Merely setting a long-term goal was a trap. She devised a "decades" plan, with a goal of 10 pounds at a time. Each "9" was a big number— 239, 229, 219. When she reached 190, she was hooked on the changes and she just kept going.

How did she do it? She started very slowly examining her portion sizes. Like many of the people I counsel, Lynn was blind to the incremental ways weight piles on. She was shocked to find out how huge her portions were. For example, at breakfast she used to eat a giant bagel with cream cheese, a plate of waffles with syrup, or a huge bowl of cereal—each three to four times an appropriate portion for one person. She became diligent about calorie counting and portion sizes.

Lynn didn't incorporate exercise until she had lost 100 pounds. She suffered from arthritis and was worried about the strain. She started very slowly, walking and then adding strength training, taking care to listen to her body and not push too hard. (Now, her doctor tells her, she has the bones of a 30-year old.)

TODAY: A PICTURE OF CONFIDENCE

With new energy and a renewed spirit, Lynn returned to writing, and she started a blog to share her experiences. She is currently studying to become a public health dietary technician and hopes to work with low-income individuals with secondary conditions like arthritis and diabetes. When her grandkids came along, she realized that she could keep up with them much better than she'd been able to do with her daughters. The first time she went down the slide with her granddaughter, she felt like she was flying. "I missed out on so much of life," she says, reflecting on her years in hiding. "But now I'm making up for it."

"ODE TO MY SIZE 28 STRETCH PANTS"

I was very touched by Lynn's poignant piece about her size 28 stretch pants. She wrote it after someone asked her what she did with all of her large clothes. Those particular pants, favorites of Lynn's, appeared on *Today's* Joy Fit Club segment, and Lynn later wrote: "I kept one lone item of clothing from my 300-pound days: my size 28 black stretch pants. I wore them every day. They were my constant companion. . . . My size 28 black stretch pants were literally stretched to their limit. As I grew larger, holes began to form. Stains no longer washed out. I didn't know it at the time, but those holes and stains reflected how I felt about myself, namely that I wasn't worth taking care of. My size 28 black stretch pants are my friend. . . . And as my friend, my pants help me through those days when I wonder: Why am I doing this? Why do I journal my food? Why do I eat the way I do? Why do I (usually) say no to chocolate cake, mac 'n' cheese, and half-and-half in my coffee? I love those things! 'Ah,' says the size 28 black stretch pants, 'but you love yourself even more.' See why we're BFF?"

THREE EVERYDAY CHANGES THAT ADDED UP FOR LYNN

Before	After	Annual calories saved	Annual pounds lost
2 lattes a day, made with ½ cup half-and-half	Tea, plain or sweetened with sugar substitute	116,800	33
Large bagel with cream cheese for breakfast	Egg white omelet with reduced-fat cheese	131,400	37
Snack: large bowl of buttered popcorn with Parmesan cheese topping	100-calorie pack of plain popcorn with a dusting of Parmesan	161,200	46

Curried Lentils and Veggies

BY Lynn Haraldson
MAKES 4 servings
SERVING SIZE 1¼ cups

Lynn says: "I like to play around with different kinds of curry, adjusting the heat to the mood of the food and the palate of the consumer. I don't like super spicy food, but I like a nice kick. When I originally made this, I used ¾ teaspoon hot curry and ¾ teaspoon Maharajah curry."

- 1 oil spray
- 1 medium onion, diced (about 1 cup)
- 2 medium carrots, diced (about 1 cup)
- 1 small zucchini or summer squash, diced (about 1 cup)
- 4 cloves garlic, minced
- 1½ teaspoons curry powder
- ¾ teaspoon ground ginger
- ½ teaspoon cayenne pepper
- ¼ teaspoon turmeric
- ¼ teaspoon ground cumin
- 2 cups plus 3 tablespoons unsalted or low-sodium vegetable broth
- 1 15-ounce can diced tomatoes, preferably no-salt-added (with liquids)
- 1 cup French (green) lentils
- 2 cups fresh spinach
- ½ teaspoon kosher salt (optional)
  Hot cooked brown rice, for serving (optional)

1 Liberally coat a large saucepan with oil spray and heat over medium heat. Add the onion and carrots and cook, stirring, for 2 minutes. Add the zucchini, garlic, spices, and 3 tablespoons of the vegetable broth; cook, stirring frequently, for 5 minutes. Add the tomatoes, lentils, and the remaining 2 cups vegetable broth. Bring the mixture to a boil. Reduce the heat to low and simmer for 30 to 40 minutes or until the lentils are tender. Add the spinach and salt (if using); stir until the spinach has wilted. If desired, serve the lentils over brown rice.

NUTRITION INFORMATION Calories: 246, Protein: 15 g, Total Fat: 1 g, Saturated Fat: 0 g, Cholesterol: 0 mg, Sodium: 300 mg, Carbohydrate: 45 g, Fiber: 19 g

Sundried Tomato and Curry Hummus with Baked Pita Chips

BY Lynn Haraldson
MAKES 16 servings (2 cups total)
SERVING SIZE 2 tablespoons

1 15-ounce can chickpeas, preferably no-salt-added or low-sodium, drained and rinsed (reserve the drained liquid from the can)
5 sundried tomato halves (sold in the bag; not packed in oil)
4 cloves garlic, peeled
2 tablespoons tahini (sesame seed paste)
3 tablespoons lemon juice
⅓ cup nonfat plain Greek yogurt
1 teaspoon curry powder
½ teaspoon ground cumin
½ teaspoon ground coriander
¼ teaspoon black pepper
¼ teaspoon kosher salt

1 Place all the ingredients except the reserved chickpea liquid in a food processor and process for 1 minute. Add a little of the reserved liquid and process for 1 to 2 minutes. Check for consistency and add more liquid if you prefer a thinner hummus. Continue processing until you reach the desired consistency. Serve immediately or chill. Enjoy with baked pita chips (recipe, below) or sliced vegetables.

NUTRITION INFORMATION Calories: 45, Protein: 2 g, Total Fat: 1 g, Saturated Fat: 0 g, Cholesterol: 0 mg, Sodium: 40 mg, Carbohydrate: 7 g, Fiber: 1.5 g

Baked Pita Chips

BY Lynn Haraldson
MAKES 8 servings
SERVING SIZE 6 wedges (1 pita)

Oil spray
8 whole wheat pitas

1 Preheat the oven to 375°F. Liberally coat 2 baking sheets with oil spray.

2 Cut each pita into 6 triangular wedges. Arrange the wedges in a single layer on the baking sheets. Bake for 4 minutes. Flip the wedges and bake for 4 minutes. Cool and serve with hummus.

NUTRITION INFORMATION Calories: 170, Protein: 6 g, Total Fat: 2 g, Saturated Fat: 0 g, Cholesterol: 0 mg, Sodium: 340 mg, Carbohydrate: 35 g, Fiber: 5 g

TODAY

BEN DAVIS

FROM Little Rock, Arkansas
AGE 25 | HEIGHT 5' 11½"
BEFORE WEIGHT 365 | AFTER WEIGHT 231 | POUNDS LOST 134

AFTER

BEFORE

Ben is a handsome, motivated young man, wise beyond his years. His weight loss journey is especially inspirational because obesity has become such a crisis for youth, and Ben is determined to do something about it. His story is a common one for an entire generation of computer- and fast food-dependent youth. He is very happy that he didn't wait until he was in his forties, plagued with medical problems, before he took action.

Ben grew up in Arkansas with two parents who worked full time. He and his siblings learned to fend for themselves when it came to food. They ate lots of cereal and snacks, usually sitting in front of the television. "I thought it was awesome to have access to all the food I wanted," Ben says, "but it wasn't too long before the other kids started teasing me for being overweight." Ben's story illustrates how important it is for parents to take charge of their family's food environment by providing balanced meals, setting limits around portions and treats, and being healthy role models themselves.

In fifth grade Ben had a crush on a girl, and he got up the courage to ask her to be his girlfriend. She replied, "You're funny, but you're way too fat for me." He laughed it off, but the rejection hurt a lot, and he still remembers it vividly. By eighth grade Ben was deeply depressed. He spent many nights crying to his mother about how unhappy he was, but he didn't have a clue about how to change things. Sometimes he would do sit-ups in bed, thinking it would make him skinny—and thus happy—but it didn't work. He became more of an introvert, spending all his free time playing computer games. This introverted lifestyle followed him to college.

Ben remembers taking solace in losing himself in the computer. "There was something satisfying about sitting down at the computer with music blaring and a pizza and giant soda beside me," he said. But the satisfaction he felt was superficial and short-lived. At one point he made an effort to be more social and had a girlfriend. It wasn't so much his weight that ended the relationship as his total sense of apathy and depression. One night stands out—he went to the movies with his girlfriend and her friend. The girls had already taken their seats when Ben realized he couldn't fit into the movie seat. They had to move to the back so he could sit in the handicap chair. The girls didn't seem to mind, but Ben became sullen and despondent. This was the beginning of a deep depression for Ben, and eventually his relationship with his girlfriend ended.

When Ben did venture out, he headed for his favorite fast-food restaurant, where he would sit in the parking lot and eat, too ashamed to go inside where people could see him. Sometimes he'd have dinner at the local diner, but he always went early, when not many people were there.

By the time he hit 350 pounds, Ben was aware that he was hurting himself physically, but at that point he felt like a hopeless case. He had almost resigned himself to the idea that being fat was just who he was—that he would probably die young but couldn't do anything about it. He always thought about it, but the task of changing seemed too daunting. It was the difference between owing $5 and owing $500,000.

A GRANDMOTHER'S INTERVENTION

In December 2008, Ben was visiting his grandmother (Meemaw) over Christmas, and sensing his inner turmoil she asked him, "Ben, are you happy?" He instantly replied, "Yeah, of course I'm happy." But later that night, lying in bed, he realized, "Ben, you are not happy. You have to get your life together."

PEP TALK

BEN'S STRATEGIES FOR SUCCESS

BE PUBLIC. If you keep it to yourself, it will be easy to quit.

GET INVOLVED IN SOMETHING OFFICIAL. The feeling of being involved in something bigger will keep you motivated. Join a local running club, cycling group, or other activity. Being around people with like-minded goals will keep you coming back.

DO SOMETHING THAT YOU ENJOY. Running isn't for everyone, so don't do it if you don't like it. Instead, try cycling, rollerblading, walking, or whatever it is you like to do.

The very next morning Ben started a website, Ben Does Life. He wrote the address on a card and gave it to Meemaw for Christmas, explaining that it was his commitment to her to become healthy and happy. He told her she could follow his progress by checking into the website. She was thrilled. Here's what Ben wrote as his first entry:

December 25, 2008
It's Christmas.
This is a gift to myself, and to you. Follow along and watch me lose. It's going to be good.

The next thing Ben did was call his brother Jed, who needed to lose about 60 pounds. "I need a partner," he said. "Are you in?" Jed said yes, and the two brothers set off on their joint journey to health. The first thing they did was go grocery shopping together, which was a new experience because they'd never before really paid attention to what they put in their carts. It was tempting to just load up on weight loss shakes and protein bars, but instead they concentrated on finding real foods that were satisfying and also healthy. They bought loads of vegetables, fruit, yogurt, and other healthful items. They wanted to be smart about eating, and they had to teach themselves what that meant. They exchanged toaster pastries for English muffins and eliminated frozen pizzas in favor of fresh fish and meat. The idea was to consume 1,800 to 2,000 calories per day.

The brothers started running on the track. Very slowly at first, but since they were young men

---

SHOP SMART

WHAT'S IN BEN'S BASKET?

TILAPIA. I hear that fish is a healthy thing to eat and it's relatively simple to cook.

GREEN BEANS. Very simple and very tasty.

HIGH-FIBER CEREAL. I eat 24 "mini" whole-wheat biscuits with a cup of skim milk for breakfast.

ORANGES. A staple.

PEANUT BUTTER-PRETZEL NUTRITION BARS. 200 calories and very filling. Perfect for a midday snack.

EGGS. I go three egg whites, one yolk, with salsa.

TURKEY. Usually combined with two slices of whole wheat bread.

HEALTHY SOUP CUPS. Lower-calorie version of New England clam chowder. It's pretty good.

LOTS OF WATER. Obviously.

WHOLE WHEAT FROZEN WAFFLES. Great snack. Filling and delicious. Only 80 calories per waffle.

they were still able to move, even with the excess weight. After a couple weeks, Jed said casually, "I'm going to sign us up for a 5K."

"What's a 5K?" Ben asked. He couldn't imagine running a race when he could barely stumble around the track. But he went along with the idea. "Maybe it wasn't the smartest thing to do less than a month out," he laughs, "but it lit a fire."

Ben knew he had a very long way to go, so he got clear on his goals. They weren't just about weight but about life itself and how he pictured himself. He wrote on his blog, "This is a list of fitness-related things that I would like to happen within my lifetime."

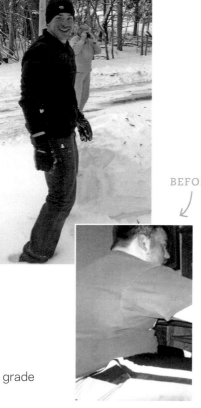

AFTER

BEFORE

- **Hit 220 pounds.** I think this would be my ideal weight. According to the BMI, it's still overweight for my height, but I disagree.
- **Size 36 (34?)** waist pants (currently 48).
- **Size Large T-shirt** (currently XXXL . . . depressing).
- **7-minute mile** (currently 11:44).
- **Go a full year and stay within 10 pounds of 220.**
- **Jog a marathon.** I'm 1/13 of the way there.
- **Complete a pull-up.** Haven't ever done one. Couldn't do one in 7th grade football; can't do one today.
- **Maintain a healthy lifestyle/dietary style.**
- **Convert myself to water-only for the most part.**
- **Touch the rim of a 10-foot basketball goal.**
- **Walk through a shopping mall and notice girls checking me out.**
- **Be competitive in some sort of triathlon or adventure race.**
- **Do 100 pushups without stopping** (currently 13).
- **Swim fast** (I don't know how to measure this, but today I did 50 meters in 49 seconds).
- **Don't die early** (currently on pace to die early).

Don't die early. The goal scrawled at the end of the list was actually the main game.

The weight came off quickly at first, and Ben found two factors really helped—his brother and his blog. Putting his journey out in the world was a form of accountability, especially from Meemaw, who logged in every day and sent him comments of love and support. Ben, who had practically become a recluse when he was overweight, now thrived on being around other people. After he'd lost his weight, he teamed up with Jed and their father, John, and ran marathons and did the Iron Man triathlon. Hugging each other afterwards, Ben felt the happiest he'd been in his life. Now Ben, Jed, and John have a company called Do Life, and they organize races and give inspirational talks to groups all over the country.

"Everything got better after I lost the weight," Ben says, "but it wasn't just the physical change. People responded to me because I was more positive, friendly, and full of the joy of life."

BEN'S DAILY DIET COMPARISONS

BEFORE	AFTER
Breakfast	**Breakfast**
Two bowls of cereal with whole milk	English muffin with peanut butter
	Banana
Lunch	**Lunch**
Fast food: Two double cheeseburgers, large fries, large sweet tea	Small bowl of soup and sandwich
Dinner	**Dinner**
Fried chicken sandwich with mayo	Spaghetti with tomato sauce
Chips and queso	Salad
Peanut butter milkshake	
Snacks	**Snacks**
Tacos	String cheese
Frozen sandwiches and entrées	Tortilla chips
Pizza	Fresh fruit

JOY'S WORDS OF ADVICE

EXERCISE TO LIFT YOUR SPIRITS

By the time Ben decided to "do life," he was in a state of depression. His instinct to focus on aerobic exercise was a good one because every time he got out on the track his body released brain chemicals that lifted his mood. Those same brain chemicals also had the effect of calming his anxieties and making him feel less stressed. On top of that, achieving new mileage or time goals was empowering and helped motivate Ben to keep going.

EXERCISE IS A MOOD-LIFTING BONANZA. While the positive chemicals are doing their job, you begin to feel better as you see results. It also helps keep you on track. When you start the day off with a workout, you don't want to undo your hard work with poor food choices.

SARAH FORD

FROM Hagerstown, Maryland
AGE 32 | HEIGHT 5' 6"
BEFORE WEIGHT 265 | AFTER WEIGHT 155 | POUNDS LOST 110

Sarah always excelled at everything she tried. She had an outgoing personality and lots of friends. She used to say to herself, "I may be fat, but I can be the best." But her drive to succeed masked a deep dissatisfaction and a low self-esteem that came from being overweight all her life. There was never a time when she wasn't concerned about her weight. As a child she was always heavier than other kids her age and even weighed more than her older brother. Food was her comfort during two major family moves. When Sarah was 7, they relocated from Massachusetts to South East Asia and then to Maryland when she was 13. As she tried to adjust to a return to life in the United States, at a very vulnerable age, Sarah increasingly turned to food for comfort and was a very emotional eater. She was ashamed that she couldn't control her eating habits or weight, and she fell into a vicious cycle of shame, which led to more overeating. During Sarah's high school years, food was the answer to feelings of boredom, sadness, anger—and even to excitement and happiness. It was her friend and companion, always there to comfort her. She gorged in secret, hiding her actual intake from others, but her weight told the true story. Her family often commented on her weight out of genuine concern, but it embarrassed her to talk about it, and she couldn't help hearing judgment in their voices. She interpreted any comment as ridicule. It was her way of putting up barriers and letting people know it wasn't safe to talk to her about this issue.

AFTER

BEFORE

During college and early adulthood Sarah threw her energies into taking care of other people, both personally and professionally, and ignored her own needs. She was passionate about helping at-risk kids achieve their full potential, but she sometimes wondered how she could inspire and motivate them to be their best if she wasn't doing it for herself. She felt like a liar. She went through many years of losing the same 30 or 40 pounds, but gained it back and then some. At age 27, she hit her highest weight of 265 pounds. She was physically and emotionally exhausted, and she felt as if she were drowning in the extra pounds. She had so many things that she wanted to do with her life, both professionally and personally, but her weight was holding her back.

"I always knew I was a good person, smart and talented, with many things to offer," Sarah says. "But I felt that people judged me based on my weight and physical appearance rather than seeing me as an interesting person who had something valuable to offer. I guess in some ways I judged myself as well, feeling that I was somehow insignificant or inadequate because I was so heavy." Sarah learned to use a quick smile or a big laugh to hide her misery. The people around her didn't see that she was so down she had trouble talking herself out of bed every day. And although she had wonderful, close friends, they, too, became a source of anxiety. When her friends asked her to be in their weddings, she was honored by the privilege but also embarrassed and ashamed by her appearance on their special day.

Sarah's biggest food problem was white, starchy carbohydrates. She craved bread and ate white starch at just about every meal—the equivalent of 20 slices of white bread a day. She'd eat pancakes for breakfast, a breaded chicken sandwich with fries for lunch, pasta and bread for dinner, and chips and cookies in between. She rarely ate fresh vegetables or fruit. And while she knew she was poisoning her body, Sarah was in such a funk that she found stopping it impossible.

A TURNING POINT

At 27, Sarah started graduate school, but she felt as if she were drowning. She was exhausted all the time and terribly uncomfortable in her body. During her first semester she watched one of her

---

PEP TALK

SARAH'S STRATEGIES FOR SUCCESS

DON'T BE A COUCH POTATO. If you're going to watch TV, move while you watch.

KEEP EATING. Eat throughout the day, with six small meals or three meals and one to two snacks to avoid hunger.

IF YOU HIT A PLATEAU. Make a change in your diet and/or exercise plan to get you right back on track.

TAKE IT ONE DAY AT A TIME.

classmates lose 50 pounds and she was awed. She felt a tiny glimmer of hope, thinking, "If she can do it, why can't I?"

She thought about it a lot and kept coming back to the same realization that her classmate's experience had showed what was possible, and she wanted to change. She felt a shiver of excitement at the thought. One morning Sarah woke up and decided to do it. She was tired of being fat, tired of being tired, and tired of missing out on her life because she was so unhealthy and unhappy with herself. It was time to stop feeling sorry for herself and blaming her problems on her weight. There was no big earth-shaking revelation, just a change in attitude and the simple will to do it. "I felt I was responsible for being overweight, and therefore it was up to me to be responsible for being healthy," she said.

HOW TO CHANGE?

The day after she made her decision, Sarah went out and bought a treadmill. She set it up in her living room and made a rule that if she was going to watch TV, she had to be walking on the treadmill, not sitting on the couch. She started very slowly and soon worked up to a 20-minute walk at 3 miles per hour.

She decided not to follow a specific diet but to become more educated and conscious about healthy eating. She cleared all the junk out of her kitchen and pantry and started from scratch. Like many people, she already knew the kinds of foods that were good for her—lean proteins and fresh fruits and vegetables—but creating a diet that worked was more complicated. Awareness was key. She began paying attention to when and why she was eating, and she trained herself to recognize when her hunger was real and when it was just the result of boredom or emotions. She would do this by pausing before she ate and examining her mood and her circumstances: What had she already eaten recently? Was it sufficient? Was she bored or feeling stressed? Was her stomach rumbling? By employing a bit of mindfulness to the process, she was able to decide whether she needed food . . . or really just needed some kind of diversion.

Sarah's main downfall had always been portion sizes. She couldn't seem to manage the amount of food she was eating. As a teenager, she would purchase boxes of donuts, cookies, or pastries and eat the entire package in one sitting. In college she always went for the high-fat and high-calorie choices in the dining hall. She'd eat large servings of fried food, ice cream, and lots of bread. During the early years of her career she relied on fast-food lunches and dinners. Even when she ate healthier foods, the portions were double or triple what they should have been. She purchased a food scale and measuring cups and spoons and began measuring her foods, retraining herself to recognize simple portions. In the beginning she felt hungry, but she was learning what real hunger felt like. "I hadn't been hungry in many years," she says. Organization was also a lifesaver for Sarah. She created menus for each day of the week and shopped only for those ingredients.

Sarah's greatest motivation was seeing how quickly the initial weight came off. Within the first month she'd lost 25 pounds, and she felt proud and satisfied with her progress. It's not that it was smooth sailing all the way. It took four years for Sarah to take off the weight, but she did it slowly and steadily, and she learned to ride the waves of change and disappointment in the process. "Life happens in the midst of losing weight," Sarah says, and her life was full of upheaval. She finished

PLATEAU MAGIC

Sarah struggled with plateaus and backtracking along the way. There are three truths about plateaus. One, everyone has them. Two, they're frustrating. Three, this too shall pass if you stick with your plan and make a few tweaks. The scale typically comes to a halt for one of two reasons: You've unintentionally become more lax with what you're eating or your metabolism has decreased in response to losing a significant amount of weight. As your body shrinks, so do your daily calorie needs, so what was working for you at your heavier starting weight may no longer be working for you at your new, slimmer weight. Unfair, but that's a scientific reality. When you hit a plateau, don't lose heart. Pat yourself on the back for what you've already accomplished, stay the course, and make some minor adjustments to get moving again.

GET MORE EXERCISE. Add an extra 10 minutes a day to your aerobic exercise and you'll burn an additional 50 to 100 calories.

EVALUATE YOUR CALORIES. Keep a detailed food journal for a few days if you're not already doing so. If your daily calories have increased because you've loosened up on the reins, it's time to hunker down and get back to your original plan. If your calories haven't changed, find a small way to shave about 100 calories off your daily total. For example, change your afternoon snack from pita chips and hummus to celery and hummus. Or replace a handful of nuts with an orange. Or eliminate one bread serving a day by eating your sandwich open-face on a single slice.

CUT A CARB. Potatoes, brown rice, and whole grain pasta can be healthy choices in moderation. But if you've hit a plateau, replacing these starchy carbs with an extra serving of veggies three or four nights a week can kick your weight loss into gear again.

DON'T GO TO EXTREMES. Sometimes the best solution is to wait out the plateau. Whatever you do, don't make any drastic changes, overexercise, or starve yourself. Being unreasonably strict could end up backfiring and cause you to abandon ship altogether.

graduate school, changed jobs, and moved, only to find that she wasn't happy with her new city. Being far away from her family made her lonely, and some of her old eating patterns started creeping back. "In the past I wouldn't have noticed that I was gaining 5 pounds here or there," she says. But the new Sarah recognized the setback and the plateau.

She moved back home. She also bumped her exercise program up a notch. She began looking for a challenge that would help her get back on track. She and her sister-in-law decided to run in a triathlon, and after six months of training they took part in the Go Diva Women's Triathlon in Philadelphia—something she would never have believed possible before.

A NEW ATTITUDE

The experience of losing more than 100 pounds gave Sarah much more than a fantastic new body. It also gave her a new attitude and outlook on life. She now views food and health as a priority. She understands that food is the fuel needed for life and something that should be enjoyed that way. In the process, Sarah's confidence and self-esteem have strengthened. "I don't believe I have changed at the core of myself," she says. "I am still—and will always be—me. But I now approach each day with the confidence and belief that I can accomplish anything that I set my mind to and have the energy and determination to follow through on that belief."

SARAH'S DAILY DIET COMPARISONS

BEFORE	AFTER
Breakfast	**Breakfast**
4-5 servings of pancakes with butter and syrup Coffee	Greek yogurt mixed with 1 cup fresh fruit and ½ cup high-fiber cereal Coffee
Lunch	**Lunch**
Fast food: Fried chicken sandwich, fries Large regular soda	Egg white and cheese on bagel thin Banana
Dinner	**Dinner**
Huge bowl of pasta Bread Large regular soda	Grilled chicken breast ½ cup brown rice 1 cup steamed vegetables
Snacks	**Snacks**
1-2 packages chocolate mini donuts 4-5 cookies Large bag of microwave popcorn with butter	Apple with 1 teaspoon peanut butter Sugar-free gelatin or pudding cup Low-fat string cheese Hard-cooked eggs

Spinach and Black Bean Enchiladas

BY Sarah Ford
MAKES 6 enchiladas
SERVING SIZE 1 enchilada

Oil spray
½ medium onion, diced
½ sweet pepper (any color), diced
1 clove garlic, minced
1 8-ounce can tomato sauce, preferably no-salt-added
¾ teaspoon chili powder
¾ teaspoon ground cumin
¼ teaspoon dried oregano
½ teaspoon kosher salt
8 cups baby spinach leaves

1 15-ounce can black beans, preferably no-salt-added or low-sodium, rinsed and drained
6 6-inch whole grain tortillas
½ cup nonfat sour cream
2 teaspoons lime juice
1 cup shredded reduced-fat Mexican cheese blend
2 plum tomatoes, diced (optional)
2 green onions, thinly sliced (optional)

1 Preheat the oven to 350°F. Coat a 9×13-inch casserole dish with oil spray.

2 Liberally coat a large sauté pan with oil spray and preheat over medium heat. Add the onion, pepper, and garlic and cook, stirring, until the veggies are soft, 5 to 7 minutes. Add the tomato sauce, chili powder, cumin, oregano, and salt and simmer over medium-low heat for 5 minutes. Add the spinach leaves and continue turning the mixture until the spinach is completely wilted down. Stir in the beans.

3 Spoon one-sixth of the spinach-bean mixture down the center of a tortilla and roll into a tube shape. Place the tortilla, seam side down, in the prepared casserole dish. Repeat with the remaining tortillas.

4 Bake, uncovered, for 15 minutes. While the enchiladas are baking, in a small bowl stir together the sour cream and lime juice.

5 Remove the enchiladas from the oven and spread the sour cream mixture evenly over the top. Sprinkle the enchiladas evenly with the cheese, tomatoes, and green onions. Bake for 5 to 10 minutes or until cheese is melted.

NUTRITION INFORMATION Calories: 271, Protein: 16 g, Total Fat: 7 g, Saturated Fat: 3 g, Cholesterol: 15 mg, Sodium: 580 mg, Carbohydrate: 36 g, Fiber: 8 g

Chicken Cutlets Italian-Style

BY Sarah Ford
MAKES 4 servings
SERVING SIZE 1 chicken breast

Oil spray
4 boneless, skinless chicken breasts
2 large egg whites
½ cup bread crumbs (preferably whole wheat)
½ cup grated Parmesan cheese
1½ cups jarred marinara sauce

1 Preheat the oven to 450°F. Liberally coat a baking sheet with oil spray.

2 Place one chicken breast between two sheets of plastic wrap or waxed paper. Pound and flatten to a ½-inch thickness using a rolling pin or a small, heavy skillet. Repeat with the remaining chicken breasts.

3 In a shallow bowl lightly beat the egg whites. In a second shallow bowl combine the bread crumbs and ¼ cup of the Parmesan cheese.

4 Dip each chicken breast in the egg whites. Allow the excess egg to drip off and then coat the chicken in the bread crumb-cheese mixture. Place the chicken on the prepared baking sheet and repeat the breading process with the remaining chicken breasts. Bake the chicken for 15 to 18 minutes, turning once about halfway through, until the chicken reaches an internal temperature of 160°F.

5 While the chicken is baking, heat the marinara sauce in a small saucepan over low heat.

6 Top the chicken breasts with the warm marinara sauce and sprinkle each chicken breast with 1 tablespoon grated Parmesan cheese.

NUTRITION INFORMATION Calories: 342, Protein: 47 g, Total Fat: 7 g, Saturated Fat: 2.5 g, Cholesterol: 105 mg, Sodium: 515 mg, Carbohydrate: 19 g, Fiber: 3 g

TAMARA FORTUNE

FROM Smyrna, Tennessee
AGE 32 | HEIGHT 5' 4"
BEFORE WEIGHT 278 | AFTER WEIGHT 137 | POUNDS LOST 141

AFTER

BEFORE

In a sense, Tamara was living a double life. At home she was surrounded by love, married to a man who adored her for herself and told her she was beautiful every day. She had two children who gave her tremendous joy. In the embrace of her family she was incredibly happy and confident. But out in the world she felt judged and dismissed because of her weight. This dichotomy tore Tamara apart emotionally because she wanted to be happy and she was an openhearted, social person by nature. But the world outside made it very hard for her to feel comfortable.

Tamara worked as a server at a restaurant, a physically demanding job but one she enjoyed. What she didn't enjoy was public attention, which often verged on ridicule. She didn't even want to go to Walmart because she knew people were staring at her. As her weight topped 250 pounds, she was very aware of the funny looks restaurant customers gave her—like how can you possibly do this job at your size? Going to stores, especially to buy clothes, was a torment. She found that some people—especially the skinny sales reps—could be just plain mean. She never got used to receiving dirty looks from people because of her weight. She felt anything but happy and confident. Instead she usually felt down and self-conscious in these settings.

For a long time Tamara tried to put her hurt feelings and shame behind her because her home life was so great. Tamara and Jason were truly a love match.

They met on the Internet, chatted for two days, and then agreed to meet in person. Tamara took her son from a previous relationship along on their first date, announcing, "We're a package deal." That was fine with Jason. Within 30 days they moved in together, and they were soon married. Jason adopted Tamara's son and they added to the family with the birth of a daughter. Their life together would have been blissful, except that Tamara was miserable about her increasing weight.

TIRED OF BEING FAT

Tamara still remembers the day, Sunday, August 17, 2008, when her life changed. It was her daughter's fourth birthday. She had worked for four hours at the restaurant, Sunday being its busiest day, and then she went to the local fast-food joint and play center, where the party was being held. She was so exhausted that she sank down onto a bench and couldn't move. She couldn't help her daughter open presents. She couldn't help her husband corral the children. She couldn't help cut the cake. She'd never felt so low, but it was the moment she decided to act.

The next day she went into work and told a friend, "I am going to lose this weight."

Her friend rolled her eyes and said, "Yeah, right. As much as you eat fast food, I'll believe it when I see it."

Tamara was truly scared to death. Was she ready? Could she do it? But she was just so tired of being fat, and that motivated her.

She started very small and told her husband, "I'm just going to make a few minor changes." She'd order grilled instead of fried chicken and add steamed vegetables or a salad. But the biggest change was getting educated. She found a website that helped her create a food log and count calories and fat grams. And once she made small, but meaningful changes, the once unmovable weight began to drop off.

PEP TALK

TAMARA'S STRATEGIES FOR SUCCESS

- Split a meal at the restaurant to save calories and money.
- Start with the little things, such as grilled chicken instead of fried.
- When you have a craving, eat a piece of fruit.
- Stick to your guns. Do it for you and no one else.

TAMARA'S DAILY DIET COMPARISONS

BEFORE	AFTER
Breakfast	**Breakfast**
Fast-food cheeseburger	1 slice whole wheat bread
Fries with white gravy	Banana
Lemon berry slushie	2 tablespoons sugar-free syrup
Lunch	**Lunch**
10-piece chicken nuggets	Sandwich-ready tuna salad pack
Large soda	Whole tomato
Apple pie	3 ounces carrots
Dinner	**Dinner**
Restaurant meal:	Home-cooked meal:
Fried chicken and mashed potatoes smothered in gravy	4 ounces lean ground turkey
Bacon-soaked collard greens and black-eyed peas	Fat-free corn tortillas
Bread and butter	4 tablespoons salsa
Large slice of pie with ice cream	Low-salt canned green beans
Snacks	**Snacks**
Chips, candy, cookies, ice cream, soda	Fresh veggies and fruit
	Low-calorie ice cream bars

TAMARA'S PANTRY

BEFORE	AFTER
2-liter bottle regular soda	Skim milk
4–5 chocolate bars	Oatmeal
Bag of chips	High-fiber bread
Bag of cheese puffs	Ground turkey breast
Chocolate sandwich cookies	Chicken breast
Cinnamon rolls (from the bakery)	Grapes
Whole milk	Strawberries
White bread	Cauliflower
Snack cakes	Bagged salad greens
Sugary breakfast cereal	Whole grain cereal
	Low-calorie ice cream bars

"CAN'T NEVER COULD"

Even with her success, Tamara realized she had to conquer those inner demons. She became more aware of how unhealthy the obsession with weight could be. One day she was going through a security line at the airport; she forgot she had a bottle of water tucked into her computer bag. The female security agent grabbed the bottle and commented, "Leave it to the skinny person to want water." Tamara laughed at the irony of it. After a lifetime of being ridiculed for her weight, she couldn't believe she was being ridiculed for being thinner! She guessed that people's obsession with weight cut both ways and thought it was a sad commentary.

But she doesn't have time for resenting small slights. Tamara has been driven to help others. A friend confessed, "I can't do what you did." Tamara encouraged her, saying, "Sure you can. Remember, can't never could." She worked with her and was gratified when the friend lost 60 pounds.

Tamara has a sense of humor about her struggle, especially when she has cravings. She imagines she has a devil on her shoulder telling her, "Go for it. You know you want it." When her husband recognizes her frame of mind during those "devil" encounters, he'll shout, "Go get a banana!"

To her surprise Tamara has discovered that she now craves wholesome foods. She enjoys eating healthfully and she loves going to the gym. "I'm at the gym every morning at 4:30, and it doesn't even open until 5," she laughs. But the best thing is being able to go outside and run and play with her children.

Tamara enjoys telling of an experience she had on *Today* when she appeared on my segment. She was in the Green Room waiting to go on, and her "before" picture flashed on the screen. "Everyone gasped. They said, 'Oh my God, look at her.' They didn't know I was sitting right there." Little did she know that they gasped even louder when I revealed her transformation on air an hour later.

NUTRITION LABEL EDUCATION

Tamara had to get educated about healthy eating. One of the best places to start is with food labels. What do all those numbers mean? Let's do a rundown.

SERVING SIZE AND SERVINGS PER CONTAINER. Pay attention to this because everything else is based on it. Package sizes can trick you. Something that looks like one serving might be listed as two, and if you don't notice you'll be eating twice as much as you thought.

CALORIES. This refers to the number of calories in one serving.

CALORIES FROM FAT. The number of calories in a single serving that come from fat.

TOTAL FAT. The amount of fat in a serving. The different types of fat are often broken down:
■ Saturated fat is mainly found in fatty cuts of meat, butter, whole milk, cheese, and other high-fat dairy foods. Eat as little as possible because this type can raise bad cholesterol.
■ Trans fat has been shown to lower HDL ("good") cholesterol and increase LDL ("bad") cholesterol. If you spot "partially hydrogenated oil," the product contains some trans fat.
■ Polyunsaturated and monounsaturated fats are healthy fats found in vegetable oils, nuts, seeds, and fatty fish. They're associated with a decreased risk of heart disease and diabetes.

CHOLESTEROL. Only animal products contain cholesterol, so plant-based foods will have a 0 in this category. The American Heart Association recommends that healthy people eat less than 300 mg per day; those with heart disease should eat less than 200 mg.

SODIUM. Everyone should aim for a total daily intake of 2,300 mg or less, and certain populations (individuals with high blood pressure, folks 40 and older, and African Americans) are advised to consume no more than 1,500 mg per day.

TOTAL CARBOHYDRATE. If you've been diagnosed with diabetes, be aware of the total number of carbohydrates you eat because carbs raise blood sugar.

DIETARY FIBER. Experts recommend 25 to 35 g total fiber daily for most people. Products are considered a good source if they have 2.5 to 4.9 grams per serving; those with 5+ grams can officially be called "high fiber."

SUGARS. This category lists total sugars, including both natural sugars (from fruit and dairy products) and added sugars (from cane sugar, corn syrup, honey, syrups, and other sweeteners). You can determine the major source(s) of sugar in a product by examining the ingredients list; if the product doesn't contain much whole fruit or unsweetened dairy (i.e., plain yogurt and skim milk), you'll know the sugar grams are coming from added sugars.

INGREDIENTS. Check here for ingredients to avoid or limit, including added sugars and partially hydrogenated vegetable oil (the main source of unhealthy trans fats).

Triple-Berry Muffins

BY Tamara Fortune
MAKES 12 muffins
SERVING SIZE 1 muffin

Oil spray

Topping
1 tablespoon butter, softened
¼ cup packed brown sugar
½ teaspoon ground cinnamon

Batter
2 cups whole wheat flour
2 teaspoons baking powder
¼ teaspoon baking soda
½ teaspoon kosher salt
½ cup granulated sugar
1 cup 100% orange juice
½ cup unsweetened (natural) applesauce
2 large eggs, lightly beaten
1 cup frozen mixed berries
½ cup walnuts, finely chopped (optional)

1 Preheat the oven to 350°F. Generously coat a 12-cup muffin pan with oil spray.

2 For the topping, in a small bowl combine the butter, brown sugar, and cinnamon.

3 For the batter, in a large bowl combine the flour, baking powder, baking soda, salt, and sugar. In another large bowl whisk together the orange juice, applesauce, and eggs. Add the orange juice mixture to the flour mixture. Fold the batter with a rubber spatula until just combined; do not overmix. Gently fold in the frozen berries and walnuts (if using). Evenly divide the batter among the prepared muffin cups. Sprinkle each muffin with the sugar-cinnamon topping mixture.

4 Bake for 20 to 25 minutes or until a toothpick inserted in the center of a muffin comes out clean. Cool for 10 minutes before removing muffins from pan.

NUTRITION INFORMATION (WITH WALNUTS) Calories: 190, Protein: 5 g, Total Fat: 5 g, Saturated Fat: 1 g, Cholesterol: 40 mg, Sodium: 135 mg, Carbohydrate: 33 g, Fiber: 3 g, Total Sugar: 17 g

Peanut Butter and Apple Oatmeal

BY Tamara Fortune
MAKES 1 serving
SERVING SIZE 1½ cups

½ cup rolled oats
½ Granny Smith apple, diced
1 tablespoon natural peanut butter
1 teaspoon sugar or sugar substitute (optional)
½ teaspoon ground cinnamon

1 Prepare the oats with water according to package directions. Stir in the apple, peanut butter, sugar or sugar substitute (if using), and cinnamon.

NUTRITION INFORMATION Calories: 340, Protein: 9 g, Total Fat: 11 g, Saturated Fat: 2 g, Cholesterol: 0 mg, Sodium: 60 mg, Carbohydrate: 53 g, Fiber: 9 g

Turkey Tostadas with Homemade Salsa

BY Tamara Fortune
MAKES 4 servings
SERVING SIZE 2 tostadas

Oil spray
1¼ pounds ground turkey (at least 90% lean)
½ teaspoon onion powder
½ teaspoon garlic powder
½ teaspoon black pepper
½ teaspoon kosher salt
8 6-inch corn tortillas

½ cup shredded reduced-fat Mexican cheese blend
1 cup shredded lettuce
1 cup chopped tomatoes
½ cup Homemade Salsa (see recipe below)
½ cup light sour cream

1 Liberally coat a large skillet with oil spray and heat over medium-high heat. Add the ground turkey, onion and garlic powders, pepper, and salt and break up the turkey with a wooden spoon. Cook, stirring occasionally, until the turkey is fully cooked, 7 to 10 minutes.

2 Preheat the broiler to high and coat 2 large baking sheets with oil spray. Place 4 corn tortillas in a single layer on each baking sheet. Mist the tops of the tortillas with oil spray and place under the broiler for 3 to 4 minutes. Flip the tortillas over and cook for 2 minutes or until golden brown and crispy. (Prepare the tortillas in two batches if your oven cannot hold 2 baking sheets on one level.)

3 Divide the ground turkey mixture among the 8 tortillas. Top each tortilla with 1 tablespoon cheese, 2 tablespoons each lettuce and tomatoes, 1 tablespoon salsa, and 1 tablespoon sour cream.

NUTRITION INFORMATION Calories: 341, Protein: 38 g, Total Fat: 12 g, Saturated Fat: 4.5 g, Cholesterol: 105 mg, Sodium: 415 mg, Carbohydrate: 19 g, Fiber: 2 g

Homemade Salsa

BY Tamara Fortune
MAKES 16 servings (about 2 cups total)
SERVING SIZE 2 tablespoons

5 plum tomatoes, roughly chopped
2 whole jalapeños, seeds and ribs removed
5 cloves garlic, peeled

½ medium white onion, roughly chopped
¼ cup fresh cilantro
½ teaspoon kosher salt

1 Combine all of the ingredients in a food processor; pulse until salsa reaches desired consistency.

NUTRITION INFORMATION Calories: 7, Protein: 0 g, Total Fat: 0 g, Saturated Fat: 0 g, Cholesterol: 0 mg, Sodium: 35 mg, Carbohydrate: 2 g, Fiber: 0 g

HOWARD DINOWITZ

FROM Morganville, New Jersey
AGE 54 | HEIGHT 5' 10"
BEFORE WEIGHT 388 | AFTER WEIGHT 170 | POUNDS LOST 218

AFTER

BEFORE

Howard grew up as part of one big, happy, food-oriented Jewish family in the Bronx. They lived in an apartment building with extended family members, and Howard's main form of exercise was running up and down the stairs for meals. He was a chubby kid and the children at school teased him, calling him "Dino the Dinosaur." His loving family always told him, "Don't listen to them. You look fine—look at that smile!" The unconditional love of his family was like a warm blanket for Howard. He could eat and not suffer. He remembers his childhood as being happy and full of support.

When he graduated high school, Howard took a good look at himself and the world around him and said, "It's time to meet a girl." So he went on an extreme diet, got his weight down to 150 pounds, and met Bonnie, who would be the love of his life for the next 30 years. They have three children—a daughter and two sons—and I adore their entire family.

One day, early in their relationship, Bonnie told him, "I think you're too thin." Howard's mother, overhearing the remark, laughed and said, "Never tell him he's too thin." She knew better. In response to Bonnie's comment, Howard loosened the diet reins and was off and running with excessive food intake. By the wedding Howard's weight had started to climb back up. That's no surprise. For one thing, his extreme, semi-starvation diet was not sustainable, and Howard had not changed his head regarding food. Why change? Howard was a happy guy, and food was a central part of that happy lifestyle.

Part of Howard's issue with eating was that he had an extremely busy practice as a podiatrist. He was up at the crack of dawn every day and didn't get home until after dark. He had a long commute, and he stocked the car with food to relieve the boredom of the drive.

Howard loved his work, and food was both a reward and a form of entertainment. He always arrived at the office with a dozen donuts or candy. If he performed a successful surgery, he'd celebrate with a cinnamon bun. He often ate in hiding, while he was driving or in his private office. Spending hours in the car every day (in what he would later refer to as his "suicide drive") was a big part of Howard's overeating. He'd stop at a 7-11 or a fast-food restaurant at the beginning of his commute, load up his car with junk food, and gorge the whole way. He came to associate driving with eating. An extra 200 pounds "snuck up" on him over a period of 30 years at a rate of six or seven pounds a year. "First you go from 200 to 250 pounds . . . then from 250 to 300 pounds . . . then from 300 to 350 pounds, and so on," he says, explaining how he grew larger and larger, almost without noticing it.

Howard had a distorted picture of himself in his mind. He calls it "a skinny head in a fat body." He thought he looked fine at all weights, and in his mind he was a lot thinner than he was. Bonnie would say, "Don't you look in the mirror?" He'd reply, "Yes, to shave—and only the top of my chin."

Howard treated around 200 patients a week in his busy practice. A 75-year-old man weighing 165 pounds might be healthy and chipper, while a 45-year-old man weighing 300 pounds would drag himself into the office. Howard noticed the difference, but he never made the connection with his own situation. A doctor once said to Howard, "How many people do you have in your practice who are over 350 pounds and over 60 years old?" He said, "None. They'd be dead if they were over 60 and more than 300 pounds. I get your point." That was a big eye-opener for Howard.

On a deep level Howard knew he was shortchanging himself and Bonnie too. He would make excuses for staying home while she went out, and then he'd drive over to a fast-food restaurant. Bonnie, who had always maintained a weight of 120 pounds, never made Howard feel

PEP TALK

HOWARD'S STRATEGIES FOR SUCCESS

- Eat slowly, giving your body 5 to 10 minutes to respond. Listen to your body.
- Fill up on the right choice as much as you would on the wrong choice.
- Try to eat a low-fat, high-fiber diet. The fat will melt off your body.
- Don't make it complicated. The trick is to find something that's tasty and filling.
- Read labels.
- Chew sugarless gum.
- Commit to making your health a priority.

uncomfortable, but he was embarrassed to be seen in public with her because he was so large. Once on a cruise—which Howard refers to as another name for "eating orgy"—he and Bonnie were dancing to the Village People song "YMCA," and he saw himself in a mirror. "I looked just like a big gorilla, jiggling like crazy," he says. He wondered, momentarily, how Bonnie could stand it.

His children also suffered. Howard gave an annual talk at their school and brought foot-shaped chocolates. The other kids would tease them unmercifully about their "fat dad"—sometimes within his hearing. Howard knew his children loved him, but what kid wants to be teased that way? They should have been proud that their dad was coming to the school; instead they probably dreaded it. That knowledge hurt Howard. Like all dads, he wanted his kids to look up to him, but he wondered how they could.

HOWARD'S AHA! MOMENT

Howard had always been especially close to his uncle, and when he died, Howard lost a great friend and anchor. His funeral was at Riverside Chapel on the Upper West Side of Manhattan, and the chapel was packed. Howard was scheduled to deliver some remarks, and he was sitting in the crowded chapel, surrounded by his family, just pouring sweat. When it came time to speak, he made a move and realized that he could not get out of the pew. So he just stood up in place and said, "I loved him dearly," and sat back down. He tried to make it appear that he was just too

HOWARD'S DAILY DIET COMPARISONS

BEFORE	AFTER

Breakfast
2 bagels with cream cheese and lox
Fried eggs
Hash browns
	Breakfast
	Egg white Western omelet with salsa,
	   mushroom, onion
	or
	Bowl of high-fiber cereal with skim milk,
	   handful of strawberries

Lunch Large order take-out Chinese or pizza at noon and a second take-out lunch at 4 p.m.	**Lunch** Turkey sandwich with one slice of bread, piled with veggies
Dinner On the way home from work around 8 p.m., stop at gas station or convenience store and buy hot dogs, chips, cookies, chocolate bars, soda, and enough food to make it home. Once home, he'd eat again.	**Dinner** Veggie burger Fruit and carrot sticks Sugar-free ice pops

emotionally distraught to go up to the microphone, but he felt horrible that he could not do this one last tribute for his uncle. As he sat glumly through the rest of the service, he thought, "I'm going to be the next one up there in a coffin if I don't do something about my weight." Just as he was thinking, "There has to be a breaking point," the pew he was sitting on actually broke from his weight.

After the service Howard and Bonnie went out for breakfast at a local coffee shop. As he ate his bagel with cream cheese and lox, Howard looked his wife in the eye and said, "This is the last time I'm going to eat anything fattening." She smiled, not knowing where he was coming from—and not believing him.

But that was really it for Howard. When he got home, he took out a piece of paper and a pen and began writing down his strategy. As a doctor he was not ignorant of nutrition; it was just a matter of applying the principles in a way that worked for him. He knew that if he cut out sugar, flour, and salt, his hunger signals, triggered by too much insulin, would readjust and he wouldn't crave food so much. He actually found that when he ate less food he was not as hungry. He also knew he had to bring consciousness to the table. He had been eating mindlessly for so long he didn't even know what he was putting in his mouth.

One day, while Howard was still formulating his plan, he was walking through a street fair when he came across an old New York City Board of Health Manual from 1948. He was intrigued by the diet formula in the book. It included a set of rules.

RULE 1: FIND YOUR IDEAL WEIGHT. For Howard, the number was deemed to be 170 pounds.

RULE 2: SET YOUR DAILY CALORIES BY MULTIPLYING YOUR TARGET WEIGHT BY 10. For Howard, that number was 1,700.

RULE 3: EAT LOW-FAT, HIGH-FIBER FOODS. Avoid fatty food, greasy food. And if you want to lose faster, eat a little less.

The manual advised that if you stuck to the plan, you'd be at your target weight in one year. Howard was intrigued. He thought it was good, old-fashioned horse sense and realized that he didn't have to do anything extravagant—just follow some basic rules. He adopted a motto: KIS—Keep It Simple.

Along the way Howard used little tricks. For example, he kept every serving of meat or fish about the size of a deck of cards to keep his portions in control. He'd divide the day into three parts and budget 500 calories for each part. He'd tell waiters he was allergic to butter and oil so they'd take him seriously about removing them from his entrée. At first he would entertain himself with the radio during his commute, although within a few weeks he noticed he wasn't hungry on the way home anymore. With his long hours, Howard didn't have time to join a health club, but he devised his own program of simple calisthenics and weights.

As Howard lost weight, he relished the positive reinforcement from patients, staff, and other doctors. Someone told him, "You just bought yourself another 20 years of life," and he knew it was true. But the biggest rewards happened in the present moment—in the new energy he had for family and work, in the complete disappearance of his medical symptoms, in looking in a full-length mirror—not just the shaving mirror anymore—and being content with the image he saw. Of course, most people thought he'd had gastric bypass surgery, which is a common assumption made about Joy Fit Club members. Howard would regularly get into arguments:

"You definitely had the surgery."

"No, I did it on my own."

"Impossible. You're lying."

At a podiatry convention, shortly after he lost the weight, people didn't recognize him. They'd ask, "Have you seen Howie?" On more than one occasion he had to show his driver's license to prove he was really Howard Dinowitz. He gets a big kick out of describing that experience.

Howard can now acknowledge that he was worried about his credibility as a doctor when he was overweight. "When you're heavy, people think you're sloppy and out of control," he says. "How could they want you to be their doctor?" He feels as if patients respond to him much better now and trust him more. And although Howard never lacked self-confidence, he experiences a new kind of confidence now. "It's nice when your wife says, 'You look hot,'" he says, smiling.

SIZING UP YOUR DINNER PLATE

Howard found that visualization was a good way to keep his portion sizes in check. Here are a few helpful visuals:

- 3 ounces of beef, pork, poultry, or a thick fish fillet: a deck of cards or the palm of your hand
- 3 ounces of a thin fish fillet: checkbook
- 5 ounces of beef, pork, poultry, or a thick fish fillet: 1½ decks of cards
- ½ cup of cottage cheese or yogurt: half a baseball
- 1 ounce of cheese: 4 dice or your thumb
- ½ cup of cooked pasta or rice: half a baseball
- 1 teaspoon of peanut butter, mayo, or salad dressing: 1 die or the tip of your thumb

JAMIE FRANCISCO

FROM Wolcott, Connecticut
AGE 35 | HEIGHT 5' 6"
BEFORE WEIGHT 230 | AFTER WEIGHT 125 | POUNDS LOST 105

As a child Jamie was known as "the chubby one." Her four
sisters were all tall and slender, and she was always about
30 pounds overweight. Growing up in an Italian household,
she was taught that it was good to have a "healthy appetite."
It was a strict requirement that everyone finish everything
on their plates, and the portions were large. In Jamie's
case this led to chronic overeating. She didn't know why
her willowy sisters didn't also gain weight. That seemed
totally unfair, as if she were the only one who was punished
for doing what everyone else did. The only other person
in the house who struggled with weight was her mother,
who often said, "You should lose weight," but Jamie had no
idea how to accomplish that. She read magazine articles
and tried various diets on her own, but as a young kid they
were hard to pull off. Unless a family commits together
to serving lighter, healthier meals for the whole gang, it's
nearly impossible for one child to be successful.

AFTER

BEFORE

When Jamie was in high school, she figured out how to reduce her calorie
intake, and started losing weight for the first time. But then disaster struck. Jamie
was 17 when her older sister Mimi developed an aggressive cancer. Mimi was only
24, and she died after 15 months. "When she lost her battle, I all but gave up on
mine," Jamie said. "I felt I had lost my place in the world. Home was not a place
where I wanted to be. It was dark and filled with grief. Looking into my mother's
wounded, empty eyes was too much to bear." Jamie started spending more time

with her boyfriend (now her husband of 10 years), and they usually dined at fast-food restaurants. Her weight loss efforts were a thing of the past. She was hurting, and food helped with the grieving process. She was embarrassed about her weight, but she couldn't help herself.

As she put on weight, Jamie stopped wanting to go out with her skinny friends. "Who wants to be the fat one in the group?" she says, recalling her embarrassment. Going out to a bar or dancing was out of the question. Meanwhile, Jamie built a shell around herself to hide her feelings. She was always the one who brought up her weight, usually in a comedic tone. Humor was her way of coping. The only person she could speak to honestly was her mother, who had struggled with her own weight her entire life. Her mother was never demeaning, just supportive. But Jamie wasn't ready to change.

On her wedding day Jamie weighed 250 pounds. "There are no pictures in my house of my wedding," she says ruefully. She didn't feel like a beautiful bride. The biggest day of her life was ruined by her weight, and she couldn't bear the thought of the picture confronting her every time she walked into a room.

Food was a main source of comfort. Everything she did seemed to revolve around food. She would never leave the table without feeling so full she was almost nauseated. It was also a way to fill up the time; with so little energy there wasn't much else she could do. When she was eating, she felt fine. It was only afterward that the depression would hit, and the cycle repeated itself over and over.

Jamie continued to gain weight after her two daughters were born, and she was heartsick that she was unable to be fully present in their lives. She didn't have the energy to keep her eyes open. They spent most of their time in the living room. The kids would watch TV and Jamie would doze on the couch. Everything hurt—her back, hips, knees, legs. Her vessels were so strained that sometimes they would just pop, and she had large bruises all over her body. Her husband, too, had adopted Jamie's poor eating habits, and he'd put on 50 pounds in the early years of their marriage.

A FRIGHTENING WAKE-UP CALL

One night Jamie came home from work to find her husband, in terrible pain, crawling up the stairs holding his chest. She froze in horror. Her worst fear was coming true. They both thought he was having a heart attack—and he was only 29 years old. At that moment Jamie got a flash of what life without him would be, and she felt devastated. This could not be happening!

It turned out that he wasn't having a heart attack. He had pulled some muscles lining his chest wall. But during the medical examination, the doctor found that his blood pressure was elevated, and he was immediately put on medication. The night when Jamie opened her cabinet and pushed food aside to make room for his medications, she faced the truth. If they didn't make some changes, their daughters could be without parents. "The battle was on," she said, describing her determination to get started on a healthy lifestyle immediately.

A CONSCIOUS DECISION

The question was, how would this time be different from all the others? She had heard me on *Today* talking about making conscious decisions, and she decided to start there. She made a deliberate choice to eat better, not to "diet"—and to move more. At first she didn't make any real changes in her eating; she strictly concentrated on becoming more aware of what she was eating. Her problem before had been mindlessness, and now she vowed she would not put anything into her mouth without thinking about it first. When she craved a fattening food, like a hamburger, instead of grabbing and gobbling it down, she and her husband put their heads together to figure out a healthier alternative.

She also prepared for the long haul. "I knew I didn't put on the weight overnight, and I wasn't going to lose it quickly either," she said. "This was going to be a journey." She told herself that she would just keep going until she hit a plateau, and then she would take it to the next level.

By practicing mindful eating, Jamie lost 20 pounds. The next phase was to cut out certain foods that were weighing her down—in particular, fried foods and soda. (This was a huge change.) She also decided to drink a lot more water. She walked 20 minutes or so on the treadmill every day—slowly, trying to add 1 minute each day—and when she hit a plateau, she adapted her food intake and exercise. She repeated that process for almost two years, and along the way her attitude about food changed. Whereas once she might have said, "This is so creamy—more gravy, please," now

---

PEP TALK

JAMIE'S STRATEGIES FOR SUCCESS

- Park at the end of the supermarket lot and walk.
- Remove one unhealthy food at a time.
- Find healthy substitutions for favorite foods. (Jamie's favorites are turkey burgers and turkey bacon.)
- Don't futurize. Live each day.
- When you hit a plateau, don't get discouraged; get moving.
- Never call it a "diet."

she was more inclined to say, "This is so fresh and crispy. It's perfectly delicious." Jamie's husband joined her, and he lost 50 pounds. Today they are a fit and healthy family. "We never slow down," Jamie says, "whether we are at the park, the bike path, or just walking around the block. We spend so much more time together as a family, and that is priceless. I find myself excited at bedtime thinking about the next day—even an ordinary day."

NO MAGIC

Jamie wanted to share her experience with others, but one of the first things she discovered was how resistant people were to the idea that a person could lose more than 100 pounds without having surgery or going to extremes. The rumor mill at the small-town hospital where she worked was in full swing, and Jamie felt hurt when she caught wind of what people were saying about how she had lost the weight. She heard everything from anorexia, bulimia, and pills to surgery. They wanted her to tell them that there was a magic solution—or a dark secret. One day at work a nurse pulled her into the stairwell and asked her in a stage whisper, "What did you do—throw up or take pills?" On another occasion someone commented, "You're healing remarkably well." He'd heard that she had had gastric bypass. At first these rumors upset Jamie. She was so proud of having done it herself. But she got over it. Now, if someone is truly interested, she will tell him or her how she did it and offer guidance, but she knows that change can't happen until you're really ready.

H$_2$0: AN UNSUNG WEIGHT LOSS HERO

Jamie was a big soda drinker who switched over to large quantities of water every day. The obvious benefit is that she saved thousands of extra calories and cups of sugar each week by ditching the pop. But drinking more water also offers up some serious weight loss advantages. People often mistake thirst for hunger, so staying hydrated can actually help prevent extracurricular nibbling. I advise people to guzzle a glass of water or sip a mug of interesting herbal tea before reaching for an extra snack, especially in the evening hours when the munchies tend to strike. And research shows that drinking water before meals can actually help you eat less food and shed more weight as a result. In one study, dieters who drank two glasses (16 ounces) of H2O before meals consumed fewer calories at meals than those who didn't and lost 44 percent more weight over the course of 12 weeks. Liquids take up space in your belly, so you feel comfortably full on smaller portions and push away your plate sooner. Though individual fluid needs are highly variable, I encourage dieters to drink at least 8 to 10 cups of water a day to aid in appetite control.

The first time Jamie celebrated her birthday after losing more than 100 pounds, her family and friends gave her a party with a big Number 1 on the cake. It was a very emotional day. The "1" was a symbol of the fact that life was just starting for her, and she was finally living the life she dreamed of.

Jamie has a fantastic sense of humor. When she reached her goal she told me, "You really are what you eat. And Joy, I'm never going to be gravy again."

JAMIE'S DAILY DIET COMPARISONS

BEFORE	AFTER
Breakfast	**Breakfast**
Large bowl of cereal	1 cup high-fiber cereal
2–3 donuts	1 cup coffee with 1 teaspoon sugar and 1 teaspoon half-and-half
	1 banana
Lunch	**Lunch**
1 foot-long buffalo chicken grinder	2 slices whole wheat bread with 1 slice turkey, 1 slice avocado, lettuce, and tomato, and balsamic vinegar spray
Chips	¼ cup walnuts or almonds
Soda	1 string cheese
Dinner	**Dinner**
Very large portion of anything fried and covered in gravy	Turkey burger on whole wheat bread with lettuce, tomato, and avocado slice, sprayed with balsamic vinegar
Mashed potatoes with sour cream and butter	Small sweet potato with cinnamon
Large piece of cheesecake	1½ cups steamed broccoli sprayed with balsamic vinegar
Snacks	**Snacks**
Potato chips with dip	3 cups air-popped popcorn
Buffalo wings with ranch dressing	4 small chocolate mint candies
Cheesecake with chocolate sauce	

Chicken with Peppers, Onions, and Olives

BY Jamie Francisco
MAKES 4 servings
SERVING SIZE 1 cup

Oil spray
1 medium onion, diced
1 sweet pepper (any color), diced
1 clove garlic, minced
1 pound boneless, skinless chicken breasts, cut into bite-size chunks
1 15-ounce can diced tomatoes, preferably no-salt-added (with liquid)
½ cup sliced pitted green olives
1 teaspoon salt-free seasoning blend
½ teaspoon kosher salt
Cooked brown rice or whole wheat pasta, for serving

1 Liberally coat a large skillet with oil spray and heat the skillet over medium-high heat.

2 Add the onion, pepper, and garlic and cook, stirring, until the onion is translucent and soft, about 5 minutes. Add the chicken and cook, stirring, until the chicken is no longer pink, about 5 minutes. Add the tomatoes, olives, seasoning blend, and salt. Bring the mixture to a boil. Reduce the heat to low and simmer, uncovered, for about 5 minutes or until thickened. Serve over brown rice or whole wheat pasta.

NUTRITION INFORMATION Calories: 189, Protein: 27 g, Total Fat: 4 g, Saturated Fat: 1 g, Cholesterol: 65 mg, Sodium: 490 mg, Carbohydrate: 10 g, Fiber: 3 g

Salsa Chicken

BY Jamie Francisco
MAKES 4 servings
SERVING SIZE 1 chicken breast with toppings

2 tablespoons ground cumin
2 tablespoons chili powder
2 large egg whites
4 chicken breast cutlets (about
   1¼ pounds)

Oil spray
1 cup jarred salsa
8 cups lettuce greens (such as spring mix)
6 ounces nonfat plain Greek yogurt

1 In a small bowl combine the cumin and chili powder. In a second small bowl lightly beat the egg whites.

2 Dip the chicken cutlets in the spice mixture. Dip the cutlets in the egg whites, then dip them in the spice mixture a second time.

3 Liberally coat a large skillet with oil spray and heat over medium-high heat. Place the chicken cutlets in the skillet and cook for 5 to 6 minutes per side or until the chicken is no longer pink.

4 While the chicken is cooking, heat the salsa in a small saucepan over medium heat until thickened, 5 to 7 minutes.

5 Arrange the lettuce on a large platter. Place the chicken breasts on the bed of lettuce. Spoon the salsa over the chicken and dollop with the yogurt.

NUTRITION INFORMATION Calories: 240, Protein: 40 g, Total Fat: 4 g, Saturated Fat: 0.5 g, Cholesterol: 80 mg, Sodium: 490 mg, Carbohydrate: 9 g, Fiber: 4 g

ROSEMARIE JEAN PIERRE

FROM Los Angeles, California
AGE 47 | HEIGHT 5' 2"
BEFORE WEIGHT 220 | AFTER WEIGHT 110 | POUNDS LOST 110

AFTER

BEFORE

Rosemarie is a very tender, emotional woman who obviously feels everything in life quite deeply. She suffered greatly from the humiliation of being overweight, and now that she has changed her life, her beaming face and new confidence are testament to how far she's come. But Rosemarie knows that in order to fully accept herself, she must also accept the parts of her life that were a terrible struggle.

In the Philippines, where Rosemarie grew up, it was very uncommon for kids to be overweight. She was 9 years old when she started gaining weight to the point of obesity. She stood out as the "fat kid," and that was a constant source of shame. The other kids bullied her relentlessly, and it was very traumatic for her. Sometimes the boys in her class would poke her with pins to see if she would deflate like a balloon. They would also pull her chair out from under her and laugh when she fell to the ground. Rosemarie couldn't understand why everyone was so mean to her. She may have been overweight, but she was a nice person who would never have dreamed of treating other children that badly. All she could do was protect herself from the ridicule by going deeper into her shell. She couldn't speak up for herself. She developed an inferiority complex and suffered from crippling migraines that plagued her over the years.

Food was her only comfort. "I loved food so much," she says. "I couldn't stop eating. It was something I could not give up. Even though I hated myself for it, I tried to fill that emotional gap inside with food." Sickened by the reflection in the mirror, Rosemarie fell into a depression. She knew there had to be something more to life than the endless shame of being overweight. She just didn't have any idea how to fix it.

When Rosemarie turned 18, she made her first attempt to lose weight. Her approach was very unhealthy; she basically starved herself and exercised too much until she had dropped 50 pounds. She soon gained the weight back, feeling sick and disgusted with herself.

Rosemarie had always wanted to be a nurse. She was a natural caretaker who just wanted to help others. When she was a nursing student, she met Kenneth through correspondence, and it was the first time any person had really understood her from the inside. They wrote back and forth for 18 months, and Rosemarie saw that they were meant for each other. They arranged to get married, and Rosemarie moved to California.

Rosemarie loved her husband, but the early period in America was very tough. She was terribly homesick, longing for her family, and she used food to comfort herself. She was always hungry, and she ate all the foods she craved, such as hamburgers, fries, shakes, and chocolate. Eventually she weighed 220 pounds, which was especially hard on her small frame. She was quiet and fearful, subject to humiliation on a regular basis. Once, standing on a crowded bus, a woman next to her said loudly, "Move over, fatso." She had grown so used to such incidents that she didn't even speak back. She wanted to disappear.

OUT OF THE COMFORT ZONE

Rosemarie finally decided to do something about her weight when she was 39 years old. Her father had died young of heart disease, and she feared she was going down the same path. As a nurse, Rosemarie saw the consequences of people making bad health choices every day, but she could not be a role model for them. She was embarrassed knowing the patients were judging her and wondering how such an overweight woman could be a health professional. She was having the kinds of health problems that usually afflict much older people—such as hypertension, high cholesterol, and prediabetes. Her doctor told her she had a serious risk of coronary heart disease.

PEP TALK

ROSEMARIE'S STRATEGIES FOR SUCCESS

- If you crave sweets, eat an apple or other sweet fruit.
- Replace sugary drinks with water or a fruit juice spritzer (sparkling water with a shot of fruit juice).
- Set aside the money you save by taking home-packed lunches to work—then buy something for yourself.

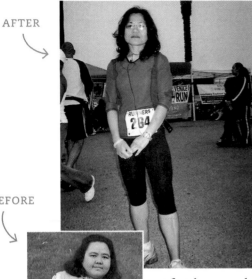

AFTER

BEFORE

She knew then that she had to step out of her comfort zone and make a change that lasted. She was determined.

Believing in Maya Angelou's statement "The more you know, the better you do," Rosemarie began by reading everything she could find about nutrition and fitness. She suddenly felt she had something to strive for, and she gave it her all. She was shocked to figure out that she was consuming between 6,000 and 7,000 calories a day, and she knew she had to cut that number drastically.

Changing her diet was difficult because it required her to completely change her ideas about food. Rosemarie ate a lot of traditional Philippine meat dishes, such as adobo, which is pork or chicken marinated in a vinegary sauce and then pan-fried to crispness. She also ate chow mein, fried chicken, and other greasy meats. And she drank up to eight cans of soda every day. Changing her diet was very difficult at first because she'd been overeating all her life, but she was highly motivated and she had a great support system. Her husband, Kenneth, her mother, Rufina, and her niece Anna-Rose were by her side giving her as much support as she needed. Her faith also played a big role. "When people ask me how I could have such self-control, I tell them I pray a lot," she says sincerely. As a nurse she had always been very compassionate toward her patients. Now she was learning to have compassion for herself. During the first month, she recalls how the smell of food would saturate her senses, but she had no second thoughts. She was happy to go on this journey, and she saw her shy, introverted self blossom into a social, happy woman.

She started walking on a treadmill in the gym at her apartment complex at the low rate of 1.5 miles per hour, gradually increasing the speed. To her surprise she found that she enjoyed it.

TWO SWAPS THAT MADE A DIFFERENCE FOR ROSEMARIE

BEFORE	AFTER
Rosemarie used to eat 3-4 cups of refined white rice for breakfast, lunch, and dinner.	Rosemarie now uses steamed greens, such as collards or spinach, as her "bed of rice."
Rosemarie's staple proteins were fatty fried chicken, fried pork chops, and high-fat marbled beef.	Today Rosemarie chooses lean options like grilled skinless chicken breast and baked salmon.

The turning point in her life was when religiously walking every day turned into running. She had never imagined herself as a runner, but she loved it. It became her passion. Rosemarie and Kenneth didn't have children, but they had four beloved dogs, and one of them, Skipper, became Rosemarie's running and training mate. Sometimes she even brought him along on races.

She realized running was something she was good at. When her nephew-in-law suggested she consider competing in the LA Marathon, she realized with amazement that she could do it. She trained every day, running at least six miles, and it became a regular thing for her to run 10K and 5K races. She didn't fully realize how good she had become until she was recognized as one of the top three runners in her division in Los Angeles. "Who would have known I'd become an athlete?" she says with wonder. "All my life I've been searching for something to ignite the passion in me, and I finally found it in running."

At half her previous size, Rosemarie feels like a new woman. The emotional hurt she suffered in childhood has become a scar on her heart that she is proud to show everyone. If she can help a single other person achieve his or her goals, she is committed to doing it. Today the formerly shy woman with the inferiority complex is bursting with enthusiasm and openness to every experience. She is happy—and running through life with a great big smile.

JOY'S WORDS OF ADVICE

LOWER YOUR CHOLESTEROL

Most overweight people struggle with high cholesterol, and Rosemarie's levels were dangerously high when she started her plan. Losing a lot of weight will substantially lower cholesterol, but you also need to target certain kinds of foods to get your numbers into a safe range. Here's a simple guide to planning a heart-healthy diet:

BAD FOR CHOLESTEROL. Avoid artery-clogging saturated and trans fats. Trans fats are found primarily in stick margarine and packaged goods that contain partially hydrogenated oils. (Read labels!) Foods rich in saturated fat include full-fat dairy products (for example, whole milk, cheese, cream, ice cream, sour cream, and butter), fatty cuts of red meat, and poultry skin.

GOOD FOR CHOLESTEROL. Monounsaturated and polyunsaturated fats can help lower LDL cholesterol (that's the bad kind) while maintaining or increasing HDL cholesterol (the good kind). Vegetable oils (such as olive, canola, and grapeseed), nuts, seeds, nut/seed butters, fatty fish, and avocados are all excellent sources of healthy fats. Omega-3 fats, a special type of polyunsaturated fat found in salmon, sardines, walnuts, and ground flaxseeds, are especially beneficial for cardiovascular health. And one of the best strategies for lowering cholesterol is to eat plenty of soluble fiber—the kind found in oatmeal, beans, lentils, and many vegetables and fruits.

Strawberry-Mango Sundae

BY Rosemarie Jean Pierre

MAKES 1 serving

½ cup frozen strawberries, thawed

1 teaspoon lemon juice

½ teaspoon granulated sugar (optional)

2 scoops vanilla frozen yogurt (about
 ¾ cup)

½ cup diced mango (fresh or frozen,
 thawed)

1 tablespoon chopped, toasted nuts

1 In a blender or food processor combine the strawberries, lemon juice, and sugar (if using); puree until smooth.

2 Scoop the frozen yogurt into a serving dish and top with the strawberry sauce. Sprinkle the sundae with the mango and chopped nuts.

NUTRITION INFORMATION Calories: 272, Protein: 5 g, Total Fat: 8 g, Saturated Fat: 2.5 g, Cholesterol: 15 mg, Sodium: 55 mg, Carbohydrate: 50 g, Fiber: 4 g, Total Sugar: 38 g

JODI DAVIS

FROM Lansing, Michigan
AGE 45 | HEIGHT 5' 7"
BEFORE WEIGHT 300 | AFTER WEIGHT 138 | POUNDS LOST 162

When Jodi was a child, she often heard people say that her mother was the spitting image of Elizabeth Taylor—a gorgeous, shapely woman who made heads turn wherever she went. By contrast, Jodi was shy and overweight, and she didn't gain much sympathy. Her grandfather, who more than anyone, liked to brag about her mother's beauty, told her straight out that she was going to be fat like her aunt, and no one would want her. He used to sing a ditty to her, lines from a 1947 song called *Too Fat Polka* by Ross MacLean and Arthur Richardson. It doesn't take too much imagination to guess at the gist of the lyrics.

AFTER

BEFORE

Jodi remembers feeling teased when her grandfather sang this song, and that she just wanted to curl up and disappear. She couldn't defend herself against this older man, and her parents didn't notice how tormented she was. Her entire family seemed to agree that her weight was a big problem.

Jodi didn't know what she had done to deserve the ugly side of the genetic lottery, but she was absolutely convinced that it was her own fault. She couldn't seem to control her eating. Jodi is an example of the way insensitivity and a lack of guidance create terrible confusion and despair for young people that only make their eating problems worse.

Jodi's mother tried her best to help her daughter lose weight, and her friends suggested that she try diet pills—something her mom was not aware of. In junior high school she managed to lose 35 pounds and fit into a size 11, but the cruel reality was that her friends were all size 6, and she still got teased.

Teasing was a daily occurrence that often left Jodi in tears. Thinking back on those years, Jodi reflects, "Teasing hurts the heart and the soul. I not only know this from my own experiences, but from others' too. Countless overweight individuals have shared these same types of stories, which they claim have caused emotional damage that won't go away. I've been there and I know what it's like to live the overweight life. I can truly say that I hated it."

She worried about her weight all the time. It was her first thought when she woke up in the morning and her last thought before she drifted off to sleep at night. Her only desire, which

---

JODI'S STRATEGIES FOR SUCCESS

Exercise was once a dirty word to Jodi. But she learned to love walking by taking baby steps.

STEP 1. Here's how to get started. Take a short walk to a specific location. If you are working in a large office building, take a short walk around the perimeter of the building. If your workplace includes a large parking lot, walk along the edge of the lot during your lunch hour. If you are at home, take a short walk to a nearby road sign of your choice.

STEP 2. Stay focused each day, making sure to take that same walk for the remainder of the week.

STEP 3. Next week, make it your goal to walk twice as far as the first week.

STEP 4. During the third week, increase the distance even more. Before long those baby steps will become big strides!

STEP 5. Do you feel you aren't eating healthy? I suggest that you begin by changing one meal per day. Consume half the portion size that you would normally eat at dinner. Do this for a week.

STEP 6. Next week, make an additional change toward healthier eating. When you snack, skip the high-calorie items and find something healthy that you can eat instead: an apple, a banana, fresh veggies, yogurt, low-fat microwave popcorn, raw almonds, or a low-fat granola bar.

STEP 7. Do you consume sugary beverages? Slowly eliminate these beverages and switch to water. Try to keep a bottle of water next to your favorite sugary beverage during your first week of baby steps. This will remind you to reach for the water first. It might help to fill your favorite sugary beverage bottle with water so it doesn't seem like such a drastic change. It works. You'll see!

STEP 8. During the second week, keep the sugary beverage out of your sight, but if you do find yourself reaching for it, take a tiny sip, savor it, close up the bottle, and put it away.

---

summoned all her passion, was to be thin and to be accepted as normal. Sometimes she thought her heart would break in two from wanting it. She imagined what it would be like to walk into a room, pretty and thin, how others would look at her with admiration and treat her as if she mattered. It was a fantasy that became an obsession. She was exhausted from it, emotionally drained from thinking only about dieting and losing weight.

When she was 16, Jodi started dating a boy from another town. He was fit and muscular, and best of all, he was nice to Jodi. It meant the world to her to have approval—to be liked for who she was. Jodi graduated high school weighing 240 pounds, and the next year she married her high school sweetheart. She lost 50 pounds for the wedding by going on a 500-calorie-a-day diet for three months and then gained 15 pounds back immediately on her honeymoon. But at least her grandfather's mean prediction wasn't going to come true. She would not be alone.

The coming years were full of family. Jodi gave birth to three children. When she was pregnant, the doctor told her she was at risk for gestational diabetes, and she stuck to a healthy diet during her pregnancies, only gaining 27 pounds each time. She was motivated by a deep love for the babies growing inside her, and for the first time she cared more about something than herself. But it didn't last. A year after her third child was born she weighed 300 pounds. Jodi compensated for her weight by being a perfectionist in other areas. She kept a spotless house. Everything had to be perfect because she wasn't. Sometimes Jodi read a magazine article or watched a TV program about someone who had lost an enormous amount of weight. She always thought it only happened to other people. She didn't believe it could ever happen to her.

AFTER

BEFORE

Looking back, it is interesting to Jodi how being fat became her identity in the family. She'd regularly hear from her overweight aunt to the effect that "We're the big ones . . . we're in this together." At family gatherings Jodi would hang out with her husband's cousin, who was a few years older than Jodi and also overweight. "We let people walk all over us," she says, "as if we didn't deserve having people be nice to us." They didn't talk too much about their weight, except to say, "We're fine with who we are." But that was not even remotely true. Then out of the blue the cousin had a heart attack and died. She was only in her early forties.

Jodi remembers being in church during the funeral and watching her cousin's son sobbing bitterly over the casket. Jodi knew that she was heavier than the other woman had been. "Oh, my gosh," she thought, "that's going to be me." She imagined her three children sobbing over *her* casket, and her heart broke with the thought of it.

DISCOVERING HEALTH

Jodi felt extremely motivated to make a change, but she didn't start right away. With a history of failed diets behind her, she knew she had to get her mind in place. She had to believe she could do it. Seeing a coworker lose more than 100 pounds, Jodi thought, "If she can do it, I can too. I have one life. I can't die!" Her girlfriend Melinda really helped. She said, "Jodi, you can do this," and Jodi saw how she thrived emotionally when someone believed in her.

She didn't start with a formal plan, except to say that this wasn't going to be a diet but a lifestyle change. Instead of following any written plan, she just concentrated on buying healthier foods at the supermarket. "It sounds simple," she says, "but why should it be complex? Complex doesn't equal success."

She ate three healthy meals a day, keeping the calorie content around 350 calories per meal. She also discovered her biggest weakness—eating before bed—and figured out how to handle it. She craved salty items, and she found that a bag of low-fat microwave popcorn or a small bowl of pretzels curbed her craving. She didn't kid herself that it would work to replace her salt craving with carrot sticks. "Been there, done that," she says. By acknowledging what she craved and finding an acceptable alternative, she didn't set herself up for failure.

Jodi realized that if she was serious about making a permanent change, the plan had to fit her lifestyle. She allowed herself to occasionally go to fast-food restaurants and have cake and ice cream at birthday parties. When she and her children went to a fast-food restaurant, she'd have a small burger plus a couple of fries—noticing that a few tasted just the same as a lot.

She realized that she had to add some form of exercise, and she dreaded it. She even hated the word "exercise." She didn't have money for fancy equipment, and she didn't want to join a gym—wearing spandex at size 24 was not an appealing idea. So she decided to walk and to keep the route manageable. She started with 1½ miles. To keep a brisk pace she imagined her house was on fire and her children were inside and needed to be saved. She walked every day—no excuses. If it was raining, she carried an umbrella. If it was cold, she wore a coat. If she was tired, she relaxed after her walk. "So many people come up with excuses for why they can't walk every day," Jodi told me. "But if I told them there was a winning lottery ticket worth millions at the end of the walk, they would find the time." It took her 22 minutes to walk every day, and that left 1,418 minutes for everything else. (Always remember that number. It's a powerful reminder of how manageable it can be to find time for exercise.)

Jodi didn't weigh herself much. She knew that if she weighed herself every day, she wouldn't see measurable results. "I looked at it this way," she says. "When driving my car, I don't check the odometer every few seconds to see how far I've driven. If I'm driving down the right path, I know I'm getting closer to my destination." When she did weigh herself after three months, she saw a 30-pound loss—and that was measurable.

It took Jodi 16 months to lose 162 pounds, and her life has been transformed. Her children marvel, "We can put our arms around you when we hug you!" In 2009 Jodi attended a high school

JODI'S MULTIPLE MINI MEALS

Jodi keeps hunger at bay and her energy high by eating seven times a day. Here is a typical rundown:

MORNING SNACK. (within first 5 minutes of waking up) Low-fat oatmeal raisin granola bar

BREAKFAST. Two pieces whole wheat toast with peanut butter and all-fruit blueberry preserves; coffee with sugar substitute and skim milk

MORNING SNACK. A piece of fresh fruit (banana, apple, nectarine, orange, pear)

LUNCH. Salad with many fresh vegetables (tomatoes, sweet peppers, sliced mushrooms, green olives, bean sprouts, broccoli, cauliflower) and a few sunflower seeds; ranch dressing on the side. A half sandwich using sliced turkey and one slice flaxseed bread with deli mustard; unsweetened iced tea with fresh lemon

AFTERNOON SNACK. A handful of soy nuts or raw almonds; unsweetened tea or coffee on ice

DINNER. Skinless chicken breast (prepared in slow cooker) with onions, potatoes, celery, and baby carrots; spray butter and low-fat sour cream on potato; ice water or green tea

EVENING SNACK. Low-fat microwave popcorn with tall glass of water with fresh lemon

class reunion, and it was an entirely different experience than her tortured years as a teenage outcast. She was aware of the irony of former beauty queens and cheerleaders asking her for weight loss advice or of seeing the football star who once teased her now overweight and looking unhealthy. She didn't take any pleasure in seeing her old classmates struggling. She realized that everyone had his or her issues, and she wished she could help them all.

The biggest breakthrough moment was the day Jodi's husband bought her a dress for the PTO Harvest Ball. He handed her the box and Jodi pulled the dress out of the tissue. It was a beautiful floor-length gown made of black stretchy material. She immediately noticed that the label read "small." She stared at her husband in disbelief. "Why did you buy a small?" she asked.

She tried it on, and it fit. "I stood looking in the mirror and the tears were rolling down my cheeks," she says, getting misty-eyed with the memory.

But more thrilling than that was the letter her daughter Kirstin wrote, which she shared with readers on her blog. Jodi wanted to reach out to obese parents and remind them of the deep feelings and fears their children have over their weight. Nothing could be more motivating, and she was proud of Kirstin for her honesty:

A LETTER FROM KIRSTIN

I was in fifth grade when I finally realized my mom wasn't like all the other mommies. Even though in so many ways she was the best mother in the world due to her strong involvement in our lives through school, sports, talent shows, and the like, it was in fifth grade when I noticed my mother wasn't normal; she was obese.

Once I noticed my mother was this overweight, it wasn't long before I understood the disadvantages that came with that fact. I soon appreciated every day with her more and more because I had no idea how many days she might have left. It wasn't like it was just her problem anymore; it was mine too. I would worry that her obesity would catch up with her. I couldn't just put it in the back of my mind either because as a child, your mother is everything.

As a child of an obese mother, I just want you to know that if you're overweight and you have children . . . they worry about it, and they worry about you.

They may not say they worry about it or even act like they notice, but I can promise you that they do. When you decided to have children, you made a commitment to do everything in your power to be there for them.

Also, know that if you're overweight, you can't compensate for it by helping at their school or buying them things. Nothing can compensate for the fact that your choices can leave them without a mother. What you may not understand is the reality that you can die from being overweight.

Is any food really worth not seeing your child walk on their graduation day or seeing them get married or holding their first child? If you had cancer, wouldn't you fight for your life? You would seek help and do whatever necessary to stay alive. Obesity is no different. It's hurting you and you really do have the choice . . . Obesity is 100 percent curable. My mom did it and you can too.

WALK IT OFF

Jodi achieved remarkable benefits from walking, and she now preaches its advantages to anyone who will listen. Walking may seem like the most natural thing in the world once we get past the toddler stage, but plenty of people still ask me, "How do I walk for fitness?" They wonder if they have to "power walk" to make it count. If you're just getting started on fitness walking, here are some things to keep in mind. First, intensity. Your walk should be challenging but not exhausting. The best way to gauge whether you're at the right intensity is to use the talk test. As you're walking, you should be able to talk without gasping for air but unable to sing without losing your breath. It might help to walk with a friend or chat with a pal using a Bluetooth headset so you know exactly when you need to slow down or speed up. You can also use a heart-rate monitor, a unit that typically consists of a watch and transmitter strap with electrodes that attach to your chest to measure your heart rate. Some models can be programmed with your target heart rate to give you feedback about how the rate you achieve compares with your goal.

You don't have to overdo the arm movements, but it's important to keep your upper body engaged as well. Keep it natural. Make loose fists with your hands and keep your arms close to your body. Bend your elbows at a 90-degree angle. Allow your arms to swing naturally. Focus on driving your elbows back and keeping your fists closed and your arms close to the sides of your body. To maintain your rhythm, think to yourself "drive, drive, drive" as you pump your arms, driving your elbows behind you.

Maintaining good posture is just as important when you're walking as it is when you're sitting. Not only does proper posture strengthen your abdominals and protect your spine from misalignment, but it also helps you move more efficiently. To walk with good posture, imagine that the top of your head is reaching toward the sky or ceiling and look straight ahead. Lift your chest while keeping your shoulders back and down. Draw in your abdominals to stabilize your core and give your arms and legs a power boost.

Turkey and Veggie Stew

BY Jodi Davis
MAKES 8 servings
SERVING SIZE 2 cups

Oil spray

1¼ pounds ground turkey (at least 90% lean)

1 small onion, diced

2 28-ounce cans diced tomatoes, preferably no-salt-added

1 10.5-ounce can condensed tomato soup, preferably low-sodium

4 cups water (or more if a thinner stew/soup is desired)

3 tablespoons Worcestershire sauce

1 teaspoon baking soda

2 medium carrots, peeled and sliced into coins (about 1 cup)

2 medium stalks celery, sliced (about 1 cup)

1 small crown broccoli, cut into small florets (about 1 cup)

1 large red potato, diced (about 1 cup)

1 sweet pepper (any color), diced (about 1 cup)

1 cup pearl barley

¾ cup lentils, picked through and rinsed

¾ cup green split peas, picked through and rinsed

½ cup brown rice

Kosher salt

Black pepper

1 Liberally coat a large soup pot with oil spray and heat over medium-high heat. Add the ground turkey and cook, stirring and breaking up the meat, until it begins to brown and crumble, about 2 minutes. Add the onion and cook, stirring, until translucent and soft, about 5 minutes.

2 Add the remaining ingredients, including salt and pepper to taste. Bring the stew to a boil, then reduce the heat to low and simmer, covered, until the lentils and split peas are tender, 45 minutes to an hour.

NUTRITION INFORMATION Calories: 449, Protein: 31 g, Total Fat: 4 g, Saturated Fat: 1 g, Cholesterol: 40 mg, Sodium: 385 mg, Carbohydrate: 73 g, Fiber: 20 g

Broccoli and Cauliflower Salad

BY Jodi Davis
MAKES 10 servings
SERVING SIZE 1½ cups

Jodi says this is delicious right after it's chilled but that it tastes even better the next day.

1½ cups low-fat mayonnaise
½ cup grated Parmesan cheese
2 tablespoons granulated sugar
¼ cup skim milk
6 slices turkey bacon, cooked and chopped
1 teaspoon dried basil (or more to taste)

1 head cauliflower, broken into bite-size florets
2 to 3 crowns broccoli, broken into bite-size florets
2 5-ounce cans sliced water chestnuts, drained
Kosher salt

1 In a small bowl combine the mayonnaise, Parmesan cheese, sugar, milk, bacon, and basil. Let the mixture stand for 15 minutes.

2 In a large bowl combine the cauliflower and broccoli florets and the water chestnuts. Pour the mayonnaise mixture over the vegetables and stir to combine. Season with salt to taste. Cover the bowl and chill in the refrigerator.

NUTRITION INFORMATION Calories: 118, Protein: 8 g, Total Fat: 5 g, Saturated Fat: 0.5 g, Cholesterol: 20 mg, Sodium: 525 mg, Carbohydrate: 14 g, Fiber: 2.5 g

White Chicken Chili

BY Jodi Davis
MAKES 7 servings
SERVING SIZE 2 cups

 2 tablespoons canola oil
 1 small onion, diced
16 ounces white button mushrooms, quartered
 1 red sweet pepper, diced
 1 green sweet pepper, diced
 2 medium stalks celery, diced
 ½ cup jarred drained mild banana peppers, roughly chopped
 6 cloves garlic, minced
 2 teaspoons dried oregano
 1 teaspoon kosher salt
 1 teaspoon black pepper
 3 boneless, skinless chicken breasts, cut into 1-inch chunks
 2 14.5-ounce cans unsalted or reduced-sodium chicken broth
 4 15-ounce cans Great Northern beans, preferably no-salt-added or low-sodium, rinsed and drained
 2 15-ounce cans black beans, preferably no-salt-added or low-sodium, rinsed and drained
 2 teaspoons white vinegar

1 In a large pot heat the oil over medium heat. Add the onion, mushrooms, sweet peppers, and celery and cook, stirring, until soft, about 10 minutes. Add the banana peppers, garlic, oregano, salt, and pepper and cook, stirring, for 1 minute. Add the chicken and cook, stirring, until no longer pink, about 5 minutes. Add the broth, beans, and vinegar. Bring the chili to a boil. Reduce the heat to medium-low and simmer, uncovered, for 1 hour.

NUTRITION INFORMATION Calories: 376, Protein: 32 g, Total Fat: 7 g, Saturated Fat: 0.5 g, Cholesterol: 40 mg, Sodium: 635 mg, Carbohydrate: 45 g, Fiber: 8 g

Slow-Cooker Pepper Steak

BY Jodi Davis
MAKES 4 servings
SERVING SIZE 1½ cups

1 pound lean top/bottom round steak, sliced against the grain into ¼-inch strips

1 medium onion, cut into chunks

1 large green sweet pepper, cut into strips

2 cloves garlic, minced

1 12-ounce can tomato paste

1 28-ounce can stewed tomatoes, preferably no-salt-added

1 cup water

2 tablespoons low-sodium soy sauce

2 tablespoons Worcestershire sauce

Black pepper

Hot cooked brown rice for serving (optional)

1 Combine the first 10 ingredients (through black pepper) in the slow cooker. Cook on the low setting for 8 to 9 hours. If desired, serve over brown rice.

NUTRITION INFORMATION Calories: 314, Protein: 32 g, Total Fat: 5 g, Saturated Fat: 1.5 g, Cholesterol: 50 mg, Sodium: 530 mg, Carbohydrate: 36 g, Fiber: 9 g

RICK GOSSER

FROM Crown Point, Indiana
AGE 52 | HEIGHT 6' 2"
BEFORE WEIGHT 310 | AFTER WEIGHT 180 | POUNDS LOST 130

AFTER

BEFORE

For many years Rick was in hiding from himself and others. He thought if people didn't see him eating, it wouldn't be so bad. So he'd buy secret food, such as giant chocolate bars, and stash them away. He'd buy six boxes of Girl Scout cookies, give three to his family, and hide the other three for himself. He'd order fast food at the drive-through, where it was easy to remain invisible and even easier to supersize. He was consumed with food. He'd put it in his pockets and go to another part of the house to eat. He'd get up in the night when everyone was sleeping and eat peanut butter right out of the jar with a spoon, sometimes consuming the entire jar. His average daily intake was around 9,000 calories.

Rick had been overweight his entire life. He graduated high school weighing 270 pounds. He had tried every diet that came along, and he had the typical experience of losing weight and gaining it back with more. Aside from his food and weight issue, Rick had a generally happy life. He adored his wife and three daughters, and he owned his own apparel company. But as he got older, his weight was taking a serious toll.

It was hard being an obese man approaching 50. Rick could see his health deteriorating. His worst problem was sleeping. He had trouble sleeping at night, but he could drift off anywhere during the day. There were times he fell asleep in the car waiting at a red light. He was afraid he had sleep apnea and would require a

sleep machine. He was tested and it was found that he didn't have sleep apnea, but the problem was most likely caused by his excessive weight. It wasn't acceptable. He had to change.

A LIFESTYLE, NOT A DIET

"The first three letters of diet are D-I-E," Rick likes to say. "I was not on a diet; I was on a lifestyle change." When he decided in December 2009 to lose weight, it was to get healthier and be in better shape. He knew that he had to exercise and watch his food consumption. All overweight people know that's what they need to do. It's just hard to make the mental decision. Rick started walking the dog daily, and those walks turned into jogs. At that time he also decided to get braces, and that jump started his program. He had the "do not eat" food list from his orthodontist, and he decided to be rigorous about not eating those foods because he didn't want to break the brackets on his braces. The added structure and rigidity helped keep him in line.

Around that time Rick's wife and one of their daughters were following the eating plan from my book *Your Inner Skinny*, and after they lost a few pounds they suggested that Rick try it. Being on the program together with his wife and daughter made all the difference. Rick never even wanted to cheat. His goal was to lose 100 pounds by Thanksgiving, and he was intensely motivated.

Rick had to force himself to eat regular meals because he was used to grazing throughout the day. He started to notice that he wasn't getting hungry in between meals, and he wasn't thinking about food all the time. His sleep problems disappeared, and his energy increased. He was even able to wear his wedding ring for the first time in 20 years.

TELL IT LIKE IT IS

Today, when Rick runs into people who knew him "when," they often say, "I don't remember you being that overweight."

"You mean fat," he counters bluntly.

He carries around postcards showing his before and after photos, which he hands out to anyone interested (I love this guy!) because a picture is worth a thousand words. "I'm just your average hometown guy that was overweight and knew I needed to do something about it," he says. "I decided to go for it (with some help from my family), and now I want people who are afraid to take that first step to know it's never too late to become healthy."

Rick began making it a point to talk to people in his business and personal life about their own struggles. One of these was a client of his apparel company named Tim, who was extremely overweight at 585 pounds. For years Tim always joked (morbidly) that he had two weeks to live. One day Tim called Rick and said that he wanted to order new embroidered shirts, but he needed to go up a size. Tim wore a 6XL shirt and he wanted a 7XL. Rick told him he would not make him 7XL shirts, but he did have a book for him to read. Not knowing how he would take it, he brought Tim my book *Your Inner Skinny* and told him he'd lost more than 100 pounds following the food plan in the book. (Did I mention that I love this guy?) After a lengthy discussion, Tim agreed to read the book. A week later Tim called Rick and said, "I hate you because everything in the book is right." He also mentioned that he was reading the book and eating two Big Macs at the same time. Rick asked him to promise that those would be the last two Big Macs that he ever ate, and he said okay. To date Tim has lost almost 100 pounds.

Rick never misses an opportunity to inspire someone else on the journey. Among his circle of friends and clients almost 1,000 pounds have been lost. Like Rick, these people did it on their own with lifestyle changes and exercise.

RICK'S DAILY DIET COMPARISONS

BEFORE	AFTER
Breakfast	**Breakfast**
6 eggs, scrambled	Bowl of high-fiber cereal
½ pound of bacon	½ banana
	½ cup skim milk
Lunch	**Lunch**
2–3 large fast-food hamburgers with the works	4 ounces turkey (no bread)
Extra-large fries	Salad
2 desserts	1 cup applesauce
1–2 soft drinks	
Dinner	**Dinner**
1–2 large steaks	Chicken breast
Baked potato loaded with butter, salt and sour cream	Broccoli or carrots
2–3 glasses of milk or 6–8 beers	Fun-size chocolate bar or gelatin cup
Half-gallon ice cream with chocolate syrup and butterscotch topping	
Snacks	**Snacks**
Chocolate bars	100-calorie packs
Cookies	Nutrition bars
Peanut butter on bread	Apples and raisins
Potato chips	

Rick's Pork Tenderloin

BY Rick Gosser
MAKES 4 servings
SERVING SIZE 4 slices

Rick says: "I make this roast for dinner and have leftovers the next day for lunch. It's even good on day two."

½ teaspoon ground sage
½ teaspoon ground thyme
½ teaspoon dried oregano
½ teaspoon onion powder
½ teaspoon garlic powder
½ teaspoon black pepper

¼ teaspoon kosher salt
¼ teaspoon cayenne pepper (or more if you prefer things spicy)
1 pork tenderloin (1 to 1¼ pounds)
2 teaspoons olive oil
Oil spray

1 Preheat the oven to 375°F.

2 Prepare the spice rub: in a small bowl combine the first 8 ingredients (through cayenne pepper).

3 Remove the silver skin from the pork tenderloin. Rub the tenderloin with the olive oil and then coat the tenderloin in the spice mixture, making sure to cover the entire piece of meat.

4 Liberally coat a large ovenproof skillet with oil spray and heat over medium-high heat. Place the tenderloin in the skillet and sear for 2 to 3 minutes per side. Transfer the skillet to the oven (if you do not have an ovenproof skillet, transfer the seared tenderloin to a baking dish before placing in the oven). Bake until the internal temperature of the roast reaches 145°F, approximately 15 minutes. Always rely on a meat thermometer, not the amount of time, to determine when the roast is done.

5 Remove the tenderloin from the oven and cover with aluminum foil. Allow to rest for 10 minutes before slicing and serving.

NUTRITION INFORMATION Calories: 159, Protein: 26, Total Fat: 5 g, Saturated Fat: 1 g, Cholesterol: 60 mg, Sodium: 380 mg, Carbohydrate: 1 g, Fiber: 0 g

---

JOY'S WORDS OF ADVICE

GET ENOUGH SLEEP

Sleep deprivation causes an imbalance in hormones that control weight and hunger. When you don't get enough sleep, ghrelin (which increases appetite) is elevated and leptin (which decreases appetite) is lowered. Plus, when you're sleep-deprived and dragging, it's easy to lose resolve and give in to temptations. Sleep is your best friend—aim for 7 to 9 hours a night.

CAROLYN LEONARD

FROM Tampa Bay, Florida
AGE 61 | HEIGHT 5' 1"
BEFORE WEIGHT 252 | AFTER WEIGHT 151 | POUNDS LOST 101

AFTER

BEFORE

I have been inspired by Carolyn's indomitable spirit since the moment I met her. She has such energy, humor, and zest for life. But I say that knowing Carolyn has come through a great deal of struggle and tragedy to reach this point. She once told me, "The winner is not the one dealt the best hand, but the one who does the most with the hand she's dealt." That's what Carolyn has done, and when you read her story you will see why I consider her to be such an inspiration.

Carolyn grew up the eldest of four children in a Polish neighborhood in Baltimore. Weight issues were common in her family, and the typical body type was, as she puts it, "compact and low to the ground." Carolyn's mother had serious weight issues, and Carolyn took after her. By the seventh grade she was wearing a size 18. However, unlike many people who struggled with their weight as children, Carolyn never felt ashamed or defeated by her size. She was very outgoing, a class leader, and a girl with ambitions. "I never felt weight stood in my way," she told me. She has thought about this anomaly a lot, and her theory is that back in the 1950s and 1960s, when she was growing up, people weren't so mean. She doesn't remember ever being teased or told she should lose weight. She felt accepted as she was and, more than that, loved and admired for her mind and her achievements. This fact may be a clue to Carolyn's wonderful personality because the truth is that people who remember being tormented about their weight as children have a much longer emotional road to travel. She does, however, acknowledge that her vivacity in high school—at size 20—was in part a defense mechanism so people wouldn't look at her size. But she was popular and she enjoyed the safety of socializing in groups.

When Carolyn was 18, she met Richard, who became her first boyfriend. The two hit it off on every level and after dating for two years they were married. Richard was a stocky man who loved to eat just as much as Carolyn did, and they always had lots of great food in the house. They were both meat and potato eaters, dessert eaters, and "prime time" eaters—if the television was on, they were eating.

Living in Baltimore, Carolyn and Richard were big fans of the Baltimore Orioles and the Baltimore Colts. They were also big fans of eating out—and they both gained weight. Carolyn soon reached her highest weight of 252 pounds. At that time, she didn't think about it a lot. Her weight didn't bother Richard, so it didn't bother her. When she was pregnant with their son, Mark, she had terrible morning sickness and couldn't tolerate rich or greasy foods. She actually lost 35 pounds and joked, "I've finally found the secret to weight loss—stay pregnant!"

Over the years, Carolyn tried various diets, and she went up and down on the scale. For her, dieting meant deprivation, and she was always miserable. It was easy to give up because Richard constantly told her he loved her just the way she was. But as they grew older they both began developing health problems. Carolyn had been diagnosed with type 2 diabetes when she was 40 and was taking oral medications. She was also taking medication for high blood pressure and pain. Simply walking was painful for her.

However, Carolyn's downfall was emotional eating. "The word 'no' didn't exist in my vocabulary," she says. Over the years, with a busy career and family life, Carolyn completely lost track of what she was doing to her health. Sadly, it took a horrifying tragedy to set her straight.

DEATH AND LIFE

It was October 6, 2005, a month before Carolyn and Richard were to celebrate their thirty-fifth wedding anniversary with a trip to California with tickets to see their favorite rock group, the Eagles. On that morning, they were in the kitchen getting ready for the day. As he was preparing to leave for work, Richard turned to Carolyn and said, "I love you." Then he fell to the floor. Carolyn dialed 911 and then collapsed beside him, cradling his body in her arms. He died before the paramedics arrived.

Carolyn walked through the funeral in a daze. She was so traumatized by her husband's sudden death that she lost the will to live. She just couldn't accept it—she even left his lunch in the refrigerator for a month, sure that one day she'd wake up from the nightmare and he would be back. She didn't know how she could go on. Although she was Catholic, she says her faith deserted her in the face of this horrible reality. She wrote a note, "Plan painless suicide," and carried it in her purse. The months followed in a blur, and many times Carolyn was convinced that she would be joining Richard soon. Her normally sunny disposition disappeared into a deep, dark despair.

Carolyn had no idea the extent to which her depression was visible to those around her. One day she was out to lunch with family members, and her 3-year-old grandson, Noah, looked at her across the table and said solemnly, "You're not going Poppy today." She was stunned, and the color completely drained from her face. How had this small child known what she was thinking? She fled the table and sat in the lobby, trying to collect herself. Suddenly a woman, a stranger, appeared before her. "You're not good, are you?"

Carolyn looked into her kind eyes and mutely shook her head. No, she was not good. It turned out that the woman was a nurse practitioner, and she told Carolyn, "I'm going to help you." They sat and talked for a long time, and Carolyn believed the stranger was an angel sent from God giving her permission to live. "The clouds parted," Carolyn says, marveling that a single moment could transform her life so completely.

JOY'S WORDS OF ADVICE

LATE-NIGHT CRAVINGS

Carolyn and her husband, Richard, were night eaters, usually plopped in front of the TV. The truth is: Late-night snacking is a major issue for most dieters. We crave foods for a number of reasons: One, environmental factors and sensory stimulation—like the smell of french fries outside a fast-food restaurant or the sight of a cheesy pizza in a TV ad—can trigger cravings. Second, hormonal fluctuations caused by stress, sleep deprivation, or a menstrual cycle can drive us to seek nutrient-dense, fatty, and sugary foods. And finally, cravings can develop because of learned behaviors. If you *always* go for cookies, chocolate, or ice cream when you're feeling stressed (or, in Carolyn's case, while watching your favorite TV shows), you come to expect these things and ultimately solidify a food habit that is very hard to break. These temptations are especially strong at night because the evening is often our first chance to relax after a long, structured, and taxing day. The urge to reward ourselves for making it through the day can trigger irresistible cravings for unhealthy comfort foods.

There are many effective strategies for crushing late-night urges. Chiefly, there's the obvious one: Don't keep tempting treats in the house. Just don't buy them! I'll admit, this isn't a foolproof strategy—I've heard stories about people who drove to the nearest gas station at 11 p.m. to get a bag of chips, a box of donuts, or some other treat they were craving. But it works most of the time. Also, eating a fiber-rich dinner will help keep you feeling full long into the evening hours and keep your blood sugar on an even keel so hunger doesn't come screaming back two hours after dinner. And last, if you typically eat dinner at 6 p.m., try moving it to 7 p.m. This will leave you with less time after dinner for snacking before bed.

AFTER

BEFORE

FROM DESPAIR TO POSSIBILITY

Once she decided to live again, Carolyn knew she had to face some hard realities. She had ignored her health for her entire adult life, and so had Richard. That might have been her on the floor. Although she had never let her weight get her down, now she viewed it in a new light. She realized that eventually it would kill her if she didn't take action. She looked back on her life with Richard and saw that they were "fat and happy" and totally ignored the signs. When they went to doctors to treat high blood pressure or diabetes, the doctors gave them pills, but Carolyn never remembered any doctor saying to lose weight. Once she started facing the truth, Carolyn saw the familial patterns that were clear as could be. There were many with diabetes in her family who dealt with their poor eating habits by eating anything and everything they wanted to and merely taking an extra pill to deal with the side effects. Her grandmother, father, and cousin had all died from complications of diabetes. She thought to herself, "I refuse to die from diabetes."

Others might have thought it was too late to change—she was well into her fifties. Not Carolyn. Looking at her children and grandchildren, who meant the world to her, she knew she had too much to live for.

But how does one take a lifetime of bad habits and make a change? The answer is, not overnight. Carolyn started by setting some ground rules for herself.

1 She did not want to spend money on programs or trainers to tell her what she already knew. She adopted a motto when going to the grocery store: DBI—Don't Buy It. On the DBI list were the chips, ice cream, and cookies that she ate while watching TV. She also made a rule: no eating while watching TV.

2 She identified her trigger foods and completely cut them out of her life. The big ones were french fries, potato chips, and cookies. French fries were a huge trigger. Carolyn didn't trust herself around them, so she cut them out of her life.

3 She called her plan Read, Write, Walk. For the first time, she started reading labels and becoming more mindful of what she was putting into her mouth. She wrote about her experience in a daily journal, which eventually turned into a blog. It was motivating to have people respond to her so personally. She walked whenever she could. Carolyn had always been a "parking lot vulture," circling the lot until a spot opened up close to the entrance. Now she deliberately parked at the back and walked. She wore a pedometer and set a goal of 10,000 steps per day.

4 Knowing that portion sizes were an issue for her, Carolyn bought smaller dinner plates to create a visual of plenty.

5 She focused on 10-pound goals, which felt much less overwhelming than 100 pounds.

6 She created a daily Calorie Bank. She could "spend" her calories any way she chose—all at once or throughout the day.

Within four months of following her own rules, Carolyn saw a difference. "I was starting to go from a pumpkin to a pear," she says. It was working. Gone were the days of the fried foods, bags of salted snacks, and sugary drinks. That being said, Carolyn was determined not to be too rigid because that was a recipe for failure. When she wanted something that was not on her new menu, she'd occasionally eat it—emphasis on occasionally. She learned that if she didn't satisfy a craving every once in a while, she'd overeat other foods. So she figured, "Just get over it, eat it, and move on." She laughs when she talks about indulging a craving, "I've learned that the sun will shine the next day and that the craving satisfaction will not be obvious to the average person." Carolyn

CAROLYN'S DAILY DIET COMPARISONS

BEFORE	AFTER
Breakfast Sugar pastry Fried eggs Bread	**Breakfast** Oatmeal with chopped apple
Lunch Fast food French fries	**Lunch** Sliced chicken breast on greens with "spritz" of red wine vinaigrette dressing Unsweetened iced tea with lemon
Dinner Fried chicken Mashed potatoes or Large portion of pasta	**Dinner** Salmon, tilapia, or tuna with half a baked potato and fresh steamed veggies Sugar-free pudding cup
Snacks Cookies Chips Anything sweet or salty	**Snacks** Oatmeal-raisin granola bar 100-calorie snack pack

jokes, "I'm no longer a food martyr, as the Catholic Church only recognizes dead martyrs."

One of the keys to Carolyn's success was her realistic idea about body size. For her entire life she had heard the gospel of sizing. You had to be a perfect 6 or 8—and in recent years even a 0. When Carolyn reached size 14, she thought she looked pretty great, but a friend confided, "I'm an 8. If I were your size, I'd kill myself." It saddened Carolyn to hear a comment like that, and she actually felt sorry for her friend instead of insulted. That point of view had everything to do with insecurity and nothing to do with health or happiness. It was all about meeting arbitrary standards. She promised herself that she would never do that—that she would be kind and reasonable with herself and make sure she felt right inside.

Today Carolyn's confidence is through the roof, and she looks and feels great. She's a force! The biggest advantage is that people take her more seriously. "It's no longer 'Oh my God, look at her thighs,'" she says with a laugh, "It's 'Oh my God, listen to what she says.'"

Carolyn's philosophy is "Why Weight? Don't DIEt . . . LIVEit."

Nani's Chick Fix

BY Carolyn Leonard
MAKES 4 servings
SERVING SIZE 1 stuffed tortilla

Oil spray
4 whole grain tortillas
1⅓ cups diced cooked chicken breast
1 cup shredded reduced-fat cheese (Carolyn recommends pepper Jack)
1 red apple, chopped
¼ cup toasted, chopped walnuts
½ cup salsa

1 Preheat the oven to 200°F. Line a baking sheet with aluminum foil.

2 Heat a large skillet coated with oil spray over medium heat. Place a tortilla in the skillet and sprinkle one half of the tortilla with ⅓ cup of the chicken and ¼ cup of the cheese. Fold the uncovered side over to fold the tortilla in half. Reduce the heat to low and cook until the cheese is melted. Open the tortilla and add ¼ of the chopped apple, 1 tablespoon of the walnuts, and 2 tablespoons of the salsa. Reclose the tortilla. Prepare the remaining 3 tortillas. Place finished tortillas in the hot oven to keep warm.

NUTRITION INFORMATION Calories: 286, Protein: 31 g, Total Fat: 14 g, Saturated Fat: 4.5 g, Cholesterol: 55 mg, Sodium: 585 mg, Carbohydrate: 20 g, Fiber: 9 g

Simple Salmon

BY Carolyn Leonard
MAKES 4 servings
SERVING SIZE 1 salmon fillet

- ½ cup low-sodium soy sauce
- ½ cup light maple syrup
- 1 teaspoon finely minced or grated fresh gingerroot
- 1 pound salmon fillet, cut into 4 portions

1 In a small bowl combine the soy sauce, maple syrup, and ginger. Pour the marinade into a large resealable bag. Add the salmon fillets, seal the bag, and thoroughly coat the fillets with the marinade. Refrigerate for 1 to 2 hours.

2 Preheat the oven to 400°F.

3 Place the salmon fillets, skin sides down, in a 9×13-inch baking dish and spoon 1 tablespoon of the leftover marinade over each fillet. Bake for 15 minutes or until the salmon flakes easily.

NUTRITION INFORMATION Calories: 201, Protein: 24 g, Total Fat: 7 g, Saturated Fat: 1 g, Cholesterol: 60 mg, Sodium: 600 mg, Carbohydrate: 9 g, Fiber: 0 g

Pucker Garlic Tilapia

BY Carolyn Leonard
MAKES 4 servings
SERVING SIZE 1 tilapia fillet

Carolyn says: "Seafood is one of my favorites. It's healthy and super easy for last-minute menu planning. I like to serve this tilapia with a side of asparagus sautéed in olive oil with minced garlic and red onion. Add a baked potato (split between two people at our house to cut calories but curb cravings) and you have a meal fit for a king—or in MY case, a QUEEN!"

Oil spray
4   6-ounce tilapia fillets
1   teaspoon butter (may substitute olive oil)
1   clove garlic, minced
Juice of 1 large lemon
Black pepper

1 Preheat the oven to 375°F. Coat a 9×13-inch baking dish with oil spray.

2 Place the tilapia fillets in the baking dish. Dot the butter over the top of the fillets. Sprinkle the fillets with the garlic, lemon juice, and pepper to taste. Bake, uncovered, for 10 to 15 minutes, or until the flesh turns opaque and flakes easily with a fork.

NUTRITION INFORMATION Calories: 177, Protein: 34 g, Total Fat: 4 g, Saturated Fat: 2 g, Cholesterol: 90 mg, Sodium: 95 mg, Carbohydrate: 2 g, Fiber: 0 g

ROSIE COATES

FROM Tacoma, Washington
AGE 44 | HEIGHT 6' 0"
BEFORE WEIGHT 300 | AFTER WEIGHT 193 | POUNDS LOST 107

AFTER

BEFORE

As a corrections officer, Rosie works primarily with female inmates. Her job brings her into daily contact with women who have lost freedom and control over their lives. She loves working with people, although she often sees the worst side of life. She feels a special compassion for the inmates because she hid the truth about her own life for so long. She realizes that while many of them are drug addicts, she was once an addict too. Her drug of choice was food.

Rosie had never fully faced the damage done to her growing up in a family that she felt was dysfunctional. She never knew her mother, and spent the first five years of her life with her grandmother, who showed love with food. When she went to live with her father and stepmother, she missed her grandmother's comforting presence and often felt out of place. Her father was in the Army, so the family moved around a lot. She felt that food was tightly controlled in her father and stepmother's home. Rosie felt ashamed and bad and even guilty for wanting more of it. As a girl, she used to sneak down and steal food from the refrigerator when everyone was asleep and hoard it under her bed. She had an insatiable appetite and ate cookies and candy bars to quiet the turmoil she felt inside.

Because Rosie was a very active child, the evidence of her bingeing wasn't there in the beginning. She had never paid any attention to her diet because she was always able to burn off the high-fat foods she loved to eat. Her dirty little secret, which was never visible before, was that she was in love with food and it helped her through any form of stress. To Rosie food was comforting, instantly gratifying, never disappointing, and like a best friend. While her household was a place of emotional deprivation, food could fill her up and ease her heartache.

Rosie longed for comfort and stability. When she was a senior in high school, she confessed to a friend that she wanted to find a military man, a guy with a stable job. And her dream came true. She got married three months after high school, and it turned into a great love match. Her husband was her biggest supporter, and he still is 25 years later. That's an especially beautiful story because children who grow up feeling like they don't belong in their own homes often don't thrive in their relationships later in life. Rosie didn't have a model of what a good marriage should be, but she created her own. It was a new experience to be loved unconditionally.

Throughout her youth Rosie had always been physically active. Sports and exercise were her antidepressants. But after she had her daughter at age 20, she began putting on more weight. She tried various diets but didn't know very much about nutrition, and they were never very healthy. She lost some weight but always put it back on. By the time she reached her thirties, she weighed 300 pounds.

On September 11, 2001, Rosie was home from work, her husband was at his job, and her daughter was at school. Staring at the television as the Twin Towers fell, she was struck by the reality that the world could end. She could not afford to waste a moment living an unconscious life. She was particularly aware of her daughter. She had strived to make sure her daughter grew up with a healthy self-image, but now she realized that she was a terrible role model, and that needed to change. She thought about it for several months, and in March 2002, while her husband and daughter were away at a high school basketball camp, she decided it was time. She felt angry at the world and at herself for getting to such a dangerously overweight point. She was 300 pounds, consuming as many as 8,000 to 10,000 calories a day. It had to stop. "I was afraid the cycle would repeat itself with my daughter," she said. "My words didn't match my actions. I was lying to myself and to everyone else."

PEP TALK

ROSIE'S STRATEGIES FOR SUCCESS

- Assess where you are and start there. Nothing is going to change until you're honest with yourself.
- Take unhealthy foods away slowly. Gradually change your habits.
- Drink plenty of water.
- Exercise if you can. Be realistic.
- Be honest about what will work for you. (My personality would have rebelled on a formal plan.)
- Start eating more salads. They're healthy, and the bulk helps fill you up.

AFTER

BEFORE

HEALTHY CHOICES

Rosie started with a choice. "I chose not to overeat," she says. She began paying attention to everything she put in her mouth and was methodical about planning her meals. She stopped ordering out at work and brought lunch from home. She told the order taker at the jail, "Don't order for me," and soon word got out. When her uniform size started changing, people took notice. "Of course, everyone wanted to feed me," she laughs.

Rosie realized right away that she had to learn to get in touch with her hunger. At first she didn't know what hunger felt like, but when she started eating on a schedule and curbed her compulsive snacking, she felt the rumbles and said, "I really am hungry. It's OK to eat now."

She began to educate herself about nutrition and kept a food log to track her daily intake, which she tried to keep at around 3,000 calories, which felt about right for her tall frame and activity level.

Through it all, an exercise regimen was Rosie's continuity. She loved to exercise, and she created a very structured plan. She walked on a treadmill and then started running on a track. Eventually Rosie added weight training, stair stepping, rowing, and biking.

Before, Rosie had a habit of weighing herself every day, but she realized that was driving her a bit crazy. She stopped weighing herself altogether, until her birthday, September 1, 2003. She got on the scale as a birthday present and saw that she had lost 100 pounds. She called for her husband and yelled, "Yes! I did it!"

REACHING OUT

Now Rosie was on a mission. People would walk up to her everywhere—especially after she appeared on the Joy Fit Club segment—and ask for advice. She saw that they trusted her because she had shared the same struggles. "I know I can accomplish anything," she says. "I have a faith in myself I didn't have before. What empowers me now is empowering others." In 2006 Rosie received certification as a personal trainer, and in addition to her job as a corrections officer she conducts fitness workshops with groups and gets tremendous satisfaction from it. She is also an avid runner and marathoner.

When she was carrying around 100 extra pounds, Rosie had a very negative perception of her body. Now? "I look at myself and I say, 'Girl, you've got it going on!'" she says enthusiastically and with pride. "I'm strong, I'm totally into life, and I'm proud of my body. The clouds are gone. I'm happy all the time."

MINDFUL EATING

It's incredibly easy to polish off a whole bag of chips or entire row of cookies if you're mindlessly snacking while watching television, driving, or plowing through work at your desk. When your attention is elsewhere, you're less apt to listen to your body's fullness cues and keep portions in check. Follow these strategies to practice mindful eating:

SLOW DOWN. Make every mouthful a pleasure. Concentrate on tasting your food. Put your fork down or take a sip of water after every bite or two.

DON'T MULTITASK. Turn off the television and the computer and set your cell phone aside. Put away the book and the newspaper. Always sit down at the table and make eating an event. When your food is your only focus, you're far less likely to eat past the point of fullness.

ROSIE'S DAILY DIET COMPARISONS

BEFORE	AFTER
Breakfast	**Breakfast**
One-half box sugary cereal	2 vegetable patties
4–6 eggs over hard	Nutrition bar (1–2 hours later)
3 sausage patties	Frozen fruits (1–2 hours later)
Lunch	Lunch
3–4 hot dogs with buns and all the trimmings	Prepared sandwich
	Salad and yogurt
Dinner	Dinner
2 large hamburgers, pan-fried with all the trimmings	4 eggs over hard with oil spray
Bag of chips (4 servings)	2 slices whole wheat toast
4–5 cups white rice	
Packaged baked goods	
Snacks	Snacks
Grazed throughout the day on snack cakes, cupcakes, and at least 2 king-size candy bars	Fruit, nutrition bar, 100-calorie snack pack

APRIL HUDSON KEATLEY

FROM Charleston, West Virginia
AGE 33 | HEIGHT 5' 9"
BEFORE WEIGHT 270 | AFTER WEIGHT 161 | POUNDS LOST 109

AFTER

BEFORE

April remembers hearing the word "fat" for the first time in the third grade. She had always been taller and bigger than the other kids, but the teasing took off after that. On one occasion a boy at church told her she was fat and ugly in front of other friends—and it's a moment she has never forgotten. She never felt good about herself or like she fit in, and she was humiliated by the frequent comment from adults, "You have such a pretty face, if only you'd lose 20 pounds." Do people realize how *mean* they sound when they say that line?

Being the tallest girl in class was always awkward, and not knowing what else to do, her mom dressed her in sweat pants and stretchy outfits. She tried to help April, but she was dealing with issues of her own. April was the youngest of six children, but her siblings were all much older than she. After her parents divorced when she was 5, it was just April and her mom. Her father was no longer in the picture. "As a young woman struggling with body issues, it would have helped to have a positive, reassuring male presence," she says now. "You always look to your father to tell you that you're beautiful." Although her mom was an extraordinary, loving parent, in retrospect, she believes that most of her self-esteem issues and feelings of being unwanted stemmed from her father's absence.

During high school April began experimenting with various diets and also tried diet pills. She always lost weight, but it came back with a vengeance. In her junior year she managed to lose 50 pounds—from 220 to 170. But by the time she graduated she was 185, and the weight kept coming back, and when she finished college she weighed 230 pounds.

It was a constant battle for April, exacerbated by stressful events in her life. She married young, and it was a mistake. "I didn't know who I was, much less how to be a wife," she says. "A lot of women forsake themselves for a man, and I wasn't confident of myself. I just wanted to be with him." On some level April felt that being married would protect her from the scorn of others. As long as she "belonged" in a family, she would not be ostracized because of her weight. When she got married in 2003, April weighed 235 pounds. She soon discovered that an unhappy marriage provides no protection whatsoever. She was lonelier than ever, and she ate to block out the feelings of misery and panic. By the time she and her husband divorced two years later, April weighed 270 pounds.

During the period when April was struggling with her marriage, her mother got sick. She had lupus and while in the hospital she contracted Legionnaires' disease and was in a drug-induced coma for two months. April lived at the hospital during that time, and as she gazed at her mother, she experienced a wake-up call. "I remember thinking, wait a minute. You only get one shot; you need to make it count." She also had a realization: "I deserve more than this." She took the first step in 2005 and ended her marriage. She started exercising out of boredom and because she wanted to lose some weight so she could be attractive enough to meet someone else. She threw herself into exercise, and between August 2005 and May 2006 she lost 50 pounds. But once again the stress of life intervened. She had a new boyfriend and they were having problems, so she chose to spend time with him instead of working out. She gained back 32 pounds—pretty much back to where she had started.

JOY'S WORDS OF ADVICE

SMART SPLURGING

April's motto is "Diets don't work, but healthy lifestyles do." So she makes sure to plan for weekday and weekend splurges that allow her to satisfy her love for sweets, pizza, and pasta—without going overboard. By strategically working them into her plan and calorie goals, she's always in control and never feels deprived of her favorite foods. During the work week, she'll have a small daily treat, such as a sugar-free pudding cup or 1 to 2 squares of dark chocolate—just enough to get her chocolate fix.

On Saturdays April typically goes out to dinner and allows herself one more elaborate planned splurge. She either enjoys a "splurge meal"—usually pasta or pizza, her favorites—or splits a decadent dessert with her husband. Even when she's indulging, she does so strategically. If she has a splurge meal, she only eats about half of the restaurant serving. When ordering pizza, she chooses thin-crust brick-oven style, topped with cheese and plenty of vegetables, such as mushrooms, spinach, and tomatoes, to make her slices more filling.

AFTER

BEFORE

A NEW KIND OF CONTROL

During this period April had never addressed her eating habits. Food was a comfort to her—"butter was like icing." April had always felt that eating was the one thing she could control. That may sound strange, given the fact that her eating habits were all over the place. But she explains it this way. "I didn't gorge, but I ate what I wanted when I wanted it. I loved to overindulge." Now she began to look at herself with an honest eye.

For April the journey to health was an emotional and psychological one. When she ate too much, she knew she was dealing with feelings. She took time to get to know herself, to be aware and reflective, because she knew that change had to come from within. She realized that she couldn't expect to meet someone and have him value her if she didn't value herself.

In the spring of 2007, weighing 252 pounds, April broke up with her boyfriend and returned to working out. It took her more than three years to get to 161 pounds, but every step of the way she was learning about herself and figuring out what it took to eat nutritionally. It took her awhile to get the connection between what she ate and how she felt. She began to see food as fuel for her body. She saw that the long process was going to be successful. "Losing weight is a marathon, not a sprint," she says. "Making small changes that become routine and integrated into your life will stick better than any kind of crash diet. With every change, I learned more and more about myself and just what I was made of." In the beginning April hated cardio because she would get so out of breath. Once exercise became a regular part of her regimen, that changed to the point where she relied upon cardio several times a week. Exercise became her time to check in with herself, to think and plan and reflect.

Throughout her journey, she was constantly heartened by the support and kindness of the people around her—from her brother telling her she looked good to random people at the gym complimenting her and telling her the hard work was really paying off. There would be days she'd walk

---

PEP TALK

APRIL'S STRATEGIES FOR SUCCESS

- If you fall off the wagon for one day, two days, or even more, don't give up.
- If you are doing everything right and you hit a plateau, keep at it—success will come.
- You're worth the time. Invest in yourself and be the best possible version of you for you.

into the gym and not want to be there. Then someone would say a kind word to her and she would find her focus. She did the same for others. If she saw someone struggling with weight working out at the gym, she'd go out of her way to say, "Good job, keep it going." A friend was intimidated about going to the gym because of her size, and April took her by the hand and showed her the ropes.

April was proud of herself. She was amazed to realize that she could work out for an hour and a half and not die or collapse. She could push herself to physical achievements she'd never thought possible. She also discovered that for the first time in her life she could balance her food intake—share a dessert or forgo a heavy entrée. It was within her power.

As she lost weight and became more in touch with herself, April met David, a tall, fit man who would happily go on runs with her. They married in 2011. April feels as if she has a whole new life—but she worked hard for it. "There is such a sense of accomplishment in being able to say I like who I am and I am going to be that person on purpose," April says. "I finally figured out that I was worth the time and effort it takes to be healthy." An old friend from high school, who had also struggled with her weight, contacted April on Facebook. "So, you've found your Prince Charming," she wrote, adding that she was still looking. April wrote back, "My best advice is to get comfortable with yourself first. Get healthy and take care of yourself. Life has a way of working out." She reminded her friend that there was no better investment she could make than in herself. These weren't just platitudes. Looking back to her first marriage, it was clear to her that she was incapable of adding value to a relationship because she didn't value herself. But now she values herself, fully and completely.

APRIL'S DAILY DIET COMPARISONS

BEFORE	AFTER
Breakfast	**Breakfast**
Yogurt	1 egg, 2 egg whites
Oatmeal	4 strips turkey bacon
Donuts	1 ounce hard cheese
Lunch	**Lunch**
Pizza or fried chicken sandwich	Grilled chicken, fish, or lean steak
Fries	Broccoli or other vegetables
"Food court" fare	Sugar-free pudding cup
Dinner	**Dinner**
Large pasta dish with cream sauce	Grilled chicken or fish
Bread	Broccoli or other fresh vegetables
Pastry	2 small pieces of chocolate
Snacks	**Snacks**
Sweets	1 cup plain Greek yogurt with mixed berries
Donuts	Orange and 1 ounce almonds
Cookies	Banana protein shake

Spinach Salad with Chicken, Pecans, and Grapes

BY April Hudson Keatley

MAKES 4 servings

Dressing

3 tablespoons raspberry vinegar

3 tablespoons balsamic vinegar

3 tablespoons extra virgin olive oil

Salad

8 to 10 cups baby spinach leaves

2 cups red grapes, sliced (may substitute other fruits, such as sliced strawberries or mandarin oranges)

¼ cup crumbled blue cheese

½ cup toasted pecans, chopped

4 6-ounce boneless, skinless chicken breasts, cooked and sliced into thin strips

1 For the dressing, in a small bowl whisk together the vinegars and olive oil.

2 For the salad, in a large bowl toss together the spinach leaves, grapes, blue cheese, and pecans. Divide the salad among 4 plates and top each plate with 1 sliced chicken breast. Drizzle the salad dressing on the salads.

NUTRITION INFORMATION Calories: 511, Protein: 46 g, Total Fat: 26 g, Saturated Fat: 5 g, Cholesterol: 110 mg, Sodium: 335 mg, Carbohydrate: 24 g, Fiber: 5 g

Blue Cheese-Bison Burgers with Sautéed Mushrooms and Onions

BY April Hudson Keatley
MAKES 6 burgers
SERVING SIZE 1 burger with toppings

Oil spray

Bison Burgers

½ teaspoon kosher or coarse sea salt
½ teaspoon black pepper
½ teaspoon crushed red pepper
½ teaspoon garlic powder
½ teaspoon onion powder
2 pounds ground bison
6 tablespoons blue cheese crumbles

Sautéed Mushrooms and Onions

1 tablespoon olive oil
2 large portobello mushroom caps, stems removed and sliced
1 medium onion, sliced
¼ teaspoon kosher salt
¼ teaspoon black pepper
½ lemon, juiced

1 Preheat the outdoor grill or heat a large skillet or indoor grill pan liberally coated with oil spray over medium-high heat.

2 For the burgers, in a small bowl combine the salt, black pepper, crushed red pepper, garlic powder, and onion powder.

3 In a large bowl break up the ground bison. Sprinkle the seasoning mixture over the bison and mix well, using your hands to ensure the seasoning is evenly distributed throughout the meat. Form the meat mixture into 6 patties.

4 Grill the burgers for 5 to 6 minutes per side or until they reach the desired doneness. Top each burger with 1 tablespoon blue cheese crumbles 1 to 2 minutes before removing it from the grill.

5 While the burgers are cooking, prepare the sautéed mushrooms and onions. In a large skillet heat the olive oil over medium heat. Add the mushrooms and onion, and sprinkle with the salt, pepper, and lemon juice. Cook, stirring, until the vegetables are soft and lightly browned, 10 to 12 minutes.

6 Top the blue cheese burgers with the sautéed mushrooms and onions and serve.

NUTRITION INFORMATION Calories: 288, Protein: 33 g, Total Fat: 16 g, Saturated Fat: 6 g, Cholesterol: 90 mg, Sodium: 365 mg, Carbohydrate: 4 g, Fiber: 1 g

DOREE KALFEN

FROM Deerfield, Illinois
AGE 52 | HEIGHT 5' 3"
BEFORE WEIGHT 230 | AFTER WEIGHT 126 | POUNDS LOST 104

AFTER

BEFORE

Doree always looked up to her older sister, who was slender, beautiful, and popular. She seemed so perfect. In contrast, Doree was chunky and awkward, and she wished she could wave a magic wand and become more like her sister. As she grew older, it only got worse. While her sister was on the cheerleading squad and having a full social life, Doree was becoming more introverted, staying home and reading, doing needlepoint, and painting. She worshipped her sister, who was 16 months older, but she felt she could never come close to emulating her. Her sister used to tell her, "Don't try to be like me. Be yourself." But to her, that sounded like choosing second best. She was happy if a boy at school talked to her. Dating was nonexistent. The thing is, she wasn't really that big in high school, and through extreme dieting she graduated at 110 pounds. But she was a classic yo-yo dieter and the weight came back. Later she would marvel that she could get so heavy over the coming decades. It happened one year at a time.

In college Doree met her husband, Alan. He was a big guy, and eating was part of their lifestyle. Alan was a very generous man, and he loved to take Doree out and splurge on her. Their life revolved around food. When Doree got pregnant, they were excited, but her eating became out of control. She gained between 70 and 80 pounds during her pregnancy, lost part of it, and then regained it—and more—with her second pregnancy.

Doree's typical eating pattern was a common one. She would skip breakfast, was starving by noon, and then didn't stop eating for the rest of the day and the evening. "I would eat until I was stuffed," she recalls. The next morning she'd wake up feeling bloated and guilty and then start the same pattern all over again.

Doree's yo-yo dieting cycles made her miserable. She would gain a few pounds, feel bad about herself, try to diet, fail, eat some more, and start another diet. And she loathed shopping for clothes. She frequently had to buy new clothes, especially pants, because the fabric in the thigh area would wear thin. She hated shopping for coats in the winter because they made her look bigger. So she would buy thinner coats that didn't keep her warm. Summer was worse. She felt she looked awful in shorts and she hated how much she sweated. She wouldn't dream of being seen in public in a swimsuit. Her friends didn't "get it." She remembers going to a store with one of her thin friends who picked out some outfits for Doree to try on. "Little did she know, there was no way I could fit into anything that she chose," Doree says. "I had to make up some excuse for not taking the outfits into the fitting room." This just increased her feelings of anger and sadness. And those feelings then became soothed with food. It was a vicious circle.

Doree's weight took a toll in other areas too. She would think about all the things she might have done were she not overweight. She lacked confidence in her abilities. In public and in her relationships, she was content to hide behind others—her husband, her parents, her siblings, her friends. She found it hard to stand up and speak for herself because she didn't want people looking at her. Her head was filled with negative self-thoughts, and physically she was just too tired to do anything about it. On the rare occasions when she would decide to go to the gym, she regretted it because she felt huge and out of place compared to the other women.

But the biggest pain came from seeing how her overeating affected her two children. Both had weight issues, and Doree knew they watched her overeat and felt they could do the same. She was filled with remorse that her problem could set her beloved children up for lifetimes of pain and humiliation. She couldn't bear the thought that one of her children would settle for a career he didn't love just because of his weight.

TIME FOR A CHANGE

The turning point for Doree came during a doctor's visit. After she got on the scale, her doctor sat her down and lowered the boom. He asked her if she wanted to spend the rest of her life on a series of medications to control blood pressure, cholesterol, and diabetes. For the first time Doree realized that overeating was making her sick, and the thought terrified her.

It was overwhelming to have to lose 100 pounds. Doree knew she had to do it, but she had to think seriously about how she would get there. She didn't want to put a lot of pressure on herself. She wanted to do it her way, with patience and small changes. Mostly Doree didn't want to be judgmental about her efforts. "I was always saying things like 'Was I bad? Was I good?' Why put this extra burden on myself?"

Doree admits that she never before got the correlation between food and health. For her, food had always been about fat and shame—so connecting it to health was a whole new way of looking at a tangible goal.

She started with two simple changes. First, she got a treadmill for the house (she was too self-conscious to go to the gym) and walked every day, very slowly at first, gradually upping the pace. Second, she decided she would not eat anything after 7 p.m. Those two changes were enough to jump-start the rest of her plan. Within two weeks she noticed her pants were getting looser. Over time she added other changes, replacing heavy dinners with lighter fare, eating something in the morning—even if only a piece of fruit or a nutrition bar—and keeping snacks at around 200 calories.

Doree had a tremendous support system from family and friends, and that made all the difference. Even her kids got into the act. Her daughter started fixing healthy meals, and her son not only ate those meals, he encouraged Doree to keep up her fitness routine.

JOY'S WORDS OF ADVICE

RESTAURANT MAKEOVER

Doree and her husband love to eat out, and really there are smart choices to be found in almost every restaurant. As I always tell clients, it's not *where* you eat; it's *what* you eat. Rather than changing her dining out routine, Doree learned to make healthy menu choices and submit special requests to cut unnecessary calories and fat. Here's a look at Doree's "before" and "after" meals at several of her favorite restaurants.

RIB/BBQ JOINT

BEFORE: Full rack of baby back ribs with BBQ sauce; loaded baked potato (topped with bacon, sour cream, cheese); mayo-based coleslaw; large piece of corn bread. 2,310 calories, 123 grams fat

AFTER: Grilled salmon (topped with BBQ sauce); steamed broccoli; baked sweet potato (plain). 550 calories, 14 grams fat

GREEK RESTAURANT

BEFORE: Gyro platter (8–10 ounces gyro meat) with toppings (lettuce/tomato/red onion/tzatziki) on side; 1 large pita bread; and french fries. 1,300 calories, 76 grams fat

AFTER: Mediterranean tilapia fillet topped with kalamata olives, capers, tomatoes (or any steamed/grilled/broiled white fish) with steamed spinach and rice pilaf. 575 calories, 17 grams fat

DINER/BRUNCH

BEFORE: 3 large pancakes with generous butter/syrup; 3 pork breakfast sausage links; hash browns. 1,175 calories, 70 grams fat

AFTER: Large egg white omelet with spinach, tomato, mushroom, onion, and feta cheese. 280 calories, 14 grams fat

It took Doree three to four years to lose over 100 pounds. She took it very slowly, and there were some bumps in the road—but she was determined, and she ultimately prevailed.

AFTER

A NEW PERSPECTIVE ON LIFE AND HEALTH

"I have lived both ways—eating unhealthfully as an obese person and being slim, healthy, and happy," Doree says. She is sold on her new reality. She has the confidence to try new things professionally and to pursue athletic ventures, such as running half marathons. Now Doree loves meeting new people. She is full of a sense of purpose—to be with people, personally or professionally. Finally she feels like she fits in.

"I love the way I look and feel," Doree says. "I am comfortable in my own skin. I have the energy to run for hours, then come home and dance to my favorite songs on the radio, then do my daily errands, and still make dinner and clean up."

Doree notices that people treat her differently, and that's a bittersweet realization. She appreciates the raves, but she also remembers that when she was a heavy person, she was rarely praised, rarely sought out for her accomplishments. Her goal is to reach out to others who are struggling as she once was. A special point of pride is to show that a woman in her fifties can change her life so dramatically. It's never too late.

DOREE'S DAILY DIET COMPARISONS

BEFORE	AFTER
Breakfast	**Breakfast**
No breakfast	High-protein cereal with skim milk
	Fruit
Lunch	**Lunch**
Anything drive-through—hamburgers, fries, sandwiches, chips, and lots of sweets	1 slice whole wheat bread topped with peanut butter and sliced banana
	Greek yogurt with berries
Dinner	**Dinner**
Pizza, fried chicken, lots of bread	Fish, chicken, or turkey
	Vegetables
	Frozen yogurt
Snacks	**Snacks**
Sweets such as candy, cake, cookies	Apples, popcorn, almonds, homemade muesli

Mustard-Dill Salmon en Papillote

BY Doree Kalfen
MAKES 4 servings
SERVING SIZE 1 salmon fillet with vegetables

Doree says: "This super easy recipe locks in all the juices for a moist, delicious taste!"

2 tablespoons olive oil
4 sheets heavy-duty aluminum foil, about 20 inches long
1 pound salmon fillet, cut into 4 pieces
4 tablespoons Dijon mustard

2 tablespoons chopped fresh dill
1 red sweet pepper, sliced
1 green sweet pepper, sliced
1 medium onion, sliced
6 button mushrooms, sliced

1 Preheat the oven to 400°F.

2 Lightly brush each sheet of aluminum foil with 1½ teaspoons olive oil. Place 1 salmon portion in the center of each foil sheet. Top each salmon portion with 1 tablespoon mustard and sprinkle with ½ tablespoon dill. Divide the sliced peppers, onion, and mushrooms evenly among the four salmon portions, placing the vegetables on top of the fish.

3 Fold the foil sheets around the salmon and vegetables and crimp the edges to make foil packets, making sure the packets are completely sealed. Place the packets on an ungreased baking sheet. Bake for 16 to 18 minutes. Carefully unwrap one packet to test for doneness; if the fish flakes easily with a fork, it is done. If the fish is not cooked through, reseal the packet and continue baking for an additional 2 to 4 minutes.

4 Remove the packets from the oven and let cool for 5 minutes before opening and serving.

NUTRITION INFORMATION Calories: 273, Protein: 26 g, Total Fat: 14 g, Saturated Fat: 2.5 g, Cholesterol: 50 mg, Sodium: 415 mg, Carbohydrate: 7 g, Fiber: 2 g

Grandma Sadie's Chicken in the Pot

BY Doree Kalfen

MAKES 6 servings

Doree says: "This recipe is a modified version of a recipe from my beloved grandmother—created from love. This healthy, low-fat dish may take some time to cook, but it's worth it!"

- 1 roasting chicken, cut into 8 pieces and skin removed
- 3 sweet potatoes, cut into large chunks
- 2 russet potatoes, cut into large chunks
- 2 sweet onions, cut into large chunks
- 1 carrot, peeled and cut into 1-inch pieces
- 1 10-ounce package white button mushrooms, halved
- 2 bay leaves
- 1½ tablespoons paprika
- 1 tablespoon dried basil
- 2 teaspoons onion powder
- 1 teaspoon garlic powder
- 1 teaspoon kosher salt
- 1 teaspoon black pepper
- 1 red sweet pepper, cut into large chunks

1 In a large pot combine the chicken pieces and ½ cup water. Cover the pot and simmer on medium-low heat for 20 minutes. Stir in the potatoes, onions, carrot, mushrooms, and seasonings (through black pepper); rearrange the chicken as necessary to make sure it's not sticking to the bottom of the pot. Allow the water to come back up to a simmer, cover the pot, and cook for 20 minutes, stirring once about halfway through. Stir in the sweet pepper and simmer for an additional 10 minutes.

2 Remove the lid and simmer, uncovered, for 20 to 30 minutes to reduce the sauce. Transfer the vegetables and sauce to a large platter and arrange the chicken pieces on top.

NUTRITION INFORMATION Calories: 305, Protein: 29 g, Total Fat: 4 g, Saturated Fat: 1 g, Cholesterol: 75 mg, Sodium: 335 mg, Carbohydrate: 39 g, Fiber: 6 g

---

PEP TALK

DOREE'S STRATEGIES FOR SUCCESS

- Eat an apple a day, especially if you have a sweet tooth.
- A nutrition bar is perfect for the 3 p.m. munchies.
- A handful of almonds is a quick and satisfying protein burst.
- 100-calorie popcorn packs work great for popcorn lovers.
- Make a box of sugar-free gelatin and pour it into individual cups for the next day.

ROCHELLE CULP

FROM Ridgeland, Mississippi
AGE 47 | HEIGHT 5' 2"
BEFORE WEIGHT 230 | AFTER WEIGHT 126 | POUNDS LOST 104

AFTER

BEFORE

Joy Fit Club members often tell me that once they lose the weight, there are people who just assume they'll gain it back. In fairness, that's the experience most people have with dieting. But those who may have harbored that idea about Rochelle would still be waiting 19 years later. Rochelle changed her life, and the evidence shows it was for good.

Rochelle grew up in the small Mississippi town of Durant. Her grandmother owned a country store, and all the kids worked in the store. The family diet was typical heavy Southern fare. As Rochelle puts it, "Gravy was a condiment."

When Rochelle was growing up, she and her three sisters all had nicknames: "small," "medium," "large," and "extra-large." Rochelle was "large."

Obesity and health problems were a common theme with her family. Her father, who was obese and also a smoker, died of a blood clot when Rochelle was 12. It was a terrible blow. Rochelle was a daddy's girl. As an active child, Rochelle managed to keep her weight somewhat in check, but that ended when she hit college. Both her activity levels and her eating habits changed for the worse. At the cafeteria she loaded her plate with fried foods and drank a six-pack of soda every day. And like many college kids, she ate pizza day and night.

After she finished college, Rochelle continued to gain weight. She got a job at an insurance company, and she ate in the cafeteria, mindless about what she was putting in her mouth. On one occasion the company sponsored a 3-mile charity walk. All the employees who participated got a day off as a reward, so Rochelle decided to do it. She was shocked when she couldn't finish the walk and then had to spend her day off recuperating. She thought to herself, "If I can't do this at 26, what will I be like at 36 or 46?"

Rochelle had many friends at work, but her weight created some embarrassing moments. She had learned—she thought—to camouflage the pounds, but she was only fooling herself. Her desk was near a window, and one day she got up to look out and the back of her blouse caught in one of the folds of fat. Everyone in her department started laughing. Rochelle was mortified. For the most part, though, Rochelle lived in denial. She banned full-length mirrors, and when she gained more weight she'd just buy clothes in the next size up without thinking about what she was doing to herself. By the time she was 26 she weighed over 230 pounds.

But reality was starting to seep in. She was only in her twenties, but she had joint problems and felt exhausted and plain lousy most days. Diabetes ran in her family, and she just assumed that would eventually be her fate. This was a dark period for Rochelle, and she knew if she didn't change she'd be like her father, dying at an early age.

Rochelle's sister, who was in nursing school and into fitness, convinced Rochelle to go walking with her. She began walking regularly and that inspired her to finally look at her diet. She was not educated about healthy eating, so she read her sister's nursing school nutrition book and began slowly making simple changes—like switching from whole milk to 2%, then 1%, and then skim. She started drinking more water and found it helped her feel full. She made sure that she never felt deprived, and she always focused on what worked for her personally.

Her regular walking outings were a great stress reliever, a time alone when she could troubleshoot problems and think about herself. Within three months people started to notice that Rochelle was losing weight. Soon her ever-nudging sister was encouraging her to join a gym. This was a step too far, in Rochelle's opinion. Gyms were full of sleek bodies who knew what they were doing. She didn't want to make a laughingstock of herself. She was especially intimidated by the idea of men at the gym watching her. But her sister persisted, and Rochelle started taking

ROCHELLE'S STRATEGIES FOR SUCCESS

DON'T GO COLD TURKEY. That's why people fall off the wagon. Begin by cutting back on your current portions and then start making healthier choices.

DON'T DO IT FOR A REASON OR A SEASON. It has to be a lifetime change.

DON'T SWEAT THE COST. You either pay now and eat healthy foods or pay later in medical costs.

DO YOUR OWN THING. One size does not fit all. It has to work for you.

an aerobics class, which she really enjoyed. To her astonishment, exercise was turning out to be the easiest part of the program. In fact, she became passionate about it. One of her greatest motivations to continue was how much better she felt. She went from being sluggish and tired all the time to having energy and confidence.

A big breakthrough for Rochelle was learning not to put so much pressure on herself. "People make it seem like it's so impossible to change," she says, "and even when you do, they're sure it won't last." During the first year after she lost the weight, she'd run into friends who would look her up and down and ask, "Are you still keeping the weight off?"—as if it were only a matter of time until she crashed. Rochelle understood that they weren't wishing for failure. They'd just never seen good examples of success.

Over the years, Rochelle has continued to challenge herself. She has competed in bodybuilding competitions, spin marathons, and boot camp programs. She has also run several full and half marathons. As she celebrates her 47th birthday, she says she lives an abundant, blessed, healthy lifestyle, and her goal is to bring others into that light. She made a career transition into tobacco prevention and health advocacy. She gets tremendous satisfaction from teaching people about making healthy lifestyle changes through seminars and workshops. She always tells people that they must find the path that works for them or they won't keep up with it.

Living in "the most overweight state in the nation," Rochelle is now on a mission to set Mississippi on a healthier course. She's a walking example of endless possibility—and she means business!

ROCHELLE'S DAILY DIET COMPARISONS

BEFORE	AFTER
Breakfast	**Breakfast**
Sausage biscuit with gravy	1 slice whole wheat toast
Scrambled eggs	Fruit or yogurt
Grits	or
	Oatmeal with apples, walnuts, and raisins
Lunch	**Lunch**
Cheeseburger with the works	Grilled chicken salad
Fries	or
Soda	Protein shake
Dinner	**Dinner**
3-4 slices of pizza with sausage, pepperoni, ham, and bacon	Grilled chicken or fish
Soda	Salad
Pastries and ice cream	Vegetables
Snacks	**Snacks**
Vending machine snacks	½ piece of fruit
Ice cream	Handful of nuts
Soda	Lots of water

JOY'S WORDS OF ADVICE

THE RIGHT BREAKFAST

HEAVY BREAKFAST. Back in her overweight days, Rochelle's typical breakfast was a sausage biscuit with gravy, 3 scrambled eggs, and a large portion of grits. That's a total of 1,200 calories and 68 grams of fat. To burn off those calories, Rochelle would have to walk for 4 hours at 3 m.p.h. or swim 2 straight hours of vigorous breast stroke in the pool.

THIN BREAKFAST. Rochelle's new and improved breakfast is a bowl of oatmeal (½ cup dry oats made with water) topped with ½ apple, diced; 1 tablespoon chopped walnuts; and 2 tablespoons raisins. One filling bowl is only 290 calories and 8 grams of fat.

Or, Rochelle whips up her Sensational Spicy Omelet (see Sensational Spicy Omelet recipe, page 148) for a slimming 183 calories and 7 grams of fat, plus 19 grams filling protein.

Sensational Spicy Omelet

BY Rochelle Culp
MAKES 1 serving

Rochelle says: "Great dish for breakfast, lunch, or dinner! Chicken breast or ground turkey breast can be added to the omelet."

Oil spray

1 to 2 tablespoons diced green sweet pepper

1 to 2 tablespoons diced onion

2 tablespoons sliced mushrooms

½ cup chopped fresh spinach

1 whole large egg

2 large egg whites

½ cup stewed tomatoes, preferably no-salt-added, well drained

1 tablespoon grated Parmesan cheese

Crushed red pepper

Black pepper

1 Liberally coat a small skillet with oil spray and heat over medium heat. Add the sweet pepper, onion, mushrooms, and spinach and cook, stirring, until the vegetables are soft, 5 to 8 minutes.

2 In a small bowl beat the whole egg and egg whites. Pour the eggs into the skillet and cook until set. Gently fold one half of the omelet over the other. Slide the omelet out of the skillet and onto a plate. Top the omelet with the stewed tomatoes and sprinkle with the cheese. Microwave for 20 to 30 seconds or just long enough to warm the tomatoes. Season the omelet with the crushed red pepper and black pepper to taste.

NUTRITION INFORMATION Calories: 183, Protein: 19 g, Total Fat: 7 g, Saturated Fat: 2.5 g, Cholesterol: 215 mg, Sodium: 300 mg, Carbohydrate: 14 g, Fiber: 2 g

LEXI MAJORS

FROM Toms River, New Jersey
AGE 25 | HEIGHT 5' 4"
BEFORE WEIGHT 253 | AFTER WEIGHT 131 | POUNDS LOST 122

For Lexi, every day was a new start to a new diet. She would starve, then binge, then starve again. She felt as if she'd been on a diet her entire life, and she had nothing to show for it. Weighing 230 pounds in high school subjected her to endless ridicule and embarrassment. She was either teased or ignored, and she often prayed that people wouldn't notice her.

AFTER

BEFORE

After being laid off from her first job, an event that was deeply emotional and depressing, her weight peaked at 253 pounds. Lexi barricaded herself in her house, only going out for essentials, mainly food. She ate enormous amounts of everything. Even though the components of her diet—hummus, vegetable stir-fry, raisin bran—weren't in themselves unhealthy, the quantities were over the top. Lexi couldn't control herself. "I would keep telling myself, 'Just STOP,'" she says, "but I couldn't stop the frenzy."

When Lexi's cousin asked Lexi to be a bridesmaid at her wedding, she dreaded the occasion. Not only would she have to come out of seclusion, but also she would have to showcase her body in a fitted gown and have it forever captured in pictures. Shopping for the dress was excruciating. "I weighed 255 pounds and she picked out a strapless gown," Lexi recalls. "I know she really thought I looked fine, but the wedding was a humiliating day for me." It was that event (and the wedding photos), with all its accompanying pain, that finally convinced Lexi to make a change. She couldn't take the shame anymore.

AFTER

BEFORE

REGAINING CONTROL

Lexi knew that to lose weight she had to find a way to control the quantities, and she began by doing the most obvious thing—counting calories. She gave herself a calorie limit, and once she reached that limit she was done for the day. Calorie counting forced her into healthier choices because she was looking for foods that she could eat *more* of. And so, slowly but surely, a diet turned into a lifestyle change.

Once she hit her first plateau, Lexi made additional changes, also cutting down on fat. At the next plateau she added more fiber and decreased the amount of sodium. Then she eliminated processed foods and finally stopped using animal products altogether. "Little by little, I was changing my diet for the better, almost without realizing what I was doing," she says. "I wanted to keep losing weight, so I incorporated different changes." It took her a year to lose 100 pounds and another half year to lose an additional 22 pounds. Probably the most important aspect, in addition to calorie control, was that she stopped eating processed foods. "Before, I was the poster child for processed foods," she says, "and now if it's from God's green earth, it's for me." Also important was becoming a vegan—a lifestyle change she has fully embraced.

She began to notice how most social engagements revolved around food, and she adopted a motto, "If you fail to plan, you plan to fail." She began strategizing in advance of family functions, when she knew there would be loads of food, deciding before she arrived how much she was going to eat and which dishes she was going to stay

---

PEP TALK

LEXI'S STRATEGIES FOR SUCCESS

- Shop the perimeter of the grocery store for fresh foods, being careful with cheese and processed meats.
- If you fail to plan, you plan to fail.
- Research the menu before going to a restaurant and decide what to order or plan to ask for substitutions.
- Never make it about deprivation, only about a healthy lifestyle.
- Find ways to add vegetables in main courses, such as stir-fries and stews.
- Know your support system: Who will help you and who will try to sabotage your diet?

away from. Or she would bring a healthy offering for everyone and eat from that. Before heading out to a restaurant, she would go online and figure out exactly what she planned to order based on the nutritional stats.

In time she added exercise. Although Lexi had always hated exercising with a passion, she found that little by little it became one of her favorite things. She started with walking and worked up to cardio machines. When she discovered yoga, it became a crucial part of her daily lifestyle. Lexi lost most of her weight within a year, and then she faced a new challenge—dating. Having never dated, she felt like an awkward teenager at first, but she's getting the hang of it. Lexi feels better than she ever has in her life—as if a huge boulder has been lifted from her shoulders. She no longer wants to be invisible. In fact, quite the contrary, she loves being out in the world. Some of her favorite things about being slimmer and healthy: shopping anywhere she likes for clothes, walking up a flight of stairs without being out of breath, finding a comfortable seat on the train. And best of all, she can live a longer life. She especially enjoys being able to look people in the eye as they pass her on the street and give them a big smile.

LEXI'S DAILY DIET COMPARISONS

BEFORE	AFTER
Breakfast	**Breakfast**
2 huge bowls of raisin bran	Small cup of whole grain cereal with almond milk
	Lunch
Lunch	**Lunch**
Turkey burger with cheese	Wild rice with edamame, seaweed, and lemon/lime juice
Fries	(Twice, one serving at noon and one at 2 p.m.)
Dinner	**Dinner**
2 huge bowls of vegetable stir-fry with rice or pasta	Buckwheat with vegetables (zucchini, cauliflower, asparagus)
Snacks	**Snacks**
Lots of crackers and hummus	Butternut squash
Popcorn	Apples
Pretzels	
Huge helpings of frozen yogurt	

STAY MOTIVATED TO EXERCISE

Lexi had always hated exercise with a passion, so she had to find a way to keep motivated for the long haul. I advise people to use the following strategies to help them stick with it:

1. SET SHORT-TERM GOALS. These are goals that are attainable in a matter of weeks; they validate that your hard work is paying off. For example, aim to walk 10 minutes every day for the next two weeks. Or, if you are currently using 2-pound weights for arm exercises, strive to reach 5-pound weights within four weeks.

2. TRY NEW THINGS. Sometimes people stop exercising because they're bored. Experimenting with different activities will help reignite your interest in exercise and keep you moving in the right direction. Sign up for group classes at the gym (Zumba, yoga, boot camp, hip-hop, etc.) or start taking lessons for a new sport, such as tennis, skiing, ballroom dancing, or snowboarding.

3. SCHEDULE EXERCISE ON YOUR CALENDAR. Treat your workout like a meeting, doctor's appointment, or any other important obligation—block out time for exercise and make it nonnegotiable!

4. PAIR FITNESS WITH SOMETHING YOU LOVE. Listen to engaging audio books on your phone or MP3 player during your daily walks or watch a favorite TV show or movie while you sweat it out on the treadmill. I have a friend who ellipticized her way through all six seasons of *Sex and the City*! You'll be so invested in the story line that you'll actually look forward to your workouts.

5. GIVE YOURSELF A FINANCIAL INCENTIVE. We actually know from studies that money is the ultimate motivator, so I've come up with a great system that will make it too costly (literally!) not to work out. I call this my Burn It to Earn It strategy, and here's how it works: "Loan" your mom (or a good friend or coworker, someone you trust!) $100 of your own money. Each time you complete a workout, your mom will give you back $5 (of course, you have to be 100% honest; no lying about your workouts). You have 30 days (one month) to earn back your $100, which means you have to fit in 20 workouts by the end of the month to recover the full amount. Anything you haven't earned back by the end Mom gets to keep. Of course, you can adjust the amount of money and the number of workouts to align with your own exercise goals, but stick with this basic system and I promise you'll be back in shape in no time!

Quinoa and Chickpea Salad

BY Lexi Majors
MAKES 8 servings
SERVING SIZE 2 cups

Lexi says: "I like to try to stick to a macrobiotic/vegan type of diet, which isn't for everyone, but I find others enjoy this recipe, so I hope you do too!"

1½ cups quinoa, rinsed (see Note, below)
1¼ teaspoons kosher salt, divided
2 15-ounce cans chickpeas, preferably no-salted-added or low-sodium, rinsed and drained
2 large zucchini, diced
1 small crown broccoli, roughly chopped
1 bunch scallions, sliced

1 bunch watercress (or 4-ounce bag), roughly chopped
½ cup chopped fresh parsley
2 lemons, juiced
2 cloves garlic, finely minced
2 teaspoons ground cumin
2 teaspoons paprika
1 teaspoon turmeric
1 teaspoon black pepper

1 In a 2- to 3-quart saucepan combine the quinoa, 2¾ cups water, and ¼ teaspoon of the kosher salt. Bring the water to a boil, then reduce the heat to low and simmer the quinoa, covered, for 15 minutes or until all of the water is absorbed. Remove the pan from the heat, remove the lid, and fluff the quinoa with a fork. Cool to room temperature (at least 20 minutes).

2 In a large bowl combine the quinoa, chickpeas, zucchini, broccoli, scallions, watercress, and parsley.

3 In a small bowl whisk together the lemon juice, garlic, the remaining 1 teaspoon kosher salt, cumin, paprika, turmeric, and pepper. Pour the dressing over the salad and stir until well combined.

NOTE Quinoa has a naturally occurring, bitter coating that must be rinsed off prior to cooking. To rinse quinoa, place it in a fine-mesh strainer or a colander lined with a paper towel. Rinse thoroughly and drain. Many brands now sell prerinsed quinoa, which allows you to skip this rinsing step, so check the package before using.

NUTRITION INFORMATION Calories: 265, Protein: 13 g, Total Fat: 3 g, Saturated Fat: 0 g, Cholesterol: 0 mg, Sodium: 225 mg, Carbohydrate: 47 g, Fiber: 9 g

KIM DIMONDO

FROM Stamford, Connecticut
AGE 39 | HEIGHT 5' 4"
BEFORE WEIGHT 258 | AFTER WEIGHT 148 | POUNDS LOST 110

AFTER

BEFORE

When she was a child, a burn trauma led Kim to seek security and comfort in food, a pattern she followed for the next 25 years. She was suffering from a form of post traumatic stress disorder, but there wasn't a lot of consciousness then about the aftereffects of trauma. Despite loving parents, family, and friends who desperately wanted to help, she was never able to obtain a healthy body weight. "From childhood into adulthood I was on a perpetual archeological dig, hunting for a treasure map to a thin body," she says now. She tried everything, starting each new diet on Monday morning. She ate low calorie, low carb, no carb, and food that tasted like cardboard. She exercised, took diet pills, went to diet doctors, and starved herself. But all the hard work ended in failure and emotional anguish. She had career ambitions, but she often wondered if she could put on an acceptable showing in the business world. With her weight, she didn't fit the mold of the slim, effective young businesswoman.

After college Kim met Mark, a guidance counselor, and they dated for seven years before getting married. To prepare for the wedding, Kim put herself on a strict diet and used ephedra, a dangerous diet supplement that has since been banned by the FDA. She didn't lose much weight because although it was an appetite suppressant, it didn't suppress her emotions. After the wedding Kim gained 30 more pounds.

Kim was relieved to get a job with a large company but soon found herself unhappy working in corporate America. She had no idea what career would suit her, and she lacked the motivation and self-esteem to find out. She was an overachiever who disguised her pain with a cheery smile and a friendly personality. She tried to dress herself well—at least from the waist up—and she avoided looking in mirrors except "to use a compact mirror to admire my thin ears and fat-free blue eyes." The irony is that Kim was so big and yet she felt invisible. Even so, people felt free to comment on her weight, often telling her that she was so beautiful—if only she'd lose a few pounds.

But food was the love of her life and her best friend. It picked her up when she was sad, celebrated with her when she was happy. "It was the only one who knew all of my pain—even though it ended up turning on me. It totally cut me off from having relationships with people. I learned at a very young age that food would numb feelings, and it felt like the easiest way to deal with life. Little did I know the damage it was causing."

She'd start each day with a new resolve and great intentions, but it would fall apart by lunchtime, and at dinner she could eat a whole box of pasta. She'd start with 1 cup, measure, cook, and eat it. Then she'd boil more water and make a second cup. When she still wasn't satisfied, she'd cook the rest of the box.

JOY'S WORDS OF ADVICE

TRIGGER FOODS

Kim is honest about her triggers—those foods she can't trust herself around. She has found healthful replacements to eliminate their power over her.

TRIGGER 1. PASTA

BEFORE: Kim would eat a gigantic portion of pasta—it was a major binge food for her.

NOW: Kim chooses other healthy whole grain starches, such as brown rice or quinoa that don't set off a binge, to enjoy with dinner. She hasn't had pasta in 7 years.

TRIGGER 2. FRESHLY BAKED COOKIES

BEFORE: If someone put a plate of cookies in front of her, Kim couldn't stop at just one.

NOW: She still enjoys cookies on occasion, but she chooses 100-calorie packs, which are preportioned, to help her stay in control.

TRIGGER 3. CHIPS (especially at Mexican restaurants)

BEFORE: If she was dining at a Mexican restaurant, Kim could easily finish off a whole basket of tortilla chips (before she even got to her entrée).

NOW: She brings a few large popped rice cakes to Mexican restaurants with her and dips them in the salsa. Or she portions out a few of the cakes for a snack at home.

AFTER

BEFORE

THE END—AND THE BEGINNING

In April 2003 Kim finally gave up. She resigned herself to living at 260 pounds. But then something happened. She had been shopping for clothes for a formal event, and as usual it was a grueling experience. Afterward Kim went out to lunch with her husband at a diner. When the waitress put Kim's heaping plate in front of her, she broke down and started to wail. How would she ever fit into her new dress and eat too? Kim was completely distraught. She had hit a wall, and as the tears fell onto the table, she realized she did not have to resign herself to being overweight.

At that lunch Kim decided she had to change. The first thing she knew was that food was a symptom, not the problem. "My mind and spirit were the issue—my body was a casualty," she says. She got brutally honest with herself and faced her demons—the reasons she ate. She let go of all the failed diet approaches of the past and got serious about tailoring a plan to her wants and needs. She worked on an exercise routine that was fun and fit into her lifestyle.

Kim was all about making her own plan that worked for her. She had tried dozens of other diets, and no standard or cookie-cutter plan ever worked for her. So she had to put together an approach that was built around her strengths and weaknesses. She knew her weaknesses—trigger foods like pastas. Her strength, however, was planning, so she planned *everything*. She planned her meals the day before and wrote it out, so the day of, as Kim says, "all I had to do was execute." She used spreadsheets to track her food intake, as well as her weight loss progress. Support was also a crucial component of her plan. She got involved with groups, found workout buddies, and relied on her husband as a pillar of support.

Then for the first time in her life, Kim saw real results—not just in her weight but in her interior feelings. She was changing from the inside out.

It took Kim two years to lose 110 pounds—90 of them the first year. Whenever she hit a plateau she told herself, "You can go forward or backward"—and she always chose to go forward. Her husband was her biggest supporter. He helped her cope with the emotional aspects of her eating. Now she can truly say that he—not food—is her best friend.

KIM HAS TWO MOTTOS THAT SHE LIVES BY:

1. "MOVE A MUSCLE, CHANGE A THOUGHT." This helps keep her knowing that as long as she's taking action, good things will happen.

2. "I PLAY BY MY OWN RULES." If she's staying true to what works for her and listening to her intuition, she can't fail.

KIM'S DAILY DIET COMPARISONS

BEFORE	AFTER
Breakfast Oversize muffin or bagel with cream cheese Midmorning cookie	**Breakfast** Oatmeal with fruit
Lunch 2 slices pizza Dessert	**Lunch** Egg white salad with hummus on 2 slices 　light bread Veggie chips
Dinner 3-4 servings pasta with marinara sauce Tater tots Mozzarella sticks	**Dinner** 3 ounces chicken Sweet potato Spinach Nonfat ice cream
Snacks Mac 'n' cheese (whole meal) 1 pint ice cream Chocolate chip cookies	**Snacks** Yogurt and carrots Small portion cottage cheese Fruit

Lentil-Stuffed Peppers

BY Kim DiMondo
MAKES 6 servings
SERVING SIZE 1 stuffed pepper

6 medium sweet peppers (peppers that are short and stout are best for stuffing)

1 cup brown rice, prepared according to package directions

1 cup lentils, prepared according to package directions

½ cup whole wheat bread crumbs

2 tablespoons prepared olive tapenade

1 large egg, lightly beaten

½ cup shredded part-skim mozzarella cheese

1 cup fire-roasted diced tomatoes (may substitute 1 cup salsa)

1 Preheat the oven to 350°F.

2 Remove the tops and seeds of the peppers and place them in a large deep baking dish. If the peppers don't stand up on their own, take a very thin slice off the bottom of the peppers to allow them to balance in the baking dish.

3 In a large bowl combine the cooked rice, cooked lentils, bread crumbs, olive tapenade, and egg until thoroughly mixed. Divide the mixture evenly among the 6 peppers (you may have some stuffing leftover depending on the size of the peppers). Sprinkle the mozzarella cheese over the tops of the peppers.

4 Fill the baking dish with ½ inch of water and cover the dish with a cover or aluminum foil. Bake for 45 to 55 minutes or until the peppers are tender.

5 Top the peppers with the fire-roasted tomatoes and serve.

NUTRITION INFORMATION Calories: 343, Protein: 16 g, Total Fat: 4 g, Saturated Fat: 1.5 g, Cholesterol: 40 mg, Sodium: 240 mg, Carbohydrate: 59 g, Fiber: 14 g

JEN AND KEITH MOORE

FROM Rochester, New York
AGE Jen, 31; Keith, 33 | HEIGHT Jen, 5′ 4″; Keith, 5′ 10″
JEN'S BEFORE WEIGHT 285 pounds | AFTER WEIGHT 150 pounds | POUNDS LOST 135
KEITH'S BEFORE WEIGHT 288 pounds | AFTER WEIGHT 188 pounds | POUNDS LOST 100

Jen and Keith are one of my star Joy Fit Club couples. They are proof that positive habits are contagious—good and bad. They were both overweight when they met, but they really started to pile on the pounds as a couple. They dated for a year before marriage, and they were deeply in love. They knew they had found kindred spirits in one another, and they ate out almost every night, regularly consuming 2,000 to 3,000 calories apiece at dinner. After they were married the habits were just part of their lives. Keith worked long hours in retail and Jen nannied full time, and at the end of the day they were too tired to prepare meals, so they headed to one of their favorite restaurants. They used food to solve all of life's problems and also for entertainment. Hard day at work? The solution was a pizza and a platter of chicken wings, chased down with a 64-ounce soda.

AFTER

BEFORE

Jen and Keith's poor dietary habits didn't just spring to life in adulthood. Each had already been laying the groundwork for many years. Jen had felt self-conscious about her weight since childhood; she had always longed to know what it was like to be thin and beautiful but was resigned to her body. She never had a boyfriend in high school, and she would eat to feel better, curling up with a book and a bag of nacho pretzels to soothe her emotional distress. "I always felt less than," Jen says. It was bad enough that the other kids teased her, but the most devastating experience came in grade school when her teacher—an adult—picked on her for her weight. Seeing her eat a snack, he pointed at her and said

AFTER

BEFORE

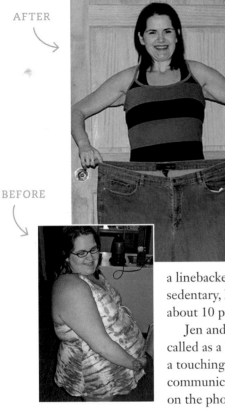

loudly, "You can't eat that. You're fat." And then he made her jump rope to work off the calories! The story of this cruelty is heartbreaking, but Jen was so cowed that it didn't even occur to her to tell anyone about it. She believed she was different from her friends. Her weight made her unworthy of proper treatment.

Jen never had a boyfriend in high school or college and never got noticed. "I was always the fat friend," she says with a sigh, "the funny one—isn't that how it goes?" She got the message that fat people can't be pretty so they have to settle for being the group comedian. Jen felt like the eternal third wheel, the perpetual matchmaker who never got to experience love herself.

In contrast, while Keith was "husky" as a child, he didn't view himself as having a weight problem. He was athletic and very active, and he thought of his physique as that of a linebacker. He dated a lot in high school. And when his lifestyle became more sedentary, he didn't even notice that he was putting on weight to the tune of about 10 pounds a year.

Jen and Keith met over a telephone chat line that Jen and some friends had called as a lark. But when Jen heard a posting by a guy with a "hot voice" reciting a touching poem that he'd written, she sent him a message. They ended up communicating on the chat line, exchanging phone numbers, and then talking on the phone for weeks before they met in person. By then Jen had a huge crush on Keith, and she was scared about their first meeting. She assumed that once he laid eyes on her it would be the same story as always, and she didn't know if she could stand to see the rejection and disgust in his eyes. But that didn't happen. They developed a deep friendship that eventually blossomed into love.

Shortly after they were married Jen was diagnosed with infertility, and in their disappointment they turned to food for comfort. Then, to their shock and amazement, Jen found out she was pregnant on her twenty-fourth birthday, and they went out for a big celebratory meal. Jen gained 60 pounds during her pregnancy, and Ken gained half that with sympathy eating.

The delivery was very difficult, and after their daughter was born Jen almost died from complications. She developed a blood clot and went into heart failure, and it took a long time to recover. Life was even more harried with a baby added to the mix, and their poor eating habits continued.

About six months after their daughter's birth, Jen decided to lose some weight, and she managed to drop 40 pounds before discovering she was pregnant again. Dieting was put on hold. In January 2007, one week past her due date, Jen went into labor and discovered that their daughter, Catriana, was stillborn. "I had to give birth to death," Jen recalls, "and there are no words to convey the depth of grief I felt."

Jen and Keith leaned on each other in the next year as they tried to heal. Their weight continued to climb—then Jen learned she was pregnant again. This time she tried to eat more healthfully and only gained 25 pounds during the pregnancy. In March 2009 their son was born and their cracked hearts began to heal.

As a couple Jen and Keith continued to be in denial about their weight and their bad habits. But that September Jen had a horrible experience that served as a revelation. They were at the amusement park, and she went on a ride with her 4-year-old daughter. The bar wouldn't fit across her stomach, and she was asked to get off. "I have never felt shame like that," Jen says, cringing at the memory. "I was soooo embarrassed." She took her daughter on another ride and she overheard the teenage attendant make a comment to his friends about her being a "fat cow." She was reeling. She'd never been called a name like that in her entire life, and it was especially painful to have it happen in front of her child. Her daughter, as it turned out, was oblivious, but Jen couldn't get the thought out of her mind that if it happened when her daughter was older, she would be ashamed of her mom. And Jen couldn't bear the thought. It was

JEN AND KEITH'S DAILY DIET COMPARISONS

BEFORE	AFTER
Breakfast	**Breakfast**
Jen: skipped breakfast	**Jen:** vanilla oatmeal, banana
Keith: 2 breakfast sandwiches, home fries, up to a pound of bacon, 3–4 donuts	**Keith:** 3-egg omelet with peppers and onions, 1 slice cheese
Lunch	**Lunch**
Jen: drive-through—2 of everything on the dollar menu	**Jen:** spinach lasagna, side salad
Keith: 2 triple-decker peanut butter and jelly sandwiches, bag of chips, quart of chocolate milk	**Keith:** whole grain wrap with turkey, avocado, lettuce, spinach
Dinner	**Dinner**
Jen: Fried appetizers and entrées with heaping side of fries, chocolate cake	**Jen:** 4-ounce pork chop with maple-mustard glaze, roasted vegetables
Keith: Fried appetizers and entrées, or steak and potatoes, cheesecake	**Keith:** 4-ounce pork chop with maple-mustard glaze, sweet potato, roasted vegetables
Snacks	**Snacks**
Jen: Large coffee drink with extra whipped cream, soda	**Jen:** Small "light" coffee drink, Greek yogurt, fruit, protein bar
Keith: 64-ounce sugary slushie drink, chips and dip	**Keith:** 1 tablespoon peanut butter with apple, fruit, Greek yogurt

AFTER

BEFORE

the first time she saw herself not just as overweight, but truly obese. "I couldn't get on a ride with my child! It made me feel terrible—and determined." That minute she vowed that she would return the following year as a hot mama, riding all the rides with her daughter, and never be called a fat cow again.

At first Keith was a little bit skeptical because Jen had tried and failed so many times before. But this time he noticed something different. She was approaching the journey in a balanced way—no more fad diets. In fact, she refused to use the word "diet," saying she was making a "lifestyle change."

Jen was absolutely determined. She realized that if she had the inner resources to transcend the pain of giving birth to a dead baby, she could find those same resources for this journey.

Jen started with evaluating her intake and deciding what she had to eat every day and what she was and was not willing to give up. She counted calories and looked for a balance of carbs, protein, and fat. She also used Facebook as a form of accountability and posted progress pictures online. Her friends rallied and kept telling her she could do it.

Jen planned ahead so that she would be eating throughout the day. Previously she had skipped breakfast and lunch and often went until 4:00 in the afternoon before her first bite of food. Then she'd be so hungry that she'd eat everything in sight. After an afternoon of heavy snacking, she and Keith would go out and consume over a day's worth of calories in one meal.

A big boost to Jen's motivation was discovering hooping. She had never been an active person, but she heard about a Beyonce video and hooping with adult-size hoops. She bought the hoop and a Hoopnotica DVD and determined to do 15 minutes a day. In the beginning, she couldn't even keep the hoop up. It took her more than two weeks to accomplish that, and then she kept getting better. She fell in love with hooping, and it was terrific exercise. In two months she lost 20 pounds.

At that point, Keith was really starting to pay attention. Jen had never nagged him, only asking that he respect her journey, but he was impressed by the change in her. Although Keith was 288 pounds, he literally did not see how big he was. "When I looked in the mirror, I saw my high school self," he says. "I'd think, 'I could stand to lose 20 pounds.'" When his clothes got tight, he thought Jen was shrinking them in the dryer. He never weighed himself, and when he finally stepped on the scale and saw the number 288 he almost fainted with horror. But because Jen was so enthusiastic and the couple always did everything together, Keith finally asked her to help him set up a food plan and hold him accountable.

FUEL UP WITH A PROTEIN-RICH BREAKFAST

Both Jen and Keith regularly skipped breakfast, setting themselves up for a crash later in the day. I can't emphasize enough the importance of taking a few minutes to start your day with a healthy, balanced breakfast. A solid morning meal helps refuel your body after a night of rest, satisfies your appetite so you're less likely to graze later, and primes you to make healthy food choices throughout the rest of the day.

But not all breakfasts have the same fill power. Research has consistently shown that including protein at breakfast is critical when it comes to weight loss. Eating a protein-rich meal in the a.m. helps to fill you up and keep you full, so you end up eating less during the afternoon and evening hours. A study published in the *International Journal of Obesity* found that dieters who dined on eggs lost more weight and reported more energy than those who had a carby bagel breakfast with the same calorie count.

HERE ARE A FEW OF MY FAVORITE HIGH-PROTEIN BREAKFASTS:

WAFFLE WITH RICOTTA AND FRUIT. Top a whole grain waffle with ½ cup part-skim ricotta cheese and 1 sliced peach or 5 sliced strawberries. The creamy ricotta provides protein and calcium. 300 calories, 15 g protein, 13 g fat, 38 g carb, 6 g fiber

GREEK YOGURT WITH FRUIT. Greek yogurt has twice as much protein as traditional yogurt, so it's the perfect base for a substantial morning meal. Enjoy a 6-ounce container of nonfat Greek yogurt (plain or flavored) topped with 1 tablespoon chopped, toasted nuts (walnuts, almonds, pecans, or any other variety) and add a banana, orange, half a grapefruit, or another piece of fruit on the side. 220–260 calories, 18–22 g protein, 5 g fat, 25–38 g carb, 3 g fiber

SPINACH-CHEESE EGG SCRAMBLE. Eggs are one of the best sources of high-quality protein at breakfast. Sauté a few handfuls of baby spinach in oil spray, then add in 1 whole egg whipped with 2 to 3 egg whites. (I use mostly egg whites to cut back on the saturated fat and calories and bump up the protein.) Sprinkle with ¼ cup shredded reduced-fat cheese and scramble away! Enjoy with a whole grapefruit alongside. 330 calories, 29 g protein, 11 g fat, 32 g carb, 7 g fiber

Like his wife, Keith was in the habit of skipping meals and then consuming large quantities later in the day. He loved sports, and while watching a ball game at the bar with friends he could easily consume 3,000 calories in pub food. He started by cutting way down on calories and eating throughout the day. "I thought of it as feeding a furnace gradually," he says. Keith made his focus "clean" eating—lots of natural, organic foods and cutting out processed and chemically altered foods.

He also had to battle "a sweet tooth a mile long." Keith confesses that his sweet tooth is never satisfied, and he'll probably battle it for the rest of his life. But he was changing his mind about the issue. Before, he felt helpless over the craving for sweets. Now he realized he could control it.

Even when he was heavy, Keith had always done a certain amount of exercise. He was passionate about weightlifting and very knowledgeable about the body's musculature. Now he had to apply that knowledge more sensibly and incorporate aerobic exercise. Every small victory—such as running a mile without stopping—was magnified and increased his motivation.

Working together, Jen and Keith's success mounted. They stopped eating out for a long time because they didn't trust their ability to navigate the restaurant world. If they went out with others, they ate beforehand and just ordered a side salad or vegetables with their friends.

COMPLETE LIFESTYLE CHANGE

Today Jen and Keith are fitness models. Jen is a certified group fitness instructor and a certified Hoopnotica instructor teaching 15 hooping classes a week. She is also a Hoopnotica Master Trainer, certifying others to teach. She was chosen as Mrs. Monroe County 2010, and she competed in the Mrs. New York pageant in a swimsuit! "I finally feel as if my outside matches my inside," she says. "I am helping my children create a strong foundation, loving being active, and trying new, healthy foods. I have never been happier."

Ken has become a certified personal trainer, a certified group fitness instructor, and a phys ed teacher, and says he is "paying it forward, helping others gain the knowledge and skills that have allowed me to change my life." He reports that he is the happiest he's been in years and in the best shape of his life. His business card has his "before" picture on the back, and he tells people, "Let me help you realize your new self." Keith is proud that he and Jen have achieved the "trifecta"—healthy minds, healthy spirits, and healthy bodies.

Moore's Meatballs

BY Jen Moore
MAKES 5 servings (25 meatballs total)
SERVING SIZE 5 meatballs

Jen says: "These meatballs freeze well and the meat mixture also makes excellent burgers."

1 large egg
1¼ pounds ground turkey (at least 90% lean) or lean ground sirloin
1 cup oats
1 cup chopped onion
1 cup finely chopped spinach
2 tablespoons reduced-fat shredded cheese (use your favorite variety)
¼ teaspoon kosher salt
¼ teaspoon black pepper
2 cups reduced-sodium broth (beef, chicken, or vegetable)

1 In a large bowl beat the egg. Add the ground turkey or beef and next 6 ingredients (through black pepper). Mix the ingredients—hands work the best—until thoroughly combined.

2 Form the meat mixture into 25 golf ball-size meatballs.

3 Bring the broth to a boil in a pot. Add the meatballs and cover the pot. Reduce the heat to low and simmer for 30 minutes, turning the meatballs every 10 minutes. Remove the meatballs from the broth with a slotted spoon.

4 To serve, mix the meatballs with marinara sauce and toss with whole wheat pasta. Or toss the meatballs into any flavorful soup.

NUTRITION INFORMATION Calories: 239, Protein: 29 g, Total Fat: 7 g, Saturated Fat: 2 g, Cholesterol: 110 mg, Sodium: 175 mg, Carbohydrate: 13 g, Fiber: 2 g

Tomato-Basil Couscous Casserole

BY Jen Moore
MAKES 12 servings

Oil spray
1½ cups unsalted or reduced-sodium
  chicken or vegetable broth
1 cup whole wheat couscous
1 tablespoon extra virgin olive oil
1 large onion, finely diced
1 (28-ounce) can diced tomatoes,
  preferably no-salt-added, drained
  (reserve ⅓ cup of the juice)

3 cloves garlic, minced
1 teaspoon dried basil
½ teaspoon kosher salt
  Black pepper
5 cups fresh spinach, finely chopped
1 cup shredded part-skim mozzarella
  cheese

1 Preheat the oven to 375°F. Liberally coat a 9×13-inch baking pan with oil spray.

2 In a medium saucepan bring the broth to a boil.

3 Add the couscous to a large bowl. Pour in the broth and stir to combine. Cover the bowl and let stand for 5 minutes. Fluff with a fork.

4 In a large skillet heat the oil over medium heat. Add the onion and cook, stirring, until translucent and soft, 5 to 7 minutes. Add the drained tomatoes, garlic, basil, salt, and pepper to taste and cook, stirring, for 10 minutes. Add the tomato mixture, reserved tomato juice, and spinach to the couscous and mix to combine. Spread half of the couscous-tomato mixture into the prepared baking pan. Sprinkle the mozzarella cheese evenly over the couscous and add the remaining couscous, creating a top layer. Cover the pan with aluminum foil and bake for 30 minutes. Allow the casserole to cool for 5 minutes to set, then cut into 12 pieces.

NUTRITION INFORMATION Calories: 126, Protein: 6 g, Total Fat: 3 g, Saturated Fat: 1 g, Cholesterol: 5 mg, Sodium: 195 mg, Carbohydrate: 20 g, Fiber: 4 g

Andrea's Pumpkin Pie

BY Jen Moore
MAKES 2 9-inch pies (16 servings)
SERVING SIZE ⅛ of 1 pie

This recipe makes two pies. Jen keeps one for her family to enjoy and either freezes the second one for another time or gives it away to friends and family.

2 cups pumpkin puree (canned or fresh) (see Note, below)	2 teaspoons pumpkin pie spice
1¼ cups skim milk	1 teaspoon ground cinnamon
3 large eggs	¼ teaspoon kosher salt
⅓ cup honey	2 unbaked 9-inch piecrusts (preferably whole wheat)
⅓ cup pure maple syrup	

1 Preheat the oven to 450°F.

2 Combine the first 8 ingredients (through salt) in a food processor and process until smooth (you can also blend the filling by hand with a whisk). Pour the filling into the crusts, dividing it evenly between the two crusts.

3 Transfer the pies to the oven and immediately reduce the oven temperature to 350°F. Bake the pies for 60 to 70 minutes or until a knife inserted halfway between the crust and the center of the pie comes out clean.

NOTE Jen sometimes uses fresh pumpkin puree for the pie. Here's how she makes the puree from scratch:

How to cook a pie pumpkin: Cut pumpkin in half, stem to bottom, and scoop out the seeds. Pour ½ cup of water on a rimmed baking sheet and set the pumpkin halves on the sheet, cut sides down. Bake at 350°F until very soft. Scoop out the flesh. Puree in a food processor until smooth.

NUTRITION INFORMATION Calories: 180, Protein: 4 g, Total Fat: 9 g, Saturated Fat: 4 g, Cholesterol: 40 mg, Sodium: 140 mg, Carbohydrate: 23 g, Fiber: 3 g, Total Sugar: 13 g

Zucchini Bread

BY Jen Moore
MAKES 2 loaves (20 servings)
SERVING SIZE ⅒ of 1 loaf

Oil spray
2 cups whole wheat flour
1 cup quinoa flour (may substitute all-purpose flour if quinoa flour is unavailable)
3 teaspoons ground cinnamon
1 teaspoon baking soda
1 teaspoon baking powder
1 teaspoon kosher salt
3 large eggs
1½ cups turbinado sugar (may substitute granulated sugar)
1 cup unsweetened applesauce
1 tablespoon vanilla extract
1 large green zucchini, grated (about 2 cups)
½ cup chopped walnuts

1 Preheat the oven to 325°F. Coat two 8×4-inch loaf pans with oil spray.

2 In a large bowl whisk together the flours, cinnamon, baking soda, baking powder, and salt.

3 In a large bowl lightly beat the eggs. Add the sugar, applesauce, and vanilla, and stir until combined. Add the dry ingredients to the wet ingredients, and stir until just combined. Stir in the zucchini and nuts. Divide the batter evenly between the two loaf pans, filling each about halfway to the top.

4 Bake for 55 to 65 minutes or until a knife or toothpick inserted in the centers of the loaves comes out clean. Cool in the pans on a rack for 20 minutes. Remove the bread from the pans and cool completely.

NUTRITION INFORMATION (1 SLICE, ⅒ OF LOAF) Calories: 160, Protein: 4 g, Total Fat: 3 g, Saturated Fat: 0 g, Cholesterol: 30 mg, Sodium: 145 mg, Carbohydrate: 30 g, Fiber: 3 g, Total Sugar: 16 g

Variation For zucchini muffins, coat two standard (12-cup) muffin pans with oil spray. Fill the muffin cups with the batter about three-fourths full and bake for 20 to 25 minutes or until a knife or toothpick inserted in the center of a muffin comes out clean. Makes 24 muffins.

ANITA MILLS

FROM Flatwoods, Kentucky
AGE 43 | HEIGHT 5'6"
BEFORE WEIGHT 382 | AFTER WEIGHT 140 | POUNDS LOST 242

AFTER

BEFORE

Anita always longed to be just like everybody else, but her weight made her stand out in the worst way. She wanted to wear cool clothes like all her friends, especially jeans, but her mom bought her stretchy pants like old people wear. ("I still have flashbacks about those pants," she admits.) In eighth grade Anita weighed 220 pounds, and her mother also weighed more than 200 pounds. It was a horrible embarrassment, and she knew people joked about them—what a pair! Her mother's weight problems made her own size seem inevitable, and this made her even more depressed.

When Anita was a freshman in high school, she and her mother joined a very restrictive high-protein diet program. Anita remembers it being horrible—endless suffering and starvation. She lost 50 pounds, but she was so hungry that she soon gained it back and more. Her senior year she weighed 250 pounds, and she lost hope that she could ever summon the discipline to take it off. In her experience, dieting meant starvation, and it was terribly unfair that she should have to starve while other girls her age were able to eat normally.

In spite of her weight problem, Anita felt like a lucky girl when she met Charlie in high school. For once in her life someone looked beneath her size and appreciated who she was. His unwavering acceptance and love made her feel cherished, and she was thrilled when he asked her to marry him. (They've now been married 25 years.) "Charlie has always told me I was beautiful, and we tell each other every day—several times—how much we love each other," Anita says. When their two sons were born, life was complete.

But being happily married and a mother didn't solve Anita's weight problem. To the contrary, it took some of the emotional pressure off and she gained even more. Anita got in the habit of eating whatever she wanted with no regard to the calories or other nutritional value of the food. It was nothing for her to eat candy bars, bags of chips, and other high-calorie snacks at any time of the day. For example, at work she'd have a candy bar and cheese curls at her 10:00 a.m. break and then another candy bar and bag of chips at her 3:00 p.m. break, along with a big lunch in between. At home she'd make high-fat dinners, and she rarely served vegetables or salads. As a result, her husband Charlie and her two sons tended to eat poorly too.

Looking back on when her children were young, Anita regrets all the things she couldn't do. She'd go to the park with them and sit on a bench and watch instead of participating. She had trouble getting up from a seated position, and when she visited friends she sometimes brought her own chair, fearing she would break theirs.

Anita's doctor, John Walz, always talked to her about her weight, and he even gave her a paper on which he'd written sure-fire diet tips, which she tucked into a purse without reading. She carried that paper around for a year, and when she changed purses, she always moved it to the next purse. It was like a talisman, but she wasn't ready to look yet. She wasn't ready to see the handwriting on the

---

HOW OFTEN SHOULD YOU EAT?

The strategy of eating every three hours worked perfectly for Anita. But keep in mind that at the end of the day, it's the total number of calories you're eating that matters most—not how many daily meals you're consuming. As long as your daily calories are appropriate for your weight loss goal, it really doesn't matter whether those calories are spread out into 5 or 6 mini meals or coming from 3 squares. My advice is to choose the eating plan that best aligns with your schedule and lifestyle—and just make sure that your total daily calories are in check.

Just a word of caution: If you do choose to eat small, mini meals every 2 or 3 hours, you'll need to be extra diligent about keeping portions small at each eating occasion. It's very easy to let those "mini meals" grow into larger meals. And then you wind up taking in too many calories and gaining weight as a result! A 2011 Purdue University study conducted with a group of overweight men compared 3 large meals per day with 6 smaller meals per day (same total daily calories). Contrary to what researchers expected, eating more frequently throughout the day didn't help curb hunger or decrease the desire to eat. The men also reported more difficulties sticking to the 6-meal plan because they couldn't keep interrupting their work day to eat another meal.

wall in the form of her mother, whose weight was taking a heavy toll on her life in the form of diabetes.

ANITA'S TURNING POINT

One day Anita was sitting with her mother in a doctor's office in Lexington, Kentucky. They were talking about her mother's diabetes. The doctor was discussing her options, and she wanted to try all of them to stay alive. Anita realized how brave her mother was, willing to do anything to keep living, while she was killing herself. She excused herself and went into the bathroom of the doctor's office and cried her eyes out. It was her breaking point. It was also her turning point.

Anita returned home and took a picture of herself. She said out loud, "I will never weigh 382 pounds again." But how could she even begin to take the first step? Suddenly she remembered Dr. Walz's paper, and she hurried to her purse and took it out. He had always told her if she followed only four steps she would lose weight. In fact, he guaranteed it. Now that she was ready, she studied the tips he'd written down for her. The note (which she still has to this day) read:

1. 8 ounces of any food every 3 hours.
2. No sugared drinks.
3. Don't skip a 3-hour meal.
4. Don't tell anyone what you are doing.

Anita talked to Dr. Walz about the steps and what they meant. He told her that step one was a way of learning about portion sizes, and she had to figure that out even before she worried about what to eat. Step two, giving up soda, was obvious. Step three, eating every three hours, was a way of keeping the metabolism going—and also a way of avoiding hunger attacks. The hardest one for Anita was step four. She asked why it was so important not to tell people what she was doing. "I thought that support was the key," she said. Dr. Walz replied that sometimes people unknowingly sabotage your efforts with a "just one won't hurt" mentality and it can cause you to falter and fail. He also said it was so much better to have someone ask, "Are you losing weight?" than to announce that you're on a new diet.

She started following the four rules, and she added exercise, walking during lunch and turning on Richard Simmons' *Sweating to the Oldies* after work.

THE 8-OUNCE MEAL

The simple act of following the first item on Dr. Walz's list—eat an 8-ounce meal every three hours—paved the way for Anita's success. She would either measure 8 ounces of food, like chicken and vegetables, on a food scale, or she would measure 8 ounces of volume for foods like oatmeal. An inexpensive food scale was a godsend.

In the beginning, Anita didn't change what she ate. She ate the same unhealthy foods as she did before—fried chicken, potato chips, and white pasta—and just focused on eating smaller portions at 3-hour intervals. As Anita's story demonstrates, it is possible to lose weight if you just cut your portions, even if you don't change the types of foods you eat.

As she continued to get results, Anita gradually began changing to less calorie-dense foods so she could eat a larger volume. She was adding in more vegetables and fruits and switching to leaner proteins, whole grains, and low-fat dairy.

After she had lost 120 pounds in about nine months, it finally sunk in for Anita that this was for real. One day, walking with her husband into Walmart, she caught a glimpse of her reflection in the window. Her first reaction was "Who's that chick walking next to my husband?" When she realized she was looking at her own reflection, all she could do was gape.

Anita's weight loss made a huge difference in her health and well-being. Her blood results are all normal, and she feels so much better. "I now can look forward to living the rest of my life with

ANITA'S DAILY DIET COMPARISONS

BEFORE	AFTER
Breakfast Sugary chocolate cereal with milk	**Breakfast** Egg whites with ham and reduced-fat cheese cooked in a mug
Lunch Pizza or fast food	**Lunch** Tuna sandwich thin with frozen veggies in cheese sauce
Dinner Deep-fried chicken or hamburgers with fries and onion rings	**Dinner** Individual chicken pizza made with a high-fiber tortilla "crust" Side salad Fat-free ice cream
Snacks Candy bar Cake Chips Cheese curls	**Snacks** Fruit—pineapple and watermelon Low-fat microwave popcorn

my family and not cutting it short because of my weight. I am now doing things I would have never dreamed of." The little things mean the most to her, such as walking up a flight of stairs. She remembers how excited she was the first time she sat on the couch and crossed her legs. She hadn't been able to do that since she was very young.

Anita enjoys the opportunities her weight loss has created for her—especially the ability to help others. "I feel God puts us on the earth to help others, and I am using that every opportunity to reach out to anyone that needs it to try to motivate them to a healthier lifestyle. It's not about getting skinny; it's about being healthy." Her immediate family hugely benefited from the overhaul Anita gave to their grocery cart, meals, and lifestyle. Her son Anthony lost 65 pounds, her son William dropped 40 pounds, and her husband, Charlie, said goodbye to 45 pounds. Anita also has friends who have started watching and exercising, motivated by seeing an actual person they know succeed.

Charlie tells everyone, "I loved her at 380 pounds. I love her at 140 pounds. The only difference is that I pick her up more often."

Black Bean Brownie Bites

BY Anita Mills
MAKES 36 to 42 mini brownies
SERVING SIZE 2 mini brownies

　　Oil spray
1　box low-fat brownie mix
1　15-ounce can black beans, preferably no-salt-added or low-sodium, rinsed and drained

1 Preheat the oven to 350°F. Coat 2 nonstick mini-muffin pans with oil spray.

2 In a blender combine the black beans and ¾ cup water and puree until smooth. Pour the bean puree into a large bowl and add the brownie mix. Beat until smooth.

3 Fill the muffin cups about three-fourths full with batter (about 1 tablespoon batter in each). Bake for 12 to 15 minutes, or until a toothpick inserted in the center of a brownie bite comes out clean. Cool for 10 minutes before removing from pan.

NUTRITION INFORMATION (FOR 2 BROWNIE BITES, ASSUMING RECIPE MAKES 36 BITES)
Calories: 151, Protein: 2 g, Total Fat: 2 g, Saturated Fat: 0.5 g, Cholesterol: 0 mg, Sodium: 130 mg, Carbohydrate: 31 g, Fiber: 2 g, Total Sugar: 19 g

SHERI HARKNESS

FROM Pocono Mountains, Pennsylvania
AGE 43 | HEIGHT 5' 8"
BEFORE WEIGHT 282 | AFTER WEIGHT 141 | POUNDS LOST 141

AFTER

BEFORE

Sheri grew up with the "eat everything on your plate or there will be no dessert" mentality. Her family life was centered on food. It was a way to show love, a way to celebrate, and a way to be together. Weekends started off with a big family breakfast, consisting of pancakes with butter and syrup, bacon and sausage, fried eggs, home fries, and biscuits. On warm nights they would barbecue huge steaks and eat her mother's homemade ice cream. When she was younger, Sheri's sports activities kept the extra weight off, and she never really had a problem, but when she was 16, her parents divorced and things changed. She was very confused and turned to food for support. Eating was like a safety net for her, a way of returning to the warm embrace of the family life she had once cherished. Her weight got out of control and continued to climb throughout her twenties. "I stopped caring about myself," she admitted. "I had no goals. I was not prepared to be on my own. I was just floating through life, and my weight helped me to not move forward."

Sheri met her husband over the phone and was attracted to the idea of being with someone. She moved to New Jersey and got married, and she was ecstatic with the birth of each of her two sons. But the marriage wasn't a good one, and Sheri felt lonely and holed up with the boys. She ate to take her mind off her troubles. By the time she was in her thirties, Sheri's weight was more than 250 pounds. She felt the effects every minute. The simplest of tasks was difficult. Walking up the steps to do laundry left her out of breath and sweating. Worst of all, she was a mere observer to the lives of her active boys. She longed for them to look up to her as a healthy, happy mom but knew that they saw her as a constantly tired, lethargic one. She hated the idea that she was an embarrassment to her sons, but she knew she was because they were present for many publicly humiliating moments.

Grocery shopping was one of Sheri's most dreaded activities. She noticed people staring at the items in her cart, as if making a mental checklist of what fat people ate so they could be sure to avoid those items.

Reflecting on those days, Sheri has empathy for her struggling self. "What I find to be so sad about being overweight," she says, "is that your pain is evident in your appearance. When people see you on the street they see someone who is disgusting. They see someone who can't get control of herself. They see a pig."

Fat and unhappy, Sheri still lacked the motivation to act until a terrible tragedy struck her family. Her mother, only 54 years old, died from pancreatic cancer. Soon after, Sheri began to suffer from panic attacks, convinced that she would get cancer as well. To add to the pressure, she was struggling in her marriage and her husband had health issues as well. She didn't know where to turn.

During that period Sheri had a routine physical, and she received some discouraging news. No, she didn't have cancer, but the doctor used the term "morbidly obese" several times during

SATISFY YOUR SWEET TOOTH

Sheri craved sweets more than any other food, and she's definitely not alone. Those of you who can relate will be happy to hear you don't necessarily have to cut out all sweet treats to be successful. Each of the following is 150 calories or less and can safely satisfy a craving.

- 1 ounce dark chocolate
- ½ cup low-fat chocolate pudding
- 1 ounce dark chocolate melted over 5 whole strawberries
- ½ cup light ice cream or frozen yogurt
- 1 low-cal ice cream pop/sandwich, frozen fruit pop, or Italian ice
- 1 sliced frozen banana
- 1 cup frozen grapes
- 1 cup berries with a squirt of whipped cream
- 1 biscotti or 2 standard store-bought cookies
- ½ sweet potato sprinkled with cinnamon and 1 teaspoon brown sugar
- 1 serving chocolate or caramel flavored mini rice cakes
- 10 small chocolate-covered pretzels

AFTER

BEFORE

her appointment and told her that her blood pressure and cholesterol levels were dangerously high. Sheri was stunned. She was only 38 years old.

After that physical, Sheri says, "I decided to have a little sit-down with Miss Mortality. We decided that enough was enough and I needed to take charge of my life."

Reflecting back on her state of mind then, Sheri notes that she didn't have a huge "aha" moment. It was more a culmination of many different life-altering events. "I believe that everyone has a dimmer switch in them, not only about weight loss but about other areas of life," she says thoughtfully. "Often times it's like we're stumbling around in the dark with our hands out in front of us feeling for the switch. On that journey in the dark we make poor decisions that can have devastating results. That is because we cannot see without the light on. For me, that series of events brought me closer to the switch until I found it and pushed it. I turned it up a little each day, making it brighter and brighter."

GETTING STARTED

Sheri decided that she was going to throw out all the old diet advice from the past and seriously create a plan just for her needs. She began with the amount of food she ate. In the beginning she kept eating the same foods, but she cut every portion in half. In restaurants she would ask to have half her portion wrapped to go before she even started eating. She also completely dropped her 2-liter-a-day soda habit—a change that saved 260,000 calories a year! It was hard getting off the sugar habit. In the early weeks, Sheri was cranky and she would have overwhelming hunger pangs for carbohydrates. But she rode it out, and soon the pangs diminished as her body grew accustomed to the new system. The longer she avoided sodas and processed foods, the less she wanted them, and when she did try to eat one of her old favorites, it didn't even taste good anymore. Hallelujah! Her taste buds had changed.

Sheri knew she had to exercise, but she resisted going to the gym for a while. She imagined herself walking past all those pretty people, and she couldn't stomach the thought. She needed positive reinforcement, not a blatant reminder of how fat she was. When she finally decided to take the leap, she vowed that she would not skulk around with her head down as if she didn't belong there. She would look everyone in the eye and smile. She started walking on the treadmill for three minutes at a time, which left her huffing and puffing and sweating profusely. It was the hardest thing she'd ever done, but she kept at it, very slowly increasing her distance.

Her biggest booster was her sister Karen, a fitness director at Bacara Resort and Spa in Santa Barbara. Karen guided her nutritional choices and exercise options, but best of all she was a loving, encouraging presence, almost as dedicated to Sheri's success as she was herself. Sheri was further supported by the spirit of her mother. "I felt her thoughts and energy moving through me daily, constantly reminding me of the task at hand, and telling me to stop and smell the roses," she says, smiling.

Sheri's weight loss journey was a mental process, as well as a physical one. While she was losing weight, she was also cleaning up her self-esteem issues and discovering who she was. With every 10 pounds lost, Sheri had to reintroduce herself to herself and check in with who she was. More and more, she was liking that person.

MILESTONES ON THE JOURNEY

Sheri is grateful for all the gifts that have been showered on her since she lost 138 pounds. She remembers with delight the first time she needed to wear a belt, the first time she crossed her legs comfortably, the first time she ran a 5K, and going to her car afterward and breaking into tears because she had never imagined such an accomplishment.

She relishes the new pride her sons take in her and sometimes catches one of them nodding in her direction as if to say, "*That's* my mom." But mostly Sheri recognizes the gift that comes each and every morning when she gets up, looks in the mirror and says, "Good morning, Sheri. You sure have been gone a long while. I've missed you. It's good to have you back. Now, let's go make a difference."

Fit, glowing with health, and looking gorgeous, Sheri says proudly, "I've found the person I was meant to be, and she's pretty darn cool."

Open-Face Lox and Tomato Sandwich with Creamy Avocado Spread

BY Sheri Harkness

MAKES 2 servings

SERVING SIZE ½ sandwich thin

- ¼ cup whipped cream cheese
- ¼ cup diced avocado
- ½ lemon, juiced
- 1 whole grain 100-calorie sandwich thin
- 2 slices tomato
- 2 ounces thinly sliced lox
- 2 leaves fresh basil, sliced into thin ribbons

1 In a small bowl combine the cream cheese, avocado, and lemon juice. Mash the ingredients together to make a smooth spread.

2 Toast the sandwich thin. Spread the avocado-cream cheese mixture evenly on one side of each half of the sandwich thin to make an open-face sandwich. Top each side with a tomato slice and 1 ounce lox and sprinkle with the basil.

NUTRITION INFORMATION Calories: 200, Protein: 11 g, Total Fat: 12 g, Saturated Fat: 4.5 g, Cholesterol: 35 mg, Sodium: 570 mg, Carbohydrate: 15 g, Fiber: 5 g

BRIAN SPAR

FROM Oceanside, New York
AGE 35 | HEIGHT 5′8″
BEFORE WEIGHT 340 | AFTER WEIGHT 185 | POUNDS LOST 155

AFTER

BEFORE

Brian admits that he was a difficult child, but when you hear his story, it's easy to feel compassion for the lost, overweight boy who didn't know how to help himself and who was too embarrassed to accept the help of others. He was overweight his entire life and remembers going to the doctor's office with his mom and being sent home with nutrition plans on sheets of paper that seemed like a punishment. He resisted change, and he felt like his parents didn't understand him. To some extent Brian blamed himself for being fat—even though he was just a kid. To this day he cites his unwillingness to give up junk food as a child for his lifetime weight problems, but of course that was far from the case. Brian's parents tried to be loving and tried to help him, but Brian became increasingly defiant. They may have been frustrated and thought, "Doesn't he want to lose weight?" But it wasn't that simple.

Brian was confronted with his weight every day at school and during every extracurricular activity, and he saw that people treated the fat kid differently from everyone else. In particular, Brian vividly remembers one time in day camp, when he was 10, being out by the pool. He was standing shirtless next to one of the male counselors and a female teenage camper. The counselor gestured to Brian and said to the girl, "That kid has bigger breasts than you do." Brian wished the ground would open and swallow him up. He was miserable, but he didn't know how to change his circumstances because food was everything.

He planned his days around eating. Going to the movies? Got to have popcorn with butter and cherry cola. Playing basketball? Stop at the convenience store for a quart of iced tea and some chips afterwards. Out with friends? This would be centered on food. He was always hungry.

Brian had wanted to be a veterinarian ever since he had found an injured baby bird at 5 years old. When it died, he grieved: "Why couldn't I help it?" He became passionate about learning to save animals, and that passion stayed with him. Brian was accepted into veterinary school in England, and he loved being on his own. But his overeating escalated once he was living away from home. He went shopping for himself, so there were no limits. He would load up on chips, soda, and frozen pizza, and those would be the staples of his diet. He usually skipped breakfast, making him ravenously hungry all day long. He was constantly snacking—bacon or sausage sandwiches, cakes, cookies, chips. For lunch he would make a couple of buttered grilled ham and cheese sandwiches accompanied by at least a half can of potato crisps and washed down with a minimum of one liter of soda. He would snack throughout the afternoon, then eat a whole pizza, more soda, and ice cream in

---

JOY'S WORDS OF ADVICE

RAISE FOOD-SAVVY KIDS

Brian is determined to teach his daughter how to eat right so she develops healthy habits and never has to struggle with a weight issue. Parents are the main teachers when it comes to nutrition. Even peer pressure doesn't stand a chance against a child who has a solid foundation. Here are some ways to get your kids excited about healthful eating.

GO GROCERY SHOPPING TOGETHER. Taking the kids to the store can be an unexpected learning experience. Shopping along with you, they'll learn about navigating a variety of foods and making the smartest choices. With older kids, demonstrate exactly why you've selected a healthy food over an unhealthy one by teaching them to read labels and make good judgment calls, such as selecting lots of fresh, colorful produce.

USE REWARDS OTHER THAN FOOD. Giving kids delicious treats because they aced their tests or cleaned their rooms makes them associate unhealthy foods with good feelings. Instead, verbally praise your kids. Give them other privileges, like a trip to the zoo or the choice of which movie the family watches tonight.

MAKE HEALTHY FOOD FUN! Dinner will become a memorable, exciting activity if you encourage your kids to help you in the kitchen. It gets them involved and makes them more willing to try new things: stews, casseroles, soups — whatever you dream up together! Another fun idea: Create theme nights of their favorite healthy foods. Maybe it's Southwestern night with grilled chicken wraps and sombreros for all to wear! Or maybe it's a Japanese theme with edamame, salmon teriyaki, chopsticks, and cushioned seating on the floor.

the evening. Going out meant fast food (he liked the 99-pence menu—two double cheeseburgers, large fries, and a large strawberry shake) or pub food (fried fish and chips) or greasy kebabs. Plus lots of beer.

Brian couldn't admit it to himself then, but realized later, that his weight held him back in every area of his life and challenged his ability to be a good veterinarian. On rotations, he was on his feet most of the day, so he was always achy. He would break out in a sweat with minimal effort. Just bending down to listen to a dog's heart would be difficult for him, let alone standing upright, completely sterile, while assisting in a five-hour surgery. Certain parts of the vet-school program were very challenging—especially going to the farms, where the vets were required to chase sheep around and handle heavy cows and horses. Brian would be exhausted and soaked with sweat after these forays.

He sometimes felt uncomfortable when he glimpsed the appraising looks of some of the pet owners. Obesity in pets is as big a problem as in people, he found, and trying to convince owners to put their dogs on diets when he was double the size of a normal human being was challenging, to say the least. He knew he lacked credibility.

Brian's social life was strained. Although he always had many friends, he often felt like an outsider. When friends wanted to go to amusement parks, water parks, or the beach, he would always decline the invitations for fear of not being able to fit on the roller coasters or for embarrassment at walking around with no shirt on. Dating just wasn't happening for him. When it came to girls, he was always "the friend." He was afraid to take things farther because he had a deep fear of rejection. It was easier not to try.

But in his third year in vet school Brian met Angela at a dingy campus pub. She was British and a year ahead of him in vet school—quiet and soft-spoken. They became friends and enjoyed hanging out together. A year after meeting they went out on their first date, and by the time Angela graduated and Brian was in his final year, they were a solid couple. They decided they would make their home in the United States and set up practices there.

As Brian flew back across the ocean, his seat belt strapped so tight he could hardly take a breath, the thought came to him: "It's time to start being an adult now. I'm a vet. I'm in a serious relationship. It's time."

THE PHOTO THAT CHANGED BRIAN'S LIFE

When Brian thinks back to the turning point that finally made him decide to lose weight, he vividly remembers one moment in particular, which came soon after he had returned to the States. He had purchased a very nice suit and had it tailored to fit for a family event, and someone had taken his picture. One day he was visiting his father's office and he saw the picture framed and sitting on his father's desk. Brian was horrified to see how he really looked—"I was huge. I looked like an engorged tick that was just about to explode," he says. He said to his dad, "Please get rid of that picture." His dad replied, "What's wrong with it?" Brian's voice shook with embarrassment. "I look huge." His dad looked at him, not unkindly, and said, "Well, that's what you look like."

Brian had known he was big, but he hadn't seen himself in such a stark way. "I could not believe I had gotten to that state," he admits, "and I started to think about changing it. I needed to take responsibility for my life and grow up. I had accomplished everything that I had set out to do. I had become a veterinarian and had found myself a wonderful, caring woman who had agreed to be my wife. The only thing I couldn't conquer, the only thing holding me back from being completely happy, was my weight."

Brian had seen a report on the news about kids who were losing weight by playing Dance Dance Revolution on the Playstation 2 game system, and he decided to try it. Maybe it would be a fun

BRIAN'S DAILY DIET COMPARISONS

BEFORE	AFTER
Breakfast	**Breakfast**
Several bowls of sugary cereal	Large bowl high-fiber, whole grain cereal with skim milk
Lunch	**Lunch**
2 buttered grilled ham and cheese sandwiches	Smoked turkey breast on whole wheat bread with mustard and a slice of fat-free cheese
½ canister potato crisps	Fat-free yogurt
1 liter soda	Apple
Dinner	**Dinner**
1 large frozen pizza	Baked or grilled salmon, tilapia, or chicken
1 liter soda	Steamed vegetables
½ pint ice cream	1 small baked sweet potato
Snacks	**Snacks**
Cakes, cookies, sandwiches, chips, candy	Nutrition bar
	Greek yogurt
	1–2 squares of 72% dark chocolate

way to get moving. He didn't lose any weight, but it had a positive psychological effect. At his dad's urging, he and Angela joined his dad's gym, and Brian started walking on the treadmill for 20 to 30 minutes three times a week. He also started to make gradual dietary changes. He switched from sugary cereals to healthier whole grains, from whole to skim milk, from regular soda to diet soda, from fried foods to grilled. These substitutions not only saved him thousands of calories, but they began to build Brian's confidence. He was now actively in the process of changing. He called it his "experiment," almost afraid to put a permanent name on what he was doing.

A few months into his experiment, Brian tried on a button-down shirt he had bought that had never fit him. He was able to button it with room to spare, and he was thrilled. It was an inflection point for Brian because he realized that he could succeed and continue to lose weight. That confidence led him to want more, and he increased the intensity, adding cardio exercises and lifting weights. He also kept tweaking his diet, choosing leaner foods and avoiding processed junk. The weight started to come off even faster. Within a year he had lost 100 pounds.

Of course, as Brian points out, if it were easy to lose weight there wouldn't be an obesity epidemic, and he had his fair share of bumps in the road. Brian was a guy who loved life, and there was always a party or wedding, a guys' night out for drinks, a Super Bowl celebration. He would sometimes give in to temptation, but the important thing is that he never let those splurges put him off course. He learned the lesson that is so important for all people trying to lose weight: Occasional digressions are not failures; they're side steps. All you have to do is step back up.

The most difficult aspect of weight loss is the plateau, and everyone experiences it. It's extremely frustrating to be dropping pounds every week and then suddenly show no loss on the scale for weeks at a time. When he hit a plateau, Brian was tempted to feel sorry for himself. "I wondered why I wasn't losing weight when I was exercising so much and eating so well," he says. It didn't feel fair to him. But once he calmed down, he'd look at his routine and figure out slight changes—like a different setting on a machine or extra time with weights, and the weight loss would kick in again.

Brian found that although he still loved to eat, the foods he found irresistibly delicious had completely changed. He no longer craved the heavy fish and chips and snack foods. Now his body wanted grilled foods and vegetables. It was telling him what it needed for energy.

It took Brian two and a half years to lose 155 pounds. He renewed his motivation when Angela gave birth to their daughter, Ella. He was determined to be fit and healthy for her. Two years in, he started running. First it was a couple minutes on the treadmill, then five to ten minutes. Then he started running the Long Beach boardwalk. In April 2006 he signed up for his first 5K, which he finished in 28:51. This progression reached its pinnacle in November 2008, when he completed the ING New York City Marathon in 4:40:21. It was one of the proudest moments of his life.

MANTRA FOR A NEW LIFE

Brian's mantra is "Do It Anyway." It's what keeps him disciplined and keeps him going. When he doesn't feel like getting up at 5 a.m. to run, he makes himself Do It Anyway. When everyone around him is ordering burgers and ribs, and he can just feel his teeth sinking into a big, juicy cheeseburger, and he really doesn't want to order the grilled salmon with steamed vegetables, he decides to Do It Anyway. When he's at a bar with friends, and they're all drinking beer and encouraging him to have one, and he could so go for a nice, cold Guinness instead of a diet soda, he chooses to Do It Anyway. When he was at mile 24 of the New York City Marathon, and he saw his sister and her fiancée, and he wanted to go over and collapse in front of them instead of running that last 2.2 miles, he chose to DO IT ANYWAY.

Brian is a new man. He has embraced his role as a husband and father and is intent on being a good role model. He wants Ella to make the right choices so she doesn't struggle like he did.

For Brian, life is a marvel. It still blows his mind to go shopping for normal-size clothes. He loves to travel—something he once dreaded—because he no longer has to worry about seat belts not fitting or the embarrassment of spilling into someone else's seat. When he attended his high school reunion, half the people had no idea who he was—a point of pride for him.

To others who are struggling with their weight, Brian says, "If a guy like me, who had been morbidly obese for the majority of his life, can run a marathon, anyone can do anything!"

Easy Turkey Meat Loaf

BY Brian Spar
MAKES 4 servings
SERVING SIZE 1 slice

Brian says: "I make this often, along with some oven-baked sweet potatoes and steamed veggies. Like this meat loaf, everything I cook is very simple and very quick."

Oil spray	½ teaspoon black pepper
1¼ pounds ground turkey (at least 90% lean)	¼ teaspoon kosher salt
1 small onion, diced	¼ cup ketchup
1 clove garlic, minced	2 tablespoons barbecue sauce (optional)
1 teaspoon dried basil	

1 Preheat the oven to 350°F. Liberally coat a 9×13-inch baking dish with oil spray.

2 In a large bowl combine first 7 ingredients (minus oil spray) until well mixed (using your hands to mix is easiest). Mound turkey mixture in a loaf shape, approximately 8×4 inches, in the prepared baking dish. Bake for 35 minutes, or until a thermometer inserted into the center of the meat loaf registers 160°F. If adding the barbecue sauce, spread it on top of the meat loaf during the last 10 minutes of baking. Allow the meat loaf to rest for 5 minutes, then cut into 4 thick slices.

NUTRITION INFORMATION Calories: 211, Protein: 31 g, Total Fat: 6 g, Saturated Fat: 1.5 g, Cholesterol: 85 mg, Sodium: 395 mg, Carbohydrate: 8 g, Fiber: 0.5 g

NICOLE DENNISON-OWENSBY

FROM Wadsworth, Ohio
AGE 34 | HEIGHT 5′8″
BEFORE WEIGHT 460 | AFTER WEIGHT 160 | POUNDS LOST 300

AFTER

BEFORE

"I just ate. That's what I did," Nicole says bluntly when she thinks about her life growing up. She doesn't remember feeling hungry. She doesn't remember feeling soothed by food. It was just there—her daily reality.

Nicole still gets emotional thinking about high school, which was a terrible four years. She was quiet and withdrawn and was usually alone, trying not to notice the happy chatter around her. She wondered enviously what it would be like to be part of a group, to belong. But every time she thought there might be a chance, something would happen to break her spirit. She'd walk into the cafeteria and the kids would moo at her, or she'd walk by a group of girls in the hall, and their giggles would follow her as she walked. She went deeper into her isolation and tried to build a wall around herself, numbing her emotions with food.

Since she was a young girl, Nicole had wanted to be a nurse after a school aptitude test said she'd be good at it, but when she graduated high school, she realized that wasn't going to happen. She couldn't fathom being able to keep up with the physical pace of nursing, and she didn't think a fat nurse would get much respect anyway. Besides, what if she couldn't fit in the desk? Going to nursing school would just be setting herself up for failure and ridicule, so she gave up the dream and started looking for jobs she could do.

Sometimes Nicole noticed her mother looking at her with a sad, regret-filled face. "She worried a lot that she didn't do enough for me and that it was her fault I turned out the way I did. I also think a part of her worried that others would think she was a horrible mother for allowing me to get so big. But I never blamed her. After all, she didn't force food down my throat."

When she was 20, Nicole got a job in a day care center, and to her surprise she found that it was enjoyable. Little kids will love you and accept you no matter what you look like. They might be curious about weight, but they're not judgmental. Nicole was content when she was at work, but the job didn't do much for her weight. The kids ate a lot—every two or three hours—and there were always snacks and meals everywhere. She'd eat with the kids and then eat again on her own. By the time Nicole was 24, she weighed 460 pounds.

Just getting out of bed in the morning was a challenge. Nicole was deeply depressed. She went to work and straight back home. She felt that everyone was embarrassed to be seen with her. Why wouldn't they be, since she was embarrassed to be seen with herself? Nicole worked hard to put a smile on her face in public but acknowledges that "when you're 460 pounds you can't say you're not depressed. I was very, very lonely."

THE BYPASS THAT WASN'T

For three years Nicole debated with herself about getting gastric bypass surgery, and the closer she came to a decision, the more she ate. On some level, she figured, why not? She was just going to lose the weight anyway. When she finally announced her decision to go ahead with the surgery, she received a great deal of support from her family and friends. Her parents had always given her unconditional love. They never ridiculed her or pushed her to lose weight. They worried about the surgery, but told Nicole that if it was what she wanted, they'd be behind her. She switched jobs so she could get insurance that would cover the surgery. But she was surprised that she couldn't just schedule the surgery and be done with it. To become eligible she had to work with a registered dietitian for six months and demonstrate that her head was in the right place. They gave her a diet plan and told her she had to lose 30 pounds before she could have the surgery. Nicole was scared. She said to herself, "You can't mess up."

During the next six months Nicole lost a lot more than 30 pounds. She was more motivated than she had ever been. By the time she went back to the gastric bypass doctor, she had lost 160 pounds. The doctor and nurses and all the staff were dumbfounded. They had never seen anything like it. But instead of being rejected by the surgical center, Nicole rejected gastric bypass surgery. She was doing so well, and she felt so good that she no longer needed it. She decided to go at it alone, and in one year she lost 200 pounds!

UPS AND DOWNS

Nicole's would turn out to be a long journey, full of ups and downs. After losing an amazing 200 pounds in her first year, her weight stabilized for a while. She was busy attending nursing school—yes, she decided that finally she could follow her dream!—and she didn't have the time or energy to worry about her weight. Slowly, she began to regain some weight. In May 2007, Nicole stepped on a scale and was very unhappy to read the number—316. She had gained 46 pounds. But amazingly, she wasn't discouraged. She reminded herself that she'd lost almost 200—and she knew that she could do it once and for all. In the next year she lost an additional 156 pounds, bringing her grand total weight loss to 300 pounds. She was so excited when she stepped on a scale (five years to the day she started) and it read 159.8 that she snapped a picture of it.

OUT IN THE WORLD

At age 30 Nicole began dating, a new experience for her. Her first real relationship only lasted a few months, and the end left her feeling a little down on herself. One night her brother invited her to tag along when he went out to get a tattoo. She figured, "Why not?" As she was sitting in the shop, a man walked in to visit some friends. His name was Nick, and they started joking around. Before she left that night Nicole decided to give Nick her phone number. They went out on their first date a week later. Nicole saw in Nick a kind, family-oriented man who appreciated her for who she was. Months later they were married, in spite of her family's warnings to take it slow, and she never regretted the decision. Soon Nicole was pregnant. She was devastated when she suffered a miscarriage and had to re-evaluate her diet and face an uncomfortable truth: She had gone overboard, starving herself of key nutrients, and had become too thin. Although rare, this obsessive extreme can sometimes happen. I have heard from people who have lost large amounts of weight about their nightmares of gorging. And some "successful losers" believe if they give in to a single craving, they'll be unable to stop, and all of their lost weight will pile back on. So they remain overly restrictive with their food intake. Nicole had to seriously consider what it took to be healthy—especially after she got pregnant again. But the effort was worth it. On April 30, 2010, she gave birth to a precious daughter.

After Nicole appeared on the Joy Fit Club, she received a call from one of her old high school tormenters. "I know we didn't get along then," she said haltingly, "but I'm struggling. Can we talk?" Nicole was generous and understanding. She said, "Of course."

Slim-Style Pizza

BY Nicole Dennison-Owensby
MAKES 1 serving
SERVING SIZE 1 individual pizza

Nicole says: "My husband *loves* pizza and has made it his ritual to have pizza while he watches any Cleveland Browns football game. So I have come up with my own slimmed-down version so I can partake in the pizza tradition too. It's an easy recipe that can be tailored to your own liking."

Oil spray
⅓ cup tomato sauce, preferably no-salt-added
2 tablespoons grated Parmesan cheese
Garlic powder, onion powder, Italian seasoning, and other preferred seasonings
1 whole grain, high-fiber flatbread or tortilla

¼ cup shredded part-skim mozzarella cheese

Toppings (optional)
Vegetables (onions, sweet peppers, mushrooms, broccoli, olives, hot peppers, etc.)
Cooked turkey sausage crumbles
Turkey pepperoni

1 Preheat the oven to 400°F. Coat a pizza pan or baking sheet with oil spray.*

2 Prepare the pizza sauce: In a small bowl stir together the tomato sauce, Parmesan cheese, and preferred seasonings to taste.

3 Place the flatbread or tortilla on the baking sheet. Evenly spread the pizza sauce on the bread and sprinkle with the mozzarella cheese. Add preferred toppings. Bake for 12 to 15 minutes or until the crust is crisp to your liking.

*NOTE Alternatively, this pizza can be cooked on a gas grill. Just place the flatbread directly on the grill; cover the grill with the lid to help the cheese melt more readily.

NUTRITION INFORMATION (CHEESE PIZZA ONLY, WITHOUT ADDITIONAL TOPPINGS) Calories: 198, Protein: 27 g, Total Fat: 9 g, Saturated Fat: 4.5 g, Cholesterol: 25 mg, Sodium: 545 mg, Carbohydrate: 18 g, Fiber: 8 g

DARREN WILLIAMS

FROM Muscatine, Iowa
AGE 35 | HEIGHT 5' 9"
BEFORE WEIGHT 452 | AFTER WEIGHT 155 | POUNDS LOST 297

AFTER

BEFORE

Darren says he has always been a modest person. He doesn't like to talk about himself, and he especially doesn't like to be in the public eye. But he agreed to share his story because he figured if he could inspire even one person to change his or her life, he couldn't pass up that opportunity.

When Darren looks back on his life, he sees struggle, pain, and shame. He is a different person now, but he still relates with great empathy to the boy with the weight problem—the boy who loved sports and wanted to be an athlete but was just too big. Sports mostly meant humiliation—having to have special uniforms made because of his size, being teased by his teammates, and finally, having his early talent come to nothing because the bigger he got, the harder it was to play.

Today, when Darren looks back at early pictures of himself, he thinks about all of the things that he missed out on as a kid—playing more sports, being able to fit onto rides at amusement parks, having a normal social life. Activities that were enjoyable to others could be agonizing for Darren. He especially hated back-to-school clothes shopping. He was never able to wear any of the latest styles. He dreaded the time of year when summer was coming to an end and it was time for his mother and him to start on the journey of finding clothes.

Darren suffered as a result of having little guidance at home about his food choices. He was allowed to eat large quantities of fast food, sweets, pizza, sugary cereals, and junky snacks. After school he'd plop in front of the TV and eat. As he entered his teen years, Darren's overeating became a way of giving him some "happiness" in his life because his weight caused him so many social problems. Every once in a while he would start an extreme starvation diet, anxious to just get rid of the pounds in one fell swoop. These diets never worked, and usually Darren ended up heavier than when he'd started.

In a real sense, Darren was merely following the family predisposition. Many family members were overweight, and it was not uncommon for relatives to die in their sixties from medical conditions associated with obesity. Ironically, his family doctor was very obese, and as a child Darren found that comforting because the doctor never confronted him about his weight.

He continued to grow in size each year and weighed about 350 pounds when he graduated high school. He put on more weight in college and was 400 pounds when he left to begin his career. He was smart and personable and confident he'd succeed in business. What he did fear was being alone. What woman would be interested in a 400-pound man? He was shocked when that woman walked into his life—a gorgeous blonde named Rhonda. They dated for two years and then were married, and Darren felt an overwhelming sense of relief. Someone loved him, in spite of his weight. He wasn't going to be alone. Rhonda recognized the real person inside. They began their married life as a happy couple, and their daughter was born in 2005. Darren was happier than he had ever been and overwhelmed with joy at the miracle of his family and the new life of his daughter.

By 2008, at 452 pounds, Darren was taking blood pressure medication, and he began to have severe anxiety attacks about his heart, which felt like heart attacks. Once, experiencing indigestion, he was convinced that he was having a heart attack. At first the stress test showed a minor blockage, but later the doctor said it was a false positive caused by skin tissue. In spite of the doctor's reassurances, Darren started behaving like a heart invalid. He really believed that he was going to have a heart attack any day. He became a homebody, feeling that he always needed to be near the hospital.

A MOMENT OF TRUTH

One day, sitting in his living room, feeling miserable, Darren hit bottom. He couldn't live like this any more. He loved his wife and daughter with all his heart, and he hated what he was doing to them. Tears came to his eyes as he imagined his daughter being fatherless, not having him around to tell her troubles to or walk her down the aisle at her wedding. She was only 3, but his macabre thoughts traveled forward to a grim future. What would people tell her about why her daddy died? Because he was fat? Because he couldn't stop eating so much?

Suddenly Darren pulled himself up from the couch and stood on shaky legs. He walked to the door and went outside. And then, very slowly, he started walking around the block. Before he had even gone halfway, he was huffing, out of breath, with sweat pouring down his face. His legs barely had the strength to hold him up, and he imagined what a sight he was for people looking out their windows. But he was back out the next day, trudging around the block, and by the second week of doing it, he noticed it was getting easier. It wasn't much, but it was a start. The power of a symbolic launch can't be underestimated. The day Darren got up off the couch was the day his life changed for good.

AGGRESSIVE YET ACHIEVABLE TARGETS

Because Darren had between 250 and 300 pounds to lose, he had to take the long view, and gradually figure out how he was going to revamp his entire lifestyle. He'd been on the fad diets, dropping his calorie intake to 1,200 calories. He knew that wouldn't work. He had to find a level that he could sustain. At the time he was eating between 4,000 and 5,000 calories a day, and he decided to start by cutting it down in the obvious places by making substitutions. He got rid of all things fried and replaced them with baked and grilled counterparts. He swapped starchy potatoes for green vegetables—something he had never eaten in the past. He had a big soda habit and couldn't give it up completely, so he allowed himself one regular soda a day and drank water the rest of the time. Eventually he stopped drinking soda altogether. Darren was a huge lunch eater who could put away several thousand calories with a buffet spread or oversize burger and fries. Packing a brown bag from home became a major driver in his success.

In October 2008 he joined a 24-hour fitness center, so there would never be an excuse for not working out. His initial regimen consisted of walking on the treadmill at 2 m.p.h. for 10 to 15 minutes. He set modest goals for himself and tracked his progress, inching up the speed and duration. When he had a sluggish day or ate more than he planned to, Darren just reminded himself of the long-term goal. Eventually he learned to use obstacles as motivational tools along the way.

Today Darren weighs 155 pounds. He's medicine-free and runs 6.5 to 7 miles per day on the treadmill at 6.5 to 7 m.p.h., lifts weights three times per week, and rides on the stationary bike.

PEP TALK

DARREN'S STRATEGIES FOR SUCCESS

- It is a lifestyle change, not a diet. Commit to the long haul. Remember, unlike a 5K or 10K race, there is no finish line.
- Set goals and hold yourself accountable. Don't go to extremes. That goes for working out, eating, or any other aspect of your plan.
- Planning is a key factor for success. Plot out in advance your workout schedule, your meals, and how you'll prepare for interruptions in routine, such as travel.
- Remind yourself every day of the joys that come from fitness.

His diet consists of between 1,800 and 2,200 calories. He continues to have favorite treats from time to time. However, he strategically plans for them by cutting back on other foods during the day or working out a little extra hard at the gym. He ran a 5K and then a 10K race, something he never imagined he could do in his wildest dreams. Being able to run that distance still feels unreal to him, but he says, "It's just proof that hard work, dedication, and a lot of mind over matter allows you to accomplish anything that you set your mind to."

Darren is happy with the big payoff to his efforts. The main thing is being able to be there for his wife and daughter, providing them the kind of enjoyable life that they deserve—not to mention being fit enough to keep up with an active little girl.

The story that best characterizes Darren's new life centers on amusement parks. Between Darren's freshman and sophomore year in college at the University of Iowa, he took a trip to Six Flags near Chicago to visit some friends he had made at school. After waiting in line for an hour with them to ride one of the rides, he sat in the seat and was too large for the bar to fasten over his belly. They asked him to get off the ride. The embarrassment was a deep, throbbing wound that stuck with him for many years. At 155 pounds, he took his family to Six Flags and was able to reap one of the proudest rewards so far of his journey. He joyfully rode all of the rides with his daughter, laughing and screaming just like everyone else.

AFTER

BEFORE

REIN IN RESTAURANT BINGES

Restaurant portions have grown exponentially over the past few decades, and that means that polishing off an entire entrée can cost you more calories than your body burns in an entire day (and that's before you factor in the drinks, bread, appetizers, and dessert). Try this technique the next time you eat out: When you've finished about half the food on your plate, take an extended pause. Stop eating for about 5 minutes and give your body a moment to decide whether it's still hungry. If after the 5 minutes you decide you're still not satisfied, it's OK to eat a bit more—at least you'll be choosing to do so out of hunger rather than habit.

DARREN'S DAILY DIET COMPARISONS

BEFORE	AFTER
Breakfast	**Breakfast**
2 sausage, egg, and cheese biscuits	Nutrition bar
Large soda	8 ounces skim milk
Lunch	**Lunch**
Combo platter appetizer	Ham and cheese sandwich
Double cheeseburger	Chips
Large fries	
Multiple sodas	
Dinner	**Dinner**
4–5 slices pizza	Grilled chicken breast
	Baked potato
	Fresh green beans
Snacks	**Snacks**
Cookies, ice cream, candy bar, chips	Apples, carrots, fat-free yogurt

TAMMEY BURNS

FROM Springfield, Missouri
AGE 53 | HEIGHT 5' 4½"
BEFORE WEIGHT 575 | AFTER WEIGHT 165 | POUNDS LOST 410

In the spring of 2002, Tammey knew she was dying. Every night she slept with five liters of oxygen, and even then she could barely move without getting breathless. She had hypertension, restrictive lung disease, sleep apnea, respiratory insufficiency, obesity hypoventilation syndrome, venous stasis insufficiency, and diabetes. The right side of her enlarged heart was failing.

At 575 pounds, Tammey could not live anything approaching a normal life. For all practical purposes she was an invalid. She had to have help from her mother for all of her personal grooming—bathing, going to the bathroom, dressing. When she took a shower she had to squeeze in sideways because the shower door was not wide enough. It was totally degrading to need assistance with her most private functions, even when the helper was her mother.

Tammey was unable to work because she was immobile and sick. She was unable to stand up for more than two or three minutes at a time without severe pain in her lower back and hips, and she was always short of breath. She couldn't get in and out of the car because the door did not open wide enough to accommodate her. She couldn't lift her leg high enough to go up even one step that was very low to the ground. It's no wonder that Tammey believed she was staring death in the face. She was almost resigned to it because she obviously couldn't go on like that.

By the time Tammey reached this severe point of crisis, she had been dealing

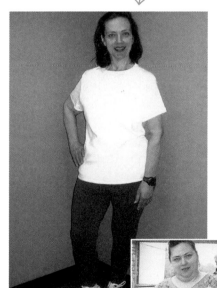

AFTER

BEFORE

with obesity her entire life. Obesity was common among her immediate and extended family members, and many of them were at least 100 pounds overweight. She saw the medical toll it took, and when she was younger, she tried every fad diet that came along, desperate to drop the pounds. She tried them all—even Overeaters Anonymous and other support groups. None were successful. The weight never stayed off. She came to view them as thumb-in-the-dike solutions.

As the years went by and her weight increased, Tammey became emotionally and physically shackled by her size. She became depressed and introverted, afraid to go out in public because of ridicule. She didn't dare go to a theater for fear the movie seat would be too small. She was even afraid to visit a friend's house because she worried she'd break a chair if she sat down—and even if she didn't break a chair, she wasn't sure she'd be able to get back up on her own. Once, when she was nearing her highest weight, she fell on the floor, and her mother and sister were unable to help her get up. Her mother ended up calling the fire department, and it took six paramedics and a special lift to get her up off the ground. She had never felt so humiliated and hopeless.

Not surprisingly, Tammey's self-esteem was nonexistent. She didn't feel that she was worthy of help. In fact, she hated herself and what she had let herself become. She could not take care of herself or of anyone else What could she possibly contribute to any relationship? She felt repulsive and believed that no one would want to be burdened with a giant beached whale. She was a "fat girl" living on the sidelines.

LOSING HOPE

By June 2002 Tammey had lost all hope, and she became obsessed with the idea that she had become an intolerable burden to her family. She just wanted a release from the suffering. One day she mentally said goodbye to the life that had been nothing but torment and tried to commit suicide. It was a loud and piercing cry for help. When she woke up and realized she was not dead, Tammey's first thought was that God had other plans for her.

The failed suicide attempt had the effect of a major wake-up call. Tammey realized she didn't want to die, and suddenly she was determined to find a way to live. She began once again a journey for answers, hoping this time she would find them. Her primary care doctor adamantly insisted on gastric bypass or lap band surgery, but she was just as adamant in her refusal. She had to find a solution for herself, and surgery was not it. In the aftermath of her suicide attempt, she turned to a psychologist who helped her define why she had such a strong addiction to food. The psychologist told her that change had to come from within. Tammey began to heal emotionally, and she also started making basic changes to her diet and counting calories. By December 2006 her weight was down to 403 pounds.

THE SLOW ROAD BACK TO LIFE

But in spite of her initial weight loss, Tammey was still finding it very difficult to breathe. Her final wake-up call came in December 2006, when she had to have a tracheotomy tube inserted to aid with her breathing. It was semi-permanent, unless she lost weight. That was it! Tammey was appalled at the idea of having a trach sticking out of her throat for the rest of her life. That was the "do or die" moment. The doctor said she could have it removed if she lost 120 pounds, and that became her goal.

Tammey joined a fitness center and worked hard, but it was a frustrating, lonely process, and results were slow in coming. She started by water-walking in the center's therapy pool because the buoyancy in the water held her up. Gradually she was able to do small spurts on an exercise bike.

One day at the center she was approached by Colleen Young, a walking coach, who challenged her to walk. Tammey took a deep breath, wondering if she could do it—and then she agreed. Colleen became her rock and her mentor. Tammey was surprised that Colleen never mentioned weight loss. She kept the focus on being dynamic and getting fit, and as Tammey lost weight, Colleen even suggested the most unimaginable thing of all—that she consider racewalking. Racewalking! For a woman who once could not even take a shower by herself. But she started doing it and loved it. (Today Tammey is Colleen's assistant coach on the USATF Master's Racewalking Team.) Tammey got so involved in her exercise program that she stopped obsessing about weight loss. She made food choices based on what would enhance her performance, including what would provide the fuel she needed for endurance and speed. It was the first time she had ever thought of food as anything other than an emotional crutch.

Tammey's weight kept coming off, and the day she had the trach removed was a huge milestone. "For the first time, I thought of food as fuel for my body and not my drug of choice. I used to 'live to eat,' and now I was 'eating to live.' It was a very exciting discovery and the weight started coming off and staying off, and the trach was removed."

She trained rigorously and started entering races. She was becoming an entirely new person, unshackled by the weight that had once made her life not worth living. Her perspective on life is positive and healthy—so different from the housebound, wounded woman she was before. "God is taking me on an amazing journey to give hope to others," she says, and this is certainly true. There are few things more inspiring than to watch a woman come back from the brink of death to be so fully alive.

Now she says, "I realized that there was no drug, no food, that could give me the joy and pride I felt when I crossed the finish line. I was no longer the fat girl on the sideline. I was the woman in the race."

Breakfast Spanakopita

BY Tammey Burns
MAKES 1 serving

Tammey says: "I don't spend a lot of time during the week in the kitchen; my day is packed with work, family, and my workouts. Weekly breakfast choices include 'power oatmeal' (with berries and whey protein powder), protein shakes, and whole grain cereal. Sundays are a slower pace, so I have time to make one of my favorite recipes, which I call Breakfast Spanakopita."

1 teaspoon olive oil
2 tablespoons chopped onion
3 white button mushrooms, sliced
⅓ 10-ounce package frozen spinach, thawed and well drained

½ teaspoon chopped fresh dill
Black pepper
½ cup egg substitute (may substitute 1 whole egg and 2 to 3 egg whites)
2 tablespoons crumbled feta cheese

1 In a small skillet heat the olive oil over medium heat. Add the onion and mushrooms and cook, stirring, until soft, about 5 minutes. Add the spinach, dill, and pepper to taste and cook, stirring constantly, for 1 minute. Transfer the vegetable mixture to a plate.

2 Return the skillet to the stove over medium heat and liberally coat with oil spray. Add the egg substitute and cook until the eggs are nearly set. Add the vegetable mixture and feta cheese to half of the omelet. Gently fold the bare side over the vegetable-cheese mixture and cook for 1 minute. Slide the omelet out of the skillet onto a plate for serving.

NUTRITION INFORMATION Calories: 187, Protein: 20 g, Total Fat: 8 g, Saturated Fat: 2.5 g, Cholesterol: 10 mg, Sodium: 450 mg, Carbohydrate: 10 g, Fiber: 4 g

---

JOY'S WORDS OF ADVICE

ANTI-DIABETES STRATEGY

Like many Joy Fit Club members, Tammey was diagnosed with type 2 diabetes, and she needs to watch her carbs, even now that she has lost so much weight. A simple way to stay on track is to choose high-protein snacks. Pairing protein with a small amount of carbohydrate helps blunt the rise in blood sugar that occurs after eating. Good snack choices include nonfat yogurt, string cheese, nuts, sunflower seeds, hummus with veggies, celery with peanut butter, edamame, and hard-cooked eggs or egg whites. Although fruit is incredibly healthy, it is pure carbohydrate and when eaten alone can elevate blood sugar levels in individuals with type 2 diabetes. For optimal diabetes control, always pair fruit with a protein food (like an apple with peanut butter or fresh berries with nonfat yogurt).

GINA PIZZO

FROM San Francisco, California
AGE 20 | HEIGHT 5' 1"
BEFORE WEIGHT 284 | AFTER WEIGHT 140 | POUNDS LOST 144

AFTER

BEFORE

From the time she was a little girl, Gina's life was controlled by two realities: her mother's breast cancer and her own weight problem. These were the only topics her parents talked about, the sole focus of everyone's concern. Even after her mother survived her first bout with breast cancer, Gina couldn't help being worried about what might happen. She loved her parents so much, but life seemed full of danger. Food was like a warm blanket that she could curl up in and soothe her worries. But she really didn't understand why she was so big. Did she really eat that much more than her friends?

Gina's parents were very proactive about her weight. They took her to numerous nutritionists and countless doctors to help her eat healthier. But Gina never had much success sticking with the plans, which made her feel deprived, hungry, and, worst of all, different than everybody else. Even her friends called her fat or chubby.

Once Gina's mother suggested they try a local weight loss group as a mother-daughter activity. Every time Gina weighed in, she had gained a pound, and it was humiliating and discouraging. She didn't like the program and felt completely defeated. She and her mother created a fiction so Gina's dad wouldn't know the truth. When he asked what she was losing every week, they'd just say, "Everything's going fine." They also hid her weekly weigh-in book so that he would not find out that she was actually gaining weight. One day, her dad found the book. "He hit the roof when he discovered how much weight I had gained," she says. "He couldn't believe I weighed 284 pounds at the age of 14!"

Gina could intellectually understand her father's concern. He had diabetes and was afraid that she would inherit it from him at an early age. He was also afraid that her heart would give out or that she would develop other life-threatening medical issues. Gina felt like a failure every step of the way, but her parents kept pushing. They kept a close eye on what she was eating and tried to get her to be more active. Her father would accompany her on fast-paced walks in the evening and had her spend some time on an exercise bike. His intentions were all out of love and concern— and this effort helped her to lose 20 pounds.

However, when Gina was 15, her mother's breast cancer returned, and the weight loss program took a back seat to caring for her. Gina was devastated by her mother's cancer, which was much more virulent and progressive than the first time. She realized her mom might not make it this time, and she was very depressed. It was extremely hard for her to keep an eye on her weight. Not only was her motivation gone, but also their house was filled with food. Friends and neighbors were constantly dropping by with dishes to help the family, and Gina lost herself in eating.

Shortly before Gina's sixteenth birthday, her mother lost her battle with cancer. Gina and her father were crushed by her death, and it took time for life to return to a semblance of normalcy. At Gina's

JOY'S WORDS OF ADVICE

STOCKING A COLLEGE DORM ROOM

When Gina went off to college feeling fit and happy, she was determined not to fall prey to the "freshman 15." Part of the strategy was to always have healthy, delicious snacks and microwavable meals handy in her dorm room, including a well-stocked mini fridge. These picks are perfect for stocking a college dorm or—for those of us who are no longer students— stashing in a desk or office fridge.

- Fruit (apples, bananas, oranges, grapes)
- Baby carrots and hummus or salsa
- Nonfat yogurt
- String cheese
- Whole grain cereal
- Oatmeal packets
- Healthy, low-sodium soups (lentil, black bean, minestrone, vegetable, etc.)

- Rice cakes and natural peanut butter
- Granola/nutrition bars
- Low-fat microwave popcorn
- 100-calorie packs
- Flavored teas
- Low-fat hot cocoa packets
- Sugarless gum

next doctor's appointment, her father found out that she had gained another 14 pounds after her mother's death. In the car driving home he turned to her, filled with frustration and said, "I've done all I can do. If you're not going to follow the plan and do this for yourself, I can't make you."

At home, Gina collapsed in her room fighting tears. She wanted to change, she really did. But how?

JUST COUNT CALORIES

At that point they had a lucky break. Gina's parents had been searching for years for a program that dealt with teenage obesity, but they'd never been able to find a program that was near their home or that they could afford. But now Gina's father got a referral to Dr. Josel Cabaccan, an endocrinologist and metabolism doctor. They went to see him, filled with guarded optimism. At first Dr. Cabaccan ran some tests to see if there was anything wrong with Gina's metabolism, but the tests found nothing. The doctor then sat her down and explained that she was eating the wrong way and he would teach her how to eat correctly. He told her, "You are not on a diet. You can eat anything you want to, but you need to count your calories."

When Gina asked him about exercise, the doctor told her that at her weight it would be too strenuous on her joints and she should just stick with diet for the time being.

Gina started out at 1,500 calories a day—and she didn't get any results! She was mortified, her father was suspicious, and the doctor was puzzled. All of his other patients did just fine on that level. "I was his only patient not getting any results," says Gina, remembering her shame. "I felt horrible that I hadn't been sticking to the program. I felt as if I was letting my father and my doctor down. Then I realized that I couldn't be losing weight to please them but that I needed to do this for myself."

Dr. Cabaccan lowered Gina's calories a bit more and had her start keeping a log to track exactly what she ate. At first she thought she would hate logging her food, but she found an online diet tracker that made it easy and even fun.

In the next year, Gina lost 150 pounds just by counting calories. It was a perfect method for a teenager. She found that she didn't feel deprived as she had on past diets—because she could eat anything she wanted in moderation. Before, she deprived herself of entire categories of her favorite foods, and then she'd fall off the wagon and overeat them. Now she could allow herself candy, chips, pretzels, or anything else she liked. She especially relied on the 100-calorie snack packs, which helped with portion control. Mostly, Gina wanted to eat what a typical teenager ate. She wanted to get together with her friends and have what they were having. Keeping the focus on calories allowed her to be one of the crowd and not feel different.

Gina became very adept at the process. At first it was difficult to stop and look up the numbers before she put something into her mouth. But with time she began to remember the information, and she almost felt as if she had a calorie index in her head.

After she lost the weight, Gina prepared for another adventure—going to college. She felt she was ready. She had lots of new confidence in herself, and as she picked out her college wardrobe, she was thrilled to feel like the other kids. She was embarking on a new life with the tools and confidence to make it a success. She looked cute in her new school outfits. No one could guess that she had been through some hard lessons in her short life or that she had enormous strength beneath her slender frame.

Cheesy Rice Cake Snack

BY Gina Pizzo
MAKES 1 serving
SERVING SIZE 1 rice cake

Gina says: "I love pizza! This is a tasty, quick, easy snack with a pizza feel that I can make in my dorm room."

1 plain rice cake
1 wedge light spreadable cheese (about 35 calories)
   Sliced fresh vegetables: sweet peppers, cucumbers, tomatoes, carrots, etc.

1 Evenly spread the cheese on the rice cake. Top with a generous amount of sliced vegetables.

NUTRITIONAL INFORMATION Calories: 112, Protein: 3 g, Total Fat: 2 g, Saturated Fat: 1 g, Cholesterol: 5 mg, Sodium: 220 mg, Carbohydrate: 20 g, Fiber: 1 g

JON STANTON

FROM Lansing, Michigan
AGE 35 | HEIGHT 5' 11"
BEFORE WEIGHT 430 | AFTER WEIGHT 201 | POUNDS LOST 229

AFTER

BEFORE

When Jon was young, he remembers being angry with God for making him the way he was. He looked around and saw mostly tall, athletic, lean types of people, but he was short, soft, and hopelessly nonathletic. He was also much heavier than the other kids, no matter what he did, and he just couldn't understand why they could eat junk food and not get fat. It was as if he was born with a fat switch that normal people didn't have.

Jon was sad and resentful. He felt unfairly burdened and ostracized by his weight problem. It was a terrible feeling being the one always singled out for being too fat. In particular, gym class was a nightmare. He was always the last one to be picked on the teams, and the group that got stuck with him moaned in disappointment. He became withdrawn because he couldn't stand being a problem for others. He didn't belong anywhere. When Jon prayed, it was for God to make him like everyone else. When he dreamed, he imagined how his life would be happy in a more attractive body.

By the time he graduated from high school, he was well on his way to 300 pounds, and his sense of self-worth was nonexistent. Deep down, he believed the judgments of others that he was not worthy of love, companionship, or even a fair break. Looking back, he can see that there were women who might have been interested in him, but he blew them off before a relationship could get started, thinking he was saving himself from inevitable rejection that way.

Jon decided that his only hope was to follow his passion. He studied music in college, and sometimes it allowed him to rise above his body and his fears and soar. But he grew increasingly self-conscious about performing in recitals. He projected his negative self-judgment to the audience, and became convinced that people couldn't hear his music because they were too busy staring at him.

Food was the only thing that provided any solace. Jon would eat huge quantities of anything that was processed. One of his favorite foods was Spam®—he'd sometimes eat two or three tins in a sitting. He'd go to Chinese buffets and gorge himself until he couldn't physically eat another bite. Buffets, he learned, are a trap for fat people. He would refill his plate multiple times and often leave the restaurant literally in pain, with an aching stomach and shortness of breath. He could easily eat an entire box of donuts. And through it all, he was disgusted with the way he looked, and demoralized by the way he felt. He was a young man, but he felt like he was breaking down from a lifetime of abuse. By the time he reached his late twenties, Jon weighed 430 pounds.

There were many times that Jon wanted to be invisible. Walking into a room of strangers nearly always elicited a few stares or raised eyebrows. Getting on an airplane was an exercise in both calisthenics and emotional fortitude. He could see the looks of panic and fear on the face of the unlucky soul who was seated next to him. He sometimes thought people were afraid that he might burst and gush fat cells all over them. How else to explain the fear in their eyes?

Worst of all, Jon's obesity robbed him of his dreams. When he was 430 pounds, he didn't think there was a chance he could ask for and receive the things he wanted and needed in life. He came to believe that he didn't deserve happiness because he had put himself in this position. At the same time, he felt robbed. Robbed of love because who would ever want to be with the Pillsbury Dough Boy? Robbed of his professional dream of becoming a college music teacher because who would ever hire him to such a prestigious and inspirational position? Robbed of peace because every social situation was filled with anxiety. Robbed of health because his life was eking away, one pound at a time. Robbed of self-esteem because he could find nothing about himself to admire.

Jon did the best he could to put on a positive front, and he kept the true level of his despair hidden from most of the people who knew him. To look at him, they might think he coped pretty well for being such an obese guy, but, he says, "I was a master of illusion."

A FATEFUL DOCTOR'S VISIT

When he was 30, Jon's weight had started to have a significant negative impact on his health. He was constantly tired, short of breath, and would break into cold sweats for no reason. His whole body ached, especially his joints. His lower legs were turning dark blue because of poor circulation. He was on medication for high blood pressure. When his hair started falling out and he felt strange flutters in his chest, he reluctantly made an appointment to see his doctor. Blood tests showed that Jon's blood sugar was out of control, and the doctor urged him to start taking an oral diabetes medication. Then, sitting across from Jon in the examination room, his doctor looked him squarely in the eye and said, "If you continue to follow the same lifestyle, you will be dead by the time you are 50, and the last 10 years of your existence will be miserable. However, if you make changes now, you can enjoy a long and happy life."

Jon was momentarily taken aback. No one had ever been so brutally honest before. He suddenly knew, deep down in his gut, that the doctor's words were true and he was being given a choice between life and death. He suddenly wanted more than anything to conquer his demons and live. He asked the doctor if he could put off starting the diabetes medication. "Give me a chance," he pleaded.

Sitting at home that night, Jon felt a new resolve. "Life is more than a sugary snack cake," he told himself. "I've had it. I'm not living this way anymore." His obesity, he realized, was a form of slow suicide.

TAKING A WALK

The next day Jon walked out his front door and slowly made his way to the end of his driveway. He was out of breath and sweating heavily by the time he got back, but it was a start. The next day he did it again, and then the next. His distance was a mere 500 feet, but his legs burned with pain, and he thought he was going to keel over at any minute, but he kept at it and within a week he was able to venture past his driveway and down the block. Step by step—Jon was determined. He poured all the energy he had previously expended on self-destruction into self-improvement.

Even with his determination, the first few weeks were hell. Jon had no idea how to construct a balanced diet for himself, so the first thing he did was cut the quantities roughly in half—from about 6,000 calories per day to 3,000 calories a day. Also, because his sweet tooth was such a big problem with overeating at night, he eliminated most sweets and desserts. Before long he adopted a diet that was heavy on fruits and vegetables. "For me it was a big change," he says, "but hearing I was going to die flipped a switch in my brain."

Jon would never tell anyone his chosen path to weight loss was easy. It wasn't. He had his fair share of setbacks. But he also gave it enough time for his taste buds to evolve. One of his early victories was having his blood sugar return to normal within three months. He kept going.

Today Jon walks an average of three to five miles a day, and he has more energy than he remembers having in his entire life. He's become used to having people ask, "What did you do? Did you have surgery? Did you join a medical weight loss group? Did you buy a gym membership?" He enjoys telling them, "No, no, and no. I changed my lifestyle, pure and simple."

Jon always enjoyed food, and it was a big revelation to him that he could still enjoy eating without letting it destroy him. There was nothing fancy about his plan. Walk a little, eat less. Nothing complicated about that.

If he has one big tip to impart it's that walking works. From a starting point of 500 feet, he now walks three to five miles a day. He gained a lot of inspiration from another Joy Fit Club member, Jodi Davis, a local woman who developed the Walking Works program through Blue Cross Blue Shield (Jodi's story is featured on page 101). He faithfully reads Jodi's blog every day for inspiration.

He also participates in activities in the Lansing area when possible, such as Community Partners in Health. He is happy that he works in downtown Lansing, which is perfect for walking during the workday. He made arrangements with his boss to eat lunch at his desk, and around 2:00 p.m. every day he takes off on a walk. His favorite loop circles the Capitol, proceeds down the boulevard between state office buildings to the Hall of Justice, circles the Hall of Justice, and returns the same way, ending at his office building for a total of about 2.5 miles. Jon also walks in the evenings at home, and on the weekends, reveling in the beauty of the environment and the new spring in his step. He has no desire—not even a temptation—to return to his former life, which he now sees was not much of a life at all.

LIFETIME SELF-ESTEEM

Sometimes Jon thinks about the past and reflects about what was going on inside his mind to allow him to get so dangerously obese. He realizes that he was completely cut off from reality. He never believed he had a problem—in fact, he thought he was invincible. Deep down, at the core of his denial, was fear that he would never be able to make the change. But now he has. When he looks in the mirror he still has a hard time recognizing himself. He sees, though, that while the physical changes have happened, the emotional scars take longer. You can't have such a deep self-loathing for so long and have it instantly disappear.

After Jon lost most of his excess weight, he began to think about dating for the first time in a decade. Just learning how to have a relationship was a big step for him. He felt emotionally immature, and why wouldn't he? He'd had hardly any experience with women, and he sometimes felt like a teenage boy in a 35-year-old body. He started online dating, met a few women, and gained confidence. Soon he was involved in a long-term relationship, with talk of marriage. However, he also realized he had a lot more work to do on his self-esteem. He'd taken 30 inches off his waist, but much of his inner negativity about himself had not gone away. Life, as they say, is a work in progress. Jon worked hard on himself, and today he and his fiancé, Janet, are happily planning their wedding. They enjoy being healthy together.

Jon is proud of his work as a Healthy Living Ambassador for the American Diabetes Association and of his fitness achievements, including two half marathons and a 100-mile century ride on his bike. He remembers the envy he felt as an obese man watching others perform similar feats, and he has made it his mission to reach out and let people like him know it's possible. He sees and relates to the pain in people. Out of his past weakness has come a great empathy. Sometimes he wants to just go up to them and say, "Look at me. You can do it." Compassion gives his life a purpose that wasn't there when his only concern was for himself. This is Jon's path to salvation, for himself and others.

JON'S DAILY DIET COMPARISONS

BEFORE	AFTER
Breakfast Leftovers from the night before or something grabbed from the gas station—donuts or a burrito	**Breakfast** Egg white omelet with vegetables
Lunch Chinese buffet	**Lunch** Soup, yogurt with fruit or salad
Dinner 4-5 double cheeseburgers, fries, diet soda	**Dinner** Salad with meat and vegetables 1 scoop sugar-free ice cream
Snacks Donuts Packaged snack cakes Beef jerky sticks	**Snacks** Fruit Veggies

Jon's Protein Powerhouse Chili

BY Jon Stanton
MAKES 7 servings
SERVING SIZE 2 cups

Jon says: "This chili tastes better if it sits on the stove after the two hours of simmering until cool, and is then put in the refrigerator for a day or two. I will often freeze single-serving portions (2 cups each) to take with me for lunch. It's a great winter treat, but it is also good year-round. I sometimes add peppers for a little bit of heat. If you like your chili hot, go for it."

Oil spray
1¼ pounds ground turkey (at least 90% lean)
8 ounces sliced mushrooms
2 tablespoons minced garlic
2 teaspoons onion powder
1 teaspoon black pepper
2 15-ounce cans kidney beans (light or dark), preferably no-salt-added or low-sodium, rinsed and drained

2 15-ounce cans black beans, preferably no-salt-added or low-sodium, rinsed and drained
46 ounces low-sodium tomato or vegetable juice
2 15-ounce cans fire-roasted diced tomatoes (with liquids)
3 tablespoons chili powder
Sliced scallions, for garnish

1 Preheat a large pot coated with oil spray over medium-high heat. Add the turkey, mushrooms, garlic, onion powder, and pepper. Sauté until the turkey is brown, about 5 minutes. Add the beans, tomato or vegetable juice, and diced tomatoes. Bring the mixture to a boil. Stir in the chili powder. Reduce the heat to low and simmer, uncovered, for 2 hours or until the chili reaches the desired consistency. Garnish with sliced scallions before serving.

NUTRITION INFORMATION Calories: 401, Protein: 35 g, Total Fat: 5 g, Saturated Fat: 1 g, Cholesterol: 50 mg, Sodium: 495 mg, Carbohydrate: 56 g, Fiber: 20 g

TODAY

JOY'S 3-WEEK MEAL PLAN

Each inspiring Joy Fit member you've come to know on these pages had his or her own approach to weight loss, but there are certainly common threads among them. To highlight the major trends, members diligently followed portion or calorie controlled-menus and ate diets rich in vegetables, fruits, lean proteins, and whole grains while minimizing sugar, unhealthy fats, and refined white starch. The similarities are no coincidence, since these tried-and-true food strategies are the perfect recipe for achieving effective, lifelong weight loss. The same healthy eating principles used by successful Joy Fit members guide the 3-week meal plan laid out here. The following menu plans are calibrated at approximately 1,400 calories per day. Breakfasts are approximately 300 calories, lunches are approximately 400 calories, dinners are approximately 500 calories, and snacks are 150 to 200 calories. You may follow the menu plans as written or substitute any meal for another meal within the same meal category (in other words, all breakfasts are interchangeable, as are all lunches, dinners, and snacks). Feel free to repeat favorite meals as often as you like. Enjoy unlimited amounts of calorie-free beverages, including water, naturally flavored seltzer, and unsweetened coffee and tea, at meals and throughout the day. Additional beverage calories (including those for sugar or milk added to coffee or tea) are not included. While there are no desserts or sweets incorporated into this menu plan, for those times when you're entertaining or feel like indulging without derailing your diet, check out the selection of light desserts that begins on page 275.

WEEK 1 MENUS

DAY 1

BREAKFAST

Oatmeal with Berries and Nuts

½ cup old-fashioned oats
1 cup fresh or frozen berries
1 to 2 tablespoons chopped walnuts or almonds
1 teaspoon sugar, honey, or pure maple syrup (optional)

1 Prepare the oatmeal with water according to package directions. Top with berries and nuts. If desired, stir in choice of sweetener. Makes 1 serving.

LUNCH

Turkey and Avocado Sandwich

1 100-calorie whole wheat sandwich thin
4 ounces sliced turkey breast
2 thin slices avocado
1 slice tomato
  Lettuce leaves
1 slice yellow onion
1 tablespoon hummus, low-fat mayonnaise, or mustard
  Baby carrots, for serving

1 On bottom half of sandwich thin, layer turkey, avocado, tomato, lettuce, and onion. Spread top half with hummus, mayonnaise, or mustard. Place on top of turkey and vegetables. Serve with baby carrots. Makes 1 serving.

SNACK

String Cheese and Fruit

1 string cheese with an orange, apple, pear—or 1 cup grapes, berries, or melon.

DINNER

Mustard-Dill Salmon with Roasted Red Potatoes

1 serving Mustard-Dill Salmon en Papillote (see Mustard-Dill Salmon en Papillote recipe, page 142). Serve with Roasted Red Potatoes (recipe below).

Roasted Red Potatoes

3 small red potatoes (about 8 ounces), cut into bite-size pieces
2 teaspoons olive oil
1 teaspoon chopped fresh dill
  Salt and freshly ground black pepper

1 Preheat oven to 425°F. Line a baking sheet with aluminum foil; generously coat the foil with oil spray.

2 In a small bowl toss potatoes with olive oil, dill, and salt and pepper to taste. Arrange potatoes in a single layer on the prepared baking sheet. Bake for 15 minutes. Stir the potatoes and bake for another 15 minutes or until crispy on the outside and soft on the inside. Makes 1 serving.

Tuna Salad with Rice Cakes

DAY 2

BREAKFAST

Spinach-Cheddar Scramble

> Oil spray
>
> 2 cups baby spinach
>
> 1 whole egg
>
> 3 egg whites
>
> ¼ cup shredded reduced-fat cheese
>
> 1 orange, peeled and separated into segments

1 Lightly spray a medium nonstick skillet with oil spray. Sauté the spinach just until wilted.

2 In a medium bowl whisk together the whole egg and egg whites. Pour eggs into pan with spinach and cook, stirring occasionally, until eggs begin to firm up but are still glossy. Add cheese and stir until cheese is melted. Transfer to a serving plate and serve with an orange. Makes 1 serving.

LUNCH

Tuna Salad with Rice Cakes

> 1 6-ounce can or pouch light tuna packed in water, drained
>
> 3 tablespoons nonfat Greek yogurt
>
> 1 tablespoon light mayonnaise
>
> ¼ teaspoon dried dillweed
>
> Pinch ground black pepper and/or onion powder
>
> 3 rice cakes
>
> Lettuce, tomato slices, thinly sliced cucumber

1 In a medium bowl stir together the tuna, yogurt, mayonnaise, dillweed, and desired seasonings.

2 Spread tuna salad over rice cakes. Top with lettuce, tomato slices, and cucumber slices. Makes 1 serving.

SNACK

Nutrition Bar

Any nutrition or granola bar with 200 calories or less.

DINNER

Chicken Cutlet Italian-Style with Garlicky Broccoli

1 Chicken Cutlet Italian-Style (see Chicken Cutlets Italian-Style recipe, page 74) with 2 to 3 cups broccoli florets sautéed in 2 teaspoons olive oil with minced garlic.

DAY 3

BREAKFAST

Triple-Berry Muffin with Hard-Cooked Egg

1 Triple-Berry Muffin (see Triple-Berry Muffins recipe, page 80) with 1 hard-cooked egg (or 4 scrambled egg whites with desired seasonings).

LUNCH

Wild Salmon Salad with Chickpeas

1 5- to 6-ounce can or pouch wild Alaskan salmon, drained
½ cup chickpeas
¼ cup chopped red sweet pepper
¼ cup chopped red onion
2 teaspoons olive oil
1 to 2 tablespoons red wine vinegar
   Salad greens

1 In a medium bowl stir together salmon, chickpeas, pepper, onion, olive oil, and vinegar. Serve on a bed of salad greens. Makes 1 serving.

SNACK

Fruit + Almonds

1 orange, banana, or apple with 10 almonds.

DINNER

Lemon-Ginger Beef and Broccoli Stir-Fry

1 serving Lemon-Ginger Beef and Broccoli Stir-Fry (see Lemon-Ginger Beef and Broccoli Stir-Fry recipe, page 238).

DAY 4

BREAKFAST

Apple with Peanut Butter

1 sliced apple with 2 level tablespoons natural peanut butter (or other nut butter).

LUNCH

Ham and Cheese Roll-Up

1 whole grain wrap or tortilla
2 teaspoons reduced-fat mayonnaise
1 teaspoon Dijon mustard
3 ounces sliced ham
1 slice reduced-fat cheese
   Lettuce, sliced tomato, sliced onion, sliced cucumbers, roasted red pepper strips
   Pickles (optional)
   Steamed sugar snap peas or green beans, for serving

1 Spread the wrap with mayonnaise and mustard. Layer with ham, cheese, lettuce, tomato, onion, cucumbers, and red peppers. If desired, add pickles. Roll up. Serve with steamed sugar snap peas. Makes 1 serving.

SNACK

Pistachio Nuts or Sunflower Seeds

½ cup pistachios in the shell (about 45 nuts) or sunflower seeds in the shell.

DINNER

Pucker Garlic Tilapia with Quinoa and Sautéed Spinach

1 serving Pucker Garlic Tilapia (see Pucker Garlic Tilapia recipe, page 124) with ¾ cup cooked quinoa or brown or wild rice. Serve with unlimited spinach sautéed in 2 teaspoons olive oil with minced garlic.

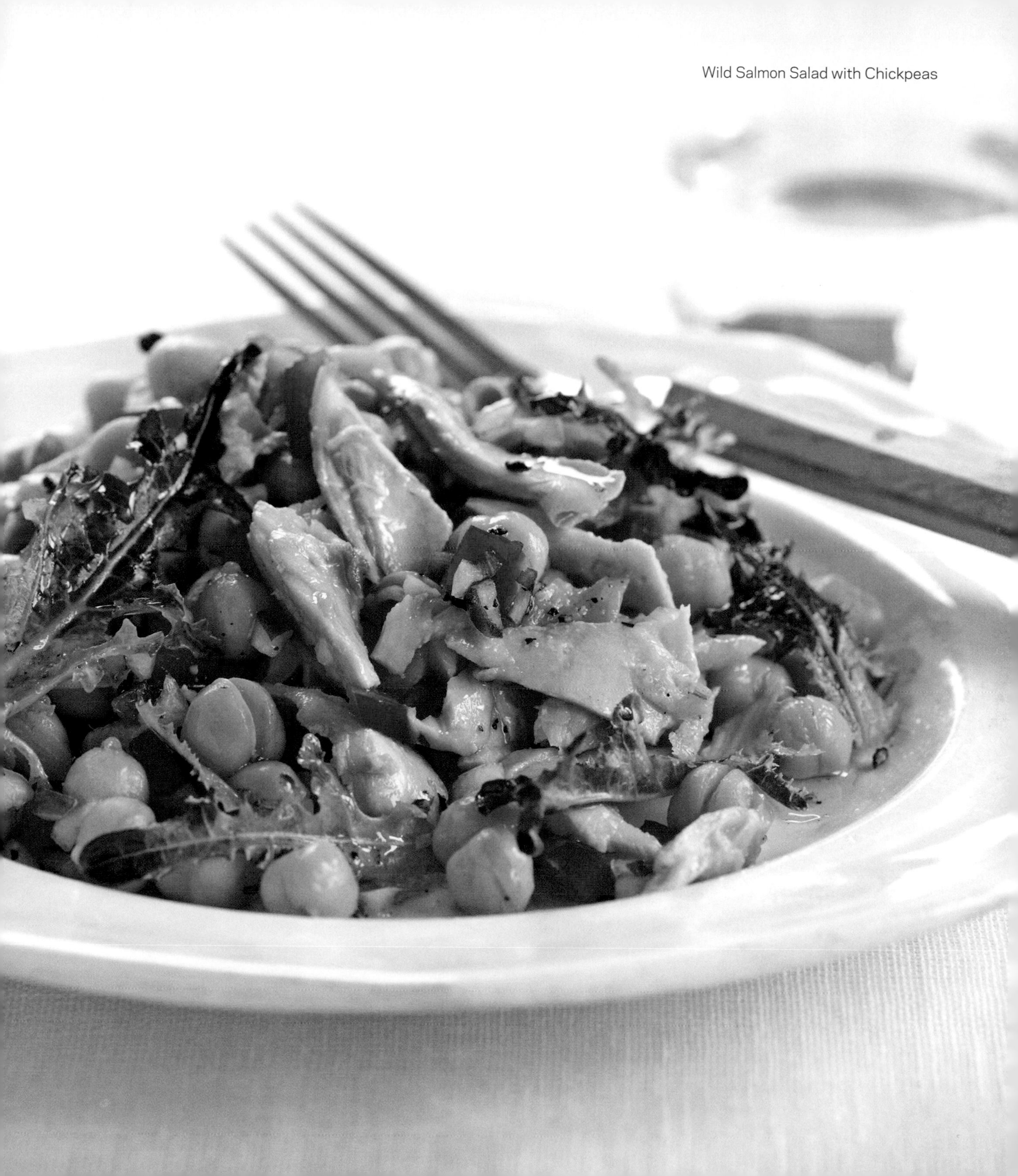

Wild Salmon Salad with Chickpeas

Chicken Caesar Salad

DAY 5

BREAKFAST

Whole Grain Waffles with Greek Yogurt

Toast 2 whole grain waffles. Top with a dollop of plain nonfat Greek yogurt and drizzle with 1 teaspoon pure maple syrup.

LUNCH

Chicken Caesar Salad

- 3 cups torn Romaine lettuce
- 4 tablespoons low-calorie Caesar salad dressing
- 3 tablespoons grated Parmesan cheese
- 4 ounces cooked boneless, skinless chicken breast, sliced thin
  Freshly ground black pepper

1 In a large bowl toss lettuce with dressing and cheese. Transfer to a serving bowl or plate. Top with chicken. Season to taste with black pepper. Makes 1 serving.

SNACK

Homemade Trail Mix

Combine ½ cup whole grain cereal with 1 tablespoon dried fruit (raisins, cranberries, or cherries), 1 tablespoon whole almonds, and 1 tablespoon dark or semisweet chocolate chips.

DINNER

Veggie Bean Burger with Avocado

1 Veggie Bean Burger topped with optional slice cheese (see Veggie Bean Burger recipe, page 262). Serve with half of an avocado sliced, drizzled with fresh lime juice, and lightly sprinkled with kosher salt.

DAY 6

BREAKFAST

Open-Face Breakfast BLT

- 1 whole grain English muffin or sandwich thin
- 2 teaspoons reduced-fat mayonnaise
- 2 slices cooked Canadian bacon or 4 strips cooked turkey bacon
  Sliced tomato, lettuce
- 1 cup grapes or fresh berries or 1 orange or apple

1 Toast the English muffin or sandwich thin. Top each half with 1 teaspoon reduced-fat mayo, 1 slice cooked Canadian bacon (or 2 strips turkey bacon), sliced tomato, and lettuce. Serve with grapes, berries, orange, or apple. Makes 1 serving.

Baked Potato with Broccoli and Cheese

LUNCH

Baked Potato with Broccoli and Cheese

- 1 medium russet potato, baked
- ½ cup cooked chopped broccoli
- ¼ cup shredded reduced-fat cheese
- 2 tablespoons light sour cream (optional)
  Salsa

1 Cut a small X in the top of potato; squeeze to open. Top with broccoli and cheese. Microwave 45 seconds or until cheese is melted. Top with sour cream, if desired, and salsa. Makes 1 serving.

SNACK

Popcorn

4 to 6 cups low-fat or air-popped popcorn.

DINNER

Crispy Turkey Skewers with Creamy Wild Rice and Sugar Snap Peas

1 serving Crispy Turkey Skewers with Creamy Wild Rice (see Crispy Turkey Skewers with Creamy Wild Rice recipe, page 251). Serve with steamed or sautéed sugar snap peas.

DAY 7

BREAKFAST

Garden Vegetable Omelet with Cheese Toast

- 2 cups choice of chopped vegetables (peppers, onions, mushrooms, spinach, Swiss chard, tomatoes, or broccoli)
- 1 whole egg
- 3 egg whites
  Pinch garlic powder and/or onion powder
  Salsa or hot sauce (optional)
- 1 slice whole wheat bread
- 1 slice reduced-fat cheese

1 Lightly spray an 8- or 10-inch omelet pan with oil spray; heat over medium heat. Sauté vegetables until soft, 4 to 5 minutes.

2 In a medium bowl whisk together whole egg, egg whites, and garlic powder and/or onion powder. Pour the egg mixture over the vegetables, swirling the egg around the pan to evenly distribute. Cook until the eggs are set on the bottom. Flip omelet over and cook the other side briefly, about 1 minute.

3 Fold omelet in half. Transfer to serving plate. If desired, top with salsa or hot sauce.

4 Toast bread. While still warm, top with cheese. Serve cheese toast with omelet. Makes 1 serving.

LUNCH

Fiery Chicken Salad

- 5 to 6 ounces cooked chicken, diced (fresh or canned)
- 1 tablespoon reduced-fat mayonnaise
  Minced jalapeño
  Minced onion
- 1 whole grain mini pita pocket bread or sandwich thin (100 calories or less)
  Baby carrots and sliced sweet pepper strips, for serving

1 In a small bowl combine chicken, mayonnaise, and jalapeño and onion to taste. Fill pita pocket with chicken salad or top sandwich thin. Serve with baby carrots and sliced sweet pepper strips. Makes 1 serving.

SNACK

Berry Smoothie

In a blender combine ½ cup skim, soy, or almond milk, ½ cup nonfat vanilla yogurt, ¾ cup fresh or frozen berries, and 3 to 5 ice cubes.

Baked Lemon-Herb Fish with
Tomato-Basil Couscous Casserole

DINNER

Baked Lemon-Herb Fish with Tomato-Basil Couscous Casserole

    Oil spray
1 6-ounce fillet of cod, sole, tilapia, or haddock
2 teaspoons fresh lemon juice
    Salt and freshly ground black pepper
1 tablespoon chopped fresh herbs, such as basil, parsley, dill, and/or thyme

1 Preheat the oven to 375°F. Line a baking sheet with aluminum foil. Generously coat foil with oil spray.

2 Place the fish on the prepared baking sheet. Season with lemon juice, salt and pepper to taste, and chopped herbs.

3 Bake for 10 to 12 minutes or until the fish is opaque and cooked through. Serve with 2 servings Tomato-Basil Couscous Casserole (see Tomato-Basil Couscous Casserole recipe, page 166). Makes 1 serving.

WEEK 2 MENUS

DAY 8

BREAKFAST

Cereal with Milk and Fruit

1 cup whole grain cereal (any brand 150 calories or less per 1-cup serving and 3+ grams fiber) with 1 cup skim, soy, or almond milk. Serve with ½ banana or ½ grapefruit or 1 orange.

LUNCH

Open-Face Tuna Melt

1 6-ounce can or pouch light tuna packed in water, drained
2 teaspoons reduced-fat mayonnaise
1 to 2 tablespoons minced onion
    Pinch ground black pepper, dried dillweed, and/or garlic powder
1 100-calorie sandwich thin, toasted
    Sliced tomato, sliced onion
2 slices reduced-fat cheese

1 Preheat oven to 350°F (or heat broiler on high).

2 In a medium bowl mash tuna with mayonnaise, onion, and desired seasonings. Spread tuna over 2 halves of sandwich thin. Top each half with sliced tomato, onion, and 1 slice reduced-fat cheese. Warm sandwich in preheated oven (or broil) until cheese is bubbly and melted. Serve immediately. Makes 1 serving.

SNACK

Warm Maple-Cinnamon Apple

Combine 1 sliced apple, 1 tablespoon water, and ½ teaspoon cinnamon. Microwave for 4 minutes and drizzle with 1 teaspoon pure maple syrup.

DINNER

Curried Lentils and Veggies

2 servings Curried Lentils and Veggies (see Curried Lentils and Veggies recipe, page 59).

DAY 9

BREAKFAST

Spicy Omelet with Toast

1 serving Sensational Spicy Omelet (see Sensational Spicy Omelet recipe, page 148) with 1 slice whole wheat toast spread with optional 1 teaspoon butter or trans fat-free soft tub spread (or 1 tablespoon all-fruit jam).

LUNCH

Pineapple Cottage Cheese

Mix 1 cup nonfat or low-fat cottage cheese with ½ cup drained crushed pineapple (canned in 100% juice). Spread the cottage cheese mixture over a toasted whole grain English muffin or 100-calorie sandwich thin.

SNACK

Zucchini Bread or Triple-Berry Muffin

1 slice Zucchini Bread (see Zucchini Bread recipe, page 170) or Triple-Berry Muffin (see Triple-Berry Muffin recipe, page 80).

DINNER

Grilled Chicken with Corn, Avocado, and Tomato Salad

1 grilled chicken breast (or 6 ounces grilled lean steak) with preferred seasonings with 2 servings Corn, Avocado and Tomato Salad (see Corn, Avocado and Tomato Salad recipe, page 44).

DAY 10

BREAKFAST

Breakfast Pumpkin Pudding

Stir together 1 6-ounce container nonfat vanilla yogurt, ½ cup canned 100% pumpkin puree, and ¼ teaspoon ground cinnamon. Top with 2 tablespoons chopped walnuts (or other nuts).

LUNCH

Lentil or Black Bean Soup

2 cups lentil or black bean soup (any brand under 400 calories per 2 cups) with unlimited baby carrots or cherry tomatoes on the side.

SNACK

Cheesy Rice Cake Snack

1 to 2 Cheesy Rice Cake Snacks (see Cheesy Rice Cake Snack recipe, page 204).

Dinner

Pork Chops with Maple-Glazed Apples and Polenta with Salad

1 serving Pork Chops with Maple-Glazed Apples and Polenta (see Pork Chops with Maple-Glazed Apples and Polenta recipe, page 241). Serve with large salad of leafy greens topped with any preferred vegetables (carrots, cucumbers, tomatoes, onions, peppers, mushrooms, etc.) and dressed with 2 tablespoons low-calorie dressing (or 1 teaspoon olive oil with unlimited fresh lemon juice or balsamic or red wine vinegar).

Protein Pancake with Strawberries

DAY 11

BREAKFAST

Egg and Cheese Sandwich

Toast 1 whole grain English muffin or sandwich thin. Top with 3 scrambled egg whites, 1 slice reduced-fat cheese, and sliced tomato.

LUNCH

Protein Pasta Salad

- ½ cup cooked whole wheat pasta (penne, rotini, or fusilli)
- 1 cup chopped nonstarchy vegetables (mushrooms, sweet peppers, cherry tomatoes, onions, cucumber, carrots, snow peas, broccoli)
- 4 to 5 ounces diced cooked chicken breast (fresh or canned) or light tuna or wild salmon OR ½ cup cooked chickpeas, black beans, kidney beans, or edamame
- 3 to 4 tablespoons low-calorie vinaigrette

1 In a medium bowl combine pasta, vegetables, and choice of protein. Toss with vinaigrette. Transfer to a serving bowl or plate. Makes 1 serving.

SNACK

Celery with Cream Cheese

Spread celery stalks with 4 tablespoons reduced-fat cream cheese.

DINNER

Chicken Thighs with Olives and Tomatoes with Green Beans

1 serving Chicken Thighs with Olives and Tomatoes served over whole wheat couscous (see Chicken Thighs with Olives and Tomatoes recipe, page 248). Serve with unlimited steamed or sautéed green beans with preferred seasonings.

DAY 12

BREAKFAST

Protein Pancake with Strawberries

- Oil spray
- ½ cup quick-cooking oats
- 4 egg whites
- 1 tablespoon sugar
- ½ teaspoon vanilla extract
- ½ teaspoon ground cinnamon
- ½ cup sliced strawberries or ½ banana, sliced

1 Generously coat a skillet with oil spray and heat over medium heat.

2 In a medium bowl whisk together the oats, egg whites, sugar, vanilla, and cinnamon.

3 Pour mixture into skillet and cook until golden brown, about 2 to 3 minutes on each side. (For a moister pancake, cover the skillet while the pancake is cooking.) Top with strawberries or banana slices. Makes 1 serving.

LUNCH

Cottage Cheese with Bananas and Walnuts

Mix 1 cup nonfat or low-fat cottage cheese with 1 sliced banana and 2 tablespoons chopped, toasted walnuts.

SNACK

Hummus and Veggies

Serve ¼ cup Sundried Tomato and Curry Hummus (see Sundried Tomato and Curry Hummus recipe, page 60) or any store-bought hummus with baby carrots, celery sticks, cucumber slices, and/or sweet pepper sticks.

DINNER

Honey-Lime Scallops with Wilted Spinach and Sweet Potato

1 serving Honey-Lime Scallops with Wilted Spinach (see Honey-Lime Scallops with Wilted Spinach recipe, page 260) Serve with 1 medium baked sweet potato topped with optional 1 tablespoon whipped butter, light sour cream, or trans fat-free soft tub spread (or try topping your potato with a dollop of tangy nonfat Greek yogurt).

DAY 13

BREAKFAST

Berry-Banana Smoothie

In a blender combine ¾ cup skim milk (or soy or almond milk), 1 6-ounce container nonfat vanilla yogurt, 1 cup fresh or frozen berries, ½ banana, optional 1 teaspoon ground flaxseed (or chia seed), and 3 to 5 ice cubes.

LUNCH

Slim-Style Pizza

1 serving Slim-Style Pizza (see Slim-Style Pizza recipe, page 191) topped with optional sautéed vegetables such as sweet peppers, onions, mushrooms, and broccoli. Enjoy with a side salad topped with 2 tablespoons low-calorie dressing (or 1 teaspoon olive oil with unlimited balsamic or red wine vinegar).

SNACK

Peanut Butter and Apple Slices

Slice 1 apple and serve with 1 level tablespoon natural peanut butter (or other nut butter).

DINNER

Chili and Chips

1 serving Jon's Protein Powerhouse Chili (see Jon's Protein Powerhouse Chili recipe, page 211) or White Chicken Chili (see White Chicken Chili recipe, page 111) with 1 serving (1 ounce) tortilla chips.

DAY 14

BREAKFAST

Breakfast Spanakopita with Grapefruit

1 serving Breakfast Spanakopita (see Breakfast Spanakopita recipe, page 200) with 1 grapefruit or 1 slice whole wheat toast spread with optional 1 teaspoon butter or trans fat-free soft tub spread (or 1 tablespoon all-fruit jam).

LUNCH

Speedy Rice and Beans

Combine 1 cup cooked brown rice, ½ cup black beans (rinsed and drained if from a can), ¼ cup salsa, and 1 to 2 tablespoons water in a microwave-safe bowl. Microwave until hot.

SNACK

Cucumber Hummus Tea Sandwich

Lightly toast 1 slice whole wheat bread and top with 2 tablespoons hummus and thinly sliced cucumbers. Cut into 4 triangles.

DINNER

Chicken and Kale with Roasted Potatoes

1 serving Chicken and Kale with Roasted Potatoes (see Chicken and Kale with Roasted Potatoes recipe, page 243).

WEEK 3 MENUS

DAY 15

BREAKFAST

Banana Bran Muffins with Cottage Cheese

2 Banana Bran Muffins (see Banana Bran Muffins recipe, page 52) with ½ cup nonfat or low-fat cottage cheese.

LUNCH

Peanut Butter and Cinnamon-Apple Sandwich

Mix 2 tablespoons natural peanut butter with ½ teaspoon ground cinnamon and spread over 2 slices of toasted whole wheat bread. Top with a thinly sliced apple.

SNACK

Spicy Turkey-Lettuce Wraps

Layer a few large lettuce leaves with 4 ounces turkey breast and top each turkey-lettuce combo with a spread of spicy mayo (mix 1 tablespoon light mayo with a few dashes of hot sauce). Roll up and enjoy.

DINNER

Roasted Pork Tenderloin with Baked Sweet Potato and Sugar Snap Peas

5 to 6 ounces roasted or grilled pork tenderloin with preferred seasonings or Rick's Pork Tenderloin (see Rick's Pork Tenderloin recipe, page 116) with 1 medium baked sweet potato and unlimited steamed or sautéed sugar snap peas.

Sweetened Ricotta Cream with Berries

DAY 16

BREAKFAST

Sweetened Ricotta Cream with Berries

½ cup part-skim ricotta cheese
1 teaspoon sugar
½ teaspoon vanilla extract
1 cup frozen berries

1 In a cereal or soup bowl stir together ricotta cheese, sugar, and vanilla extract.

2 In a microwave-safe bowl, microwave berries on high for 1 minute or until warm. Stir the berries and all of the liquids into the ricotta mixture. Makes 1 serving.

LUNCH

Entrée Salad

3 cups leafy salad greens
5 to 6 ounces cooked chicken, shrimp, salmon, or tofu OR ¾ cup cooked beans
¼ cup cubed avocado
1 cup chopped nonstarchy vegetables (tomatoes, carrots, cucumbers, broccoli, onion, sweet peppers, mushrooms, chopped hot peppers)
1 teaspoon olive oil
Fresh lemon juice, or balsamic or red wine vinegar

1 Place salad greens in an individual serving bowl or on a dinner plate. Top with choice of protein, avocado, and vegetables. Drizzle with 1 teaspoon olive oil and lemon juice or vinegar to taste. Makes 1 serving.

SNACK

Peanut Butter-Banana Freeze

Cut a banana lengthwise and spread 1 teaspoon natural peanut butter (or other nut butter) on each side. Place banana back into original position, cover with plastic wrap, and place in freezer for 4 hours.

DINNER

Easy Turkey Meat Loaf with Baked Potato and Green Beans

1 serving Easy Turkey Meat Loaf (see Easy Turkey Meat Loaf recipe, page 187). Serve with 1 medium baked potato topped with optional 1 tablespoon light sour cream and unlimited steamed or sautéed green beans.

DAY 17

BREAKFAST

Open-Face Lox and Tomato Sandwich with Fruit

1 serving Open-Face Lox and Tomato Sandwich with Creamy Avocado Spread (see Open-Face Lox and Tomato Sandwich with Creamy Avocado Spread recipe, page 180) with ½ cantaloupe or 1 cup grapes.

LUNCH

Broccoli and Cheese Omelet

    Oil spray
1 cup fresh broccoli florets
1 whole egg
3 egg whites
    Pinch of dried basil; garlic powder; and/or onion powder
¼ cup shredded reduced-fat cheese
1 slice whole wheat toast or a 100-calorie serving of whole grain crackers

1 Generously coat a skillet with oil spray and heat over medium heat. Sauté the broccoli until tender, 4 to 5 minutes.

2 In a medium bowl whisk together the whole egg and egg whites. Add desired seasonings. Pour egg mixture over the sautéed broccoli, swirling pan slightly to evenly distribute egg mixture and vegetables. When bottom is cooked, gently turn over and cook the other side for about 1 minute.

3 Sprinkle with cheese and continue to cook until eggs are done and cheese is melted, about 1 minute. Serve with toast or crackers. Makes 1 serving.

SNACK

Yogurt with Fruit

Top 1 6-ounce nonfat plain or flavored yogurt with ½ cup berries, pineapple chunks, or melon.

DINNER

Simple Salmon with Edamame and Salad

1 serving Simple Salmon (see Simple Salmon recipe, page 123) with 2 cups edamame in the pod. Serve with large salad of leafy greens topped with any preferred vegetables (carrots, cucumbers, tomatoes, onions, peppers, mushrooms, etc.) and dressed with 2 tablespoons low-calorie dressing (or 1 teaspoon olive oil with unlimited fresh lemon juice or balsamic or red wine vinegar).

DAY 18

BREAKFAST

Cinnamon Cottage Cheese with Sliced Apple

Sprinkle 1 cup nonfat or low-fat cottage cheese with cinnamon and serve with 1 sliced apple for scooping.

LUNCH

Veggie Burger on a Toasted English Muffin

Layer 1 veggie burger (any brand less than 200 calories or use Veggie Bean Burger recipe, page 262) with lettuce, tomato, onion, and 2 tablespoons ketchup or salsa on a toasted whole grain English muffin or 100-calorie sandwich thin. Serve with crunchy sweet pepper sticks on the side.

SNACK

Banana Bran Muffin with String Cheese

1 Banana Bran Muffin (see Banana Bran Muffins recipe, page 52) with 1 string cheese.

DINNER

Chicken with Creamy Garlic Pasta and Broccoli

1 serving Chicken with Creamy Garlic Pasta and Fresh Basil (see Chicken with Creamy Garlic Pasta and Fresh Basil recipe, page 244). Serve with steamed or sautéed broccoli.

DAY 19

BREAKFAST

Peanut Butter and Apple Oatmeal

1 serving Peanut Butter and Apple Oatmeal (see Peanut Butter and Apple Oatmeal recipe, page 81).

LUNCH

Sundried Tomato and Curry Hummus Pita

¼ cup Sundried Tomato and Curry Hummus (see Sundried Tomato and Curry Hummus recipe, page 60) or any store-bought hummus with 2 mini whole wheat pita breads. Serve with Cucumber-Tomato Salad.

Cucumber-Tomato Salad

- 1 cucumber, chopped
- 1 tomato, chopped
- ¼ cup chopped red onion
- 1 to 2 teaspoons olive oil
  Red wine vinegar
  Kosher salt and black pepper
  Dried oregano

1 In a medium bowl combine cucumber, tomato, and red onion. Drizzle with 1 to 2 teaspoons olive oil and vinegar to taste.

Season to taste with black pepper, kosher salt, and dried oregano. Makes 1 serving.

SNACK

Vanilla Pumpkin Pudding

Combine 1 6-ounce nonfat vanilla yogurt with ½ cup canned 100% pumpkin puree and sprinkle with cinnamon.

DINNER

Sloppy Pizza Joes with Salad

1 serving Sloppy Pizza Joes (see Sloppy Pizza Joes recipe, page 252). Serve with large salad of leafy greens topped with any preferred vegetables (carrots, cucumbers, tomatoes, onions, peppers, mushrooms, etc.) and dressed with 2 tablespoons low-calorie dressing (or 1 teaspoon olive oil with unlimited fresh lemon juice or balsamic or red wine vinegar).

DAY 20

BREAKFAST

Zucchini Bread with Yogurt

1 slice Zucchini Bread (see Zucchini Bread recipe, page 170) with 1 6-ounce container plain or flavored nonfat yogurt (any brand 150 calories or less).

Curried Chicken Salad with Green Peas

½ cup frozen peas
5 ounces cubed cooked chicken breast (fresh or canned)
1 tablespoon reduced-fat mayonnaise
1 to 2 tablespoons minced onion
1 teaspoon curry powder
Salad greens
1 mango, sliced, or 1 cup grapes, for serving

1 Place peas in a colander and hold under running water until peas are thawed.

2 In a small bowl combine chicken, mayonnaise, onion, curry powder, and thawed peas. Serve chicken salad on a bed of greens with mango or 1 cup grapes. Makes 1 serving.

SNACK

Rice Cakes with Ricotta, Tomato, and Basil

Top 2 rice cakes with ¼ cup part-skim ricotta cheese, sliced tomato, and optional fresh basil.

DINNER

Seafood Stew with Green Beans

3 cups (1½ servings) Seafood Stew with White Beans and Cilantro (see Seafood Stew with White Beans and Cilantro recipe, page 259). Serve with unlimited steamed or sautéed green beans or sugar snap peas with preferred seasonings.

DAY 21

BREAKFAST

Whole Wheat Pumpkin Pancakes

1 serving Whole Wheat Pumpkin Pancakes (see Whole Wheat Pumpkin Pancakes recipe, page 32).

LUNCH

Open-Face Tomato Grilled Cheese

Toast 2 slices whole wheat bread and top each with sliced tomato and 1 slice reduced-fat cheese. Place under broiler until cheese melts. Enjoy with unlimited steamed green beans.

SNACK

Edamame

2 cups cooked edamame in the pod.

DINNER

Mini Meat Loaves with Roasted Parmesan Cauliflower

1 serving Mini Meat Loaves (see Mini Meat Loaves recipe, page 242). Enjoy with Roasted Parmesan Cauliflower.

Roasted Parmesan Cauliflower

Preheat oven to 400°F. Coat a baking sheet with oil spray. Arrange 3 cups cauliflower florets on baking sheet. Mist florets with oil spray and sprinkle with ¼ teaspoon garlic powder and kosher salt and black pepper to taste. Bake for 25 to 30 minutes or until florets are brown and crispy, stirring once halfway through cooking. Sprinkle florets with 1 to 2 tablespoons grated Parmesan cheese and bake for an additional 5 minutes.

Curried Chicken Salad with Green Peas

BONUS RECIPES FROM JOY'S KITCHEN

Lemon-Ginger Beef and Broccoli Stir-Fry

MAKES 4 servings
SERVING SIZE ¾ cup cooked rice with a slightly rounded 1 cup of the beef and broccoli mixture
PREP TIME (START TO FINISH) 40 minutes

1 pound beef sirloin steak, trimmed of fat
1¼ cups water
3 tablespoons reduced-sodium soy sauce
2 tablespoons honey
4 teaspoons cornstarch
2 teaspoons finely chopped fresh ginger
    or ½ teaspoon ground ginger
2 teaspoons finely shredded lemon zest

¼ teaspoon crushed red pepper (optional)
3 cups fresh broccoli florets*
1 medium yellow sweet pepper, cut into
    thin bite-size strips
½ of a medium red onion, thinly sliced
    Oil spray
3 cups cooked brown rice, cooked soba
    noodles, or cooked brown rice fettuccine

1 Wrap beef with plastic wrap and place in the freezer for 20 to 30 minutes to make it easier to slice. Meanwhile, in a small bowl combine ¾ cup of the water, the soy sauce, honey, cornstarch, ginger, lemon zest, and, if desired, crushed red pepper. Set aside.

2 In a large wok or nonstick skillet combine broccoli and remaining ½ cup water. Bring to boiling over medium-high heat. Reduce heat and simmer, covered, for 3 minutes. Uncover and add the sweet pepper and red onion. Cook, uncovered, over medium heat for 3 to 5 minutes or until vegetables are crisp-tender and water is evaporated. Transfer vegetables to a large bowl and set aside.

3 Remove the beef from the freezer and slice into very thin strips. Coat the wok with oil spray and place over medium-high heat. Add half the beef strips. Cook and stir for 3 to 5 minutes or until beef is just a little pink in the center. Transfer the beef to the bowl with the vegetables and repeat with the remaining beef. Return all the beef and vegetables to the wok.

4 Stir the lemon-ginger sauce until well combined. Add to the wok. Cook and stir until thickened and bubbly. Cook and stir 1 minute more. Divide rice among four serving plates. Top evenly with beef mixture.

*TIP For quicker prep, pick up pre-cut broccoli florets in your market's produce department.

NUTRITION INFORMATION Calories: 417, Protein: 32 g, Total Fat: 7 g, Saturated Fat: 2 g, Cholesterol: 48 mg, Sodium: 508 mg, Carbohydrate: 55 g, Fiber: 5 g

Pork Chops with Maple-Glazed Apples and Polenta

MAKES 4 servings

SERVING SIZE ¾ cup polenta, 1 pork chop, and ½ cup sliced apples with sauce

PREP TIME (START TO FINISH) 35 minutes

2½ cups reduced-sodium chicken broth

1½ cups water

1 cup dry whole grain polenta

2 teaspoons snipped fresh sage or
½ teaspoon dried sage

¼ teaspoon freshly ground black pepper

4 ½- to ¾-inch-thick boneless pork loin chops (about 1¼ pounds total)

½ teaspoon smoked paprika or sweet paprika

¼ teaspoon kosher salt
Oil spray

3 medium cooking apples, such as Jonathan, Rome, or McIntosh, quartered, cored, and thinly sliced

2 tablespoons water

2 tablespoons pure maple syrup

1 In a large saucepan combine broth, 1½ cups water, and the polenta. Bring to boiling, stirring constantly. Reduce heat. Simmer, uncovered, for 25 to 30 minutes or until polenta is thick and tender, stirring frequently. Stir in the sage and ⅛ teaspoon of the pepper.

2 Meanwhile, trim any fat from the pork chops. In a small bowl combine paprika, salt, and remaining ⅛ teaspoon of the pepper. Sprinkle evenly over the pork chops.

3 Coat a large nonstick skillet with oil spray. Heat skillet over medium-high heat. Add seasoned chops to the hot skillet. Cook for 6 to 8 minutes or until chops are just light pink in the center (145°F to 150°F), turning once halfway through cooking. Remove chops from the skillet; cover to keep warm.

4 Add apples and 2 tablespoons water to the hot skillet. Bring just to boiling. Cover and cook for 3 minutes or until apples are just tender, stirring once or twice. Add syrup and toss to coat.

5 Divide polenta mixture among four serving plates. Add 1 pork chop to each plate. Spoon apples and sauce evenly over the pork chops.

NUTRITION INFORMATION Calories: 426, Protein: 37 g, Total Fat: 6 g, Saturated Fat: 2 g, Cholesterol: 93 mg, Sodium: 544 mg, Carbohydrate: 53 g, Fiber: 5 g

Mini Meat Loaves

MAKES 6 servings
SERVING SIZE 2 mini meat loaves
PREP TIME 30 minutes | **BAKE TIME** 23 minutes

1⅓ cups water
⅔ cup bulgur
Oil spray
2 cups chopped fresh button mushrooms
¾ cup chopped onion
1 stalk celery, chopped
4 cloves garlic, minced, or 2 teaspoons jarred minced garlic
2 egg whites
1½ teaspoons fresh thyme or ½ teaspoon dried thyme

1 teaspoon kosher salt
¼ teaspoon freshly ground black pepper
1¼ pounds lean ground turkey or lean ground beef (at least 90% lean)

Topping
½ of a 6-ounce can no-salt-added tomato paste (⅓ cup)
1 tablespoon water
2 teaspoons packed brown sugar
2 teaspoons white or balsamic vinegar
Dash kosher salt

1 Preheat oven to 350°F. In a small saucepan combine water and bulgur. Bring to boiling. Reduce the heat and simmer, covered, for 12 to 15 minutes or until bulgur is tender. Drain off any liquid.

2 Coat a large nonstick skillet with oil spray; heat over medium heat. Add mushrooms, onion, and celery. Cook for 8 to 10 minutes or until vegetables are tender. Stir in garlic. Remove from heat.

3 In a large bowl whisk egg whites. Stir in thyme, 1 teaspoon salt, and pepper. Add turkey or beef, bulgur, and mushroom mixture. Mix and divide among 12 standard muffin cups, patting mixture to an even layer.

4 Bake for 18 minutes or until centers of meat loaves register 145°F to 150°F on an instant-read thermometer. For the topping, in a small bowl combine tomato paste, water, brown sugar, vinegar, and dash salt. Spoon evenly over meat loaves. Bake meat loaves 5 to 10 minutes more or until centers of meat loaves register 165°F (turkey) or 160°F (beef) on an instant-read thermometer.

5 Cool meat loaves in pan on a wire rack for 5 minutes. Remove meat loaves from muffin cups.

TIP If desired, omit the 1⅓ cups water and bulgur. Combine ¾ cup boiling water and ⅔ cup quick-cooking oats. Stir and let stand for 1 minute. Add to meat mixture in place of bulgur in Step 3.

NUTRITION INFORMATION Calories: 248, Protein: 24 g, Total Fat: 8 g, Saturated Fat: 2 g, Cholesterol: 67 mg, Sodium: 451 mg, Carbohydrate: 20 g, Fiber: 5 g

Chicken and Kale with Roasted Potatoes

MAKES 4 servings

SERVING SIZE 1 chicken breast half or chicken thigh,
1 cup roasted vegetable mixture, and ¾ cup cooked kale

PREP TIME (START TO FINISH) 40 minutes

1½ pounds small red potatoes (about 2-inch diameter), scrubbed and quartered

½ of a sweet onion, cut into thin wedges

3 sprigs fresh thyme
Oil spray

¾ teaspoon kosher salt

½ teaspoon freshly ground black pepper

1 large red sweet pepper, coarsely chopped

4 small skinless, boneless chicken breast halves (about 1½ pounds total) or 4 large bone-in chicken thighs (about 1¾ pounds total), skinned

½ cup water

10 to 12 cups coarsely chopped fresh kale (about one 1-pound bunch, trimmed)

5 cloves garlic, thinly sliced

2 teaspoons chopped fresh thyme

1 Preheat oven to 400°F. Line a shallow roasting pan with parchment paper or aluminum foil. Add potatoes, onion wedges, and thyme sprigs to the prepared pan. Coat vegetables with oil spray and sprinkle with ¼ teaspoon of the salt and ¼ teaspoon of the pepper. Toss to coat. Roast for 20 minutes, stirring once. Add the sweet pepper to the pan. Toss to mix and roast for 15 to 20 minutes more or until vegetables are tender and lightly browned, stirring once.

2 Meanwhile, coat a large nonstick skillet with oil spray. Heat skillet over medium heat. Sprinkle the chicken breast halves or thighs with ¼ teaspoon of the salt and remaining ¼ teaspoon of the pepper. Add chicken to the hot pan, seasoned sides down. Cook for 8 to 10 minutes or until chicken is browned, turning once halfway through cook time. Remove skillet from the heat and carefully add the water. Return to the heat, cover, and cook for 9 to 12 minutes or until chicken is no longer pink (180°F for thighs or 170°F for breast halves). Remove the chicken from the skillet, reserving any liquid in the pan. Cover chicken and keep warm.

3 Add the kale, garlic, and remaining ¼ teaspoon salt to the same skillet, adding the kale in two batches. Cook, tossing with tongs, for 5 to 7 minutes or until kale is tender.

4 Divide the kale evenly among four serving plates. Top kale with the chicken. Remove the thyme sprigs from the roasted potato mixture and discard. Stir in the chopped fresh thyme and divide the potato mixture among the serving plates.

NUTRITION INFORMATION (USING CHICKEN BREAST HALVES) Calories: 446, Protein: 46 g, Total Fat: 7 g, Saturated Fat: 1 g, Cholesterol: 109 mg, Sodium: 615 mg, Carbohydrate: 53 g, Fiber: 8 g

Chicken with Creamy Garlic Pasta and Fresh Basil

MAKES 4 servings

SERVING SIZE about 1 cup pasta mixture with 3½ ounces cooked chicken and 2 tablespoons fresh basil

PREP TIME (START TO FINISH) 40 minutes

Oil spray

3 medium skinless, boneless chicken breast halves (about 1¼ pounds total)

½ teaspoon kosher salt

¼ teaspoon freshly ground black pepper

½ cup water

6 ounces dry whole grain linguine

½ cup reduced-sodium chicken broth (if needed)

8 ounces assorted fresh mushrooms (such as button, cremini, and stemmed shiitake), thinly sliced (about 3 cups)

1 medium onion, halved and thinly sliced

4 cloves garlic, minced, or 2 teaspoons jarred minced garlic

4 ounces reduced-fat cream cheese

¾ cup nonfat milk

½ cup jarred roasted red sweet peppers, drained and cut into thin strips

½ cup chopped fresh basil or 2 tablespoons chopped fresh oregano or thyme

1 Coat a large nonstick skillet with oil spray. Heat the skillet over medium heat. Meanwhile, season the chicken with the salt and pepper. Add chicken to the hot pan. Cook for 6 to 8 minutes or until chicken is browned, turning once halfway through cook time. Remove the skillet from the heat and carefully add the water. Return to the heat and bring the water to boiling. Reduce the heat and cover the skillet. Cook for 9 to 12 minutes more or until chicken is no longer pink (170°F).

2 Meanwhile, cook the linguine according to package directions. Drain and set aside.

3 Remove the chicken from the skillet, reserving any liquid in the pan. Cover the chicken and keep warm. If necessary, add enough of the chicken broth to the pan to make ½ cup total liquid in the pan. Add the mushrooms, onion, and garlic to the liquid in the skillet. Cover and cook over medium heat for 5 minutes or until mushrooms and onion are tender. Add the cream cheese and stir until cheese is melted and combined with the vegetables. Stir in the milk, roasted pepper strips, and drained linguine. Cook and stir about 1 minute or until mixture is heated through and well coated with the sauce.

4 Divide the pasta mixture among four serving plates. Thinly slice the chicken. Place the chicken on top of the pasta on the plates. Sprinkle with the basil, oregano, or thyme.

NUTRITION INFORMATION Calories: 446, Protein: 42 g, Total Fat: 13 g, Saturated Fat: 4.5 g, Cholesterol: 112 mg, Sodium: 534 mg, Carbohydrate: 42 g, Fiber: 7 g

Chipotle Chicken Tortilla Soup

MAKES 4 servings
SERVING SIZE about 2 cups
PREP TIME (START TO FINISH) 35 minutes

Oil spray

2 medium red and/or green sweet peppers, cut into thin bite-size strips

1 medium onion, chopped

3 cloves garlic, minced, or 1½ teaspoons jarred minced garlic

½ teaspoon ground cumin

3½ cups reduced-sodium chicken broth

1 cup water

1 to 2 teaspoons finely chopped canned chipotle pepper in adobo sauce

1 14.5-ounce can no-salt-added diced tomatoes

8 ounces cooked skinless chicken breast, shredded (about 2 cups)

Kosher salt and freshly ground black pepper (optional)

¼ cup light sour cream

3 tablespoons chopped fresh cilantro

1 ounce baked tortilla chips, crushed (½ cup)

1 lime, cut into 4 wedges

1 Coat a 4-quart pot with oil spray. Heat the pan over medium heat. Add the sweet peppers and onion. Cook for 8 minutes or until vegetables are crisp-tender, stirring occasionally. Add garlic and cumin. Cook and stir for 1 minute.

2 Add chicken broth, water, and chipotle pepper. Bring to boiling. Reduce heat and simmer, covered, for 5 minutes. Stir in tomatoes and chicken. Cover and cook for 5 minutes more. Season to taste with kosher salt and black pepper (skip the salt if you have high blood pressure).

3 In a small bowl combine sour cream and 2 tablespoons of the cilantro. To serve, divide soup among four serving bowls. Top each serving with one-fourth of the sour cream mixture and sprinkle with one-fourth of the crushed chips. Sprinkle with remaining chopped cilantro and serve with lime wedges to squeeze over the soup.

NUTRITION INFORMATION Calories: 229, Protein: 23 g, Total Fat: 7 g, Saturated Fat: 2 g, Cholesterol: 52 mg, Sodium: 595 mg, Carbohydrate: 20 g, Fiber: 5 g

Chicken Thighs with Olives and Tomatoes

MAKES 4 servings

SERVING SIZE 1 chicken thigh with ½ cup tomato mixture and about ¾ cup couscous

PREP TIME (START TO FINISH) 40 minutes

4 large bone-in chicken thighs (about 1¾ pounds total), skinned

¼ teaspoon freshly ground black pepper
   Oil spray

½ cup water

1¾ cups reduced-sodium chicken broth (one 14.5-ounce can)

1 cup dry whole wheat couscous

½ of a medium red onion, thinly sliced

4 cloves garlic, minced, or 2 teaspoons jarred minced garlic

2 cups cherry or grape tomatoes, halved

¼ cup pitted kalamata olives, halved

2 teaspoons chopped fresh oregano or rosemary

¼ cup chopped fresh flat-leaf parsley or 2 tablespoons chopped fresh oregano (optional)

2 teaspoons finely shredded lemon zest

⅛ teaspoon freshly ground black pepper

1 Trim fat off the chicken thighs. Sprinkle thighs with ¼ teaspoon pepper. Coat a large nonstick skillet with oil spray. Heat skillet over medium heat. Add chicken thighs, seasoned sides down. Cook for 6 to 8 minutes or until chicken is browned, turning once halfway through cook time. Remove skillet from the heat and carefully add the water. Return to the heat, cover, and cook for 9 to 12 minutes or until chicken is no longer pink (180°F). Transfer chicken to a plate and cover to keep warm.

2 Meanwhile, in a medium saucepan bring 1½ cups of the chicken broth to boiling. Stir in couscous and remove from the heat. Cover and let stand 5 minutes.

3 Add red onion to the hot skillet after removing the chicken. Cook over medium heat for 6 to 8 minutes or until onion is just tender, stirring occasionally. Add garlic; cook and stir for 30 seconds. Add tomatoes and the remaining ¼ cup chicken broth. Cook, covered, for about 3 minutes or until tomatoes are softened. Use a potato masher to mash tomatoes slightly. Add olives and 2 teaspoons oregano or rosemary. Stir until well combined. Place the chicken thighs on top of the tomato mixture and pour any juice that collected on the plate into the skillet. Cover and cook 1 minute to heat through.

4 Fluff the couscous with a fork and stir in the parsley or 2 tablespoons oregano, if desired, the lemon zest, and ⅛ teaspoon pepper. Divide couscous among four serving plates. Add 1 chicken thigh to each plate and spoon the tomato mixture over the chicken thighs.

NUTRITION INFORMATION Calories: 380, Protein: 32 g, Total Fat: 9 g, Saturated Fat: 1 g, Cholesterol: 94 mg, Sodium: 485 mg, Carbohydrate: 46 g, Fiber: 8 g

Crispy Turkey Skewers with Creamy Wild Rice

MAKES 4 servings
SERVING SIZE 1 turkey skewer with about ¾ cup rice mixture
PREP TIME 30 minutes | COOK TIME 45 minutes | BROIL TIME 12 minutes

Oil spray
1½ cups sliced fresh button or cremini mushrooms
3 medium carrots, thinly sliced
1 medium onion, chopped
3 cloves garlic, minced, or 1½ teaspoons jarred minced garlic
2 cups reduced-sodium chicken broth
½ cup dry wild rice, rinsed
½ cup dry brown rice

2 tablespoons nonfat milk
1 egg white, lightly beaten
1 cup whole wheat panko bread crumbs or dry whole wheat bread crumbs
1 pound turkey breast tenderloins, cut into 1½- to 2-inch pieces
½ teaspoon freshly ground black pepper
¼ teaspoon kosher salt
2 ounces reduced-fat cream cheese
¼ cup nonfat milk

1 Coat a large saucepan with oil spray. Heat the pan over medium heat. Add the mushrooms, carrots, and onion. Cook for about 8 minutes or until vegetables are almost tender, stirring occasionally. Stir in garlic. Transfer vegetable mixture to a small bowl. Add the broth, wild rice, and brown rice to the same saucepan. Bring to boiling. Reduce heat. Simmer, covered, for 40 minutes.

2 Preheat the broiler. Line a baking sheet with foil and set aside. Whisk together 2 tablespoons milk and the egg white in a shallow dish. Put bread crumbs in another shallow dish. Dip the tenderloin pieces, a few at a time, in the egg white mixture. Allow excess to drip off and then roll them in the bread crumbs to coat evenly. Skewer the coated turkey pieces onto four 10- to 12-inch skewers,* leaving a ¼-inch space between pieces. Sprinkle the turkey evenly with ¼ teaspoon of the pepper and the salt. Place the skewers on the prepared baking sheet.

3 Broil the turkey skewers 4 to 5 inches from the heat for 12 to 14 minutes or until turkey is no longer pink in the centers of the pieces, turning once halfway through cook time.

4 Meanwhile, stir the mushroom mixture into the rice. Cover and continue to cook for 5 to 10 minutes or until rice is tender and the liquid is absorbed. Stir in the cream cheese, ¼ cup milk, and remaining ¼ teaspoon pepper until well combined. Remove from the heat, cover, and let stand for 5 minutes.

5 Divide the rice mixture among four serving plates. Top each serving with one of the turkey skewers.

*NOTE If using wooden or bamboo skewers, soak the skewers in enough water to cover for 30 minutes before using to prevent them from burning.

NUTRITION INFORMATION Calories: 433, Protein: 41 g, Total Fat: 7 g, Saturated Fat: 2 g, Cholesterol: 81 mg, Sodium: 565 mg, Carbohydrate: 53 g, Fiber: 6 g

Sloppy Pizza Joes

MAKES 6 servings
SERVING SIZE 1 sandwich (1 bun, ⅔ cup turkey mixture,
  2 tablespoons cheese, and ¼ cup spinach)
PREP TIME (START TO FINISH) 30 minutes

2 Italian-style turkey sausage links (about 8 ounces total)
8 ounces ground turkey (at least 90% lean)
2 cups chopped fresh cremini mushrooms
1 large red or green sweet pepper, chopped
1 medium onion, chopped
4 cloves garlic, minced, or 2 teaspoons jarred minced garlic

2 8-ounce cans no-salt-added tomato sauce
2 tablespoons chopped fresh oregano or 2 teaspoons dried oregano
6 whole wheat hamburger buns, split
¾ cup shredded reduced-fat Italian cheese blend
1½ cups fresh baby spinach leaves

1 Remove casings from sausage links and discard. In a large nonstick skillet cook sausage, ground turkey, mushrooms, sweet pepper, onion, and garlic over medium heat until turkey is no longer pink and vegetables are tender, stirring to break up turkey as it cooks. Add tomato sauce and oregano. Bring to boiling. Reduce heat and simmer, uncovered, for 10 minutes to blend flavors and reduce the sauce.

2 Meanwhile, preheat the broiler. Line a large baking sheet with foil. Place bun halves, cut sides up, on the prepared baking sheet. Broil 3 to 4 inches from the heat for 1 to 2 minutes or until buns are toasted. Remove the bun tops from the baking sheet. Spoon the turkey mixture evenly onto the bun bottoms on the pan. Sprinkle evenly with the cheese. Broil about 1 minute or until cheese is melted.

3 To serve, divide the spinach among the sandwiches, placing it on top of the cheese. Replace the bun tops.

TIP If desired, use one 1.25-pound package of ground turkey (at least 90% lean) in place of the turkey sausage and ground turkey so that you only have to purchase one product.

NUTRITION INFORMATION Calories: 332, Protein: 26 g, Total Fat: 11 g, Saturated Fat: 3 g, Cholesterol: 59 mg, Sodium: 525 mg, Carbohydrate: 30 g, Fiber: 4 g

Sweet Sesame-Crusted Salmon

MAKES 4 servings
SERVING SIZE 1 piece of salmon
PREP TIME 15 minutes | BAKE TIME 12 minutes

1 egg white
¼ cup all-fruit apricot preserves
¾ cup whole wheat panko bread crumbs
  or dry whole wheat bread crumbs
2 tablespoons sesame seeds
1 pound fresh or frozen skinless salmon,
  thawed if frozen and cut into 4 equal
  fillets

½ teaspoon kosher salt
¼ teaspoon freshly ground black pepper
  or cayenne pepper
  Oil spray
2 tablespoons chopped fresh chives
  (optional)

1 Preheat oven to 425°F. Line a large baking sheet with foil; set aside. In a shallow dish or pie plate whisk egg white until lightly beaten. Using kitchen shears, snip any large pieces of fruit in the preserves. Whisk preserves into the egg whites. In another shallow dish or pie plate combine the panko crumbs and sesame seeds.

2 Rinse salmon fillets and pat dry with paper towels. Dip the salmon fillets, one at a time, into the egg white mixture, turning to coat evenly. Allow excess to drip off. Dip in the panko mixture, turning to coat evenly. Place the fillets on the prepared baking sheet. Sprinkle the tops with salt and black or cayenne pepper and lightly coat the tops with oil spray.

3 Bake for 12 to 14 minutes or until fish flakes easily when tested with a fork. To serve, divide salmon pieces among serving plates. If desired, sprinkle with chives.

NUTRITION INFORMATION Calories: 326, Protein: 26 g, Total Fat: 18 g, Saturated Fat: 4 g, Cholesterol: 62 mg, Sodium: 335 mg, Carbohydrate: 15 g, Fiber: 2 g

Aïoli-Smeared Fish Sandwiches

MAKES 4 servings
SERVING SIZE 1 sandwich
PREP TIME (START TO FINISH) 35 minutes

⅓ cup light mayonnaise
1 tablespoon chopped fresh chives
1 teaspoon finely shredded lemon zest
1 tablespoon lemon juice
2 small cloves garlic, minced, or
   1 teaspoon jarred minced garlic
1 pound fresh or frozen skinless tilapia or
   flounder fillets, thawed if frozen

¼ teaspoon kosher salt
¼ teaspoon freshly ground black pepper
   Oil spray
4 thin slices red onion (optional)
8 slices whole grain bread, toasted
2 leaves fresh romaine lettuce
½ cup jarred roasted red sweet peppers,
   drained and cut into thin strips

1 For aïoli, in a small bowl combine mayonnaise, chives, lemon zest, lemon juice, and garlic. Cover and chill until ready to serve.

2 Rinse fish and pat dry with paper towels. Sprinkle fish evenly with salt and black pepper. Lightly coat both sides of fish fillets with oil spray. If using red onion, lightly coat both sides of onion slices with oil spray.

3 Preheat a charcoal or gas grill, adjusting the coals or heat level to medium heat. Place the onion slices (if using) directly on the grill rack over the heat. Grill for 8 to 10 minutes or until crisp-tender and browned, turning halfway through grilling. Add the fish fillets to the grill rack after the onions have cooked for a few minutes. Grill the fish for 5 to 7 minutes or until fish flakes easily when tested with a fork, turning once halfway through grilling. Remove the fish and onions from the grill.

4 To serve, spread one side of each toasted bread slice with some of the aïoli mixture. Break the lettuce leaves into smaller pieces and arrange on top of half the bread slices. Top the lettuce evenly with the fish. Top the fish with the onions (if using) and the red pepper strips. Place the remaining bread slices on top, aïoli sides down. Cut sandwiches in half to serve.

NUTRITION INFORMATION (SANDWICH) Calories: 373, Protein: 33 g, Total Fat: 13 g, Saturated Fat: 2 g, Cholesterol: 63 mg, Sodium: 537 mg, Carbohydrate: 34 g, Fiber: 9 g

Fish Tacos with Aïoli Sauce Prepare as directed above, except cut the lettuce into thin strips and substitute 8 6-inch corn tortillas for the bread slices. To serve, warm the tortillas according to package directions and top tortillas evenly with lettuce. Break fish into large chunks and place on top of lettuce. Top with red onion, if using, and roasted pepper strips. Spoon aïoli evenly over tacos. Serves 4 (2 tacos per serving).

NUTRITION INFORMATION (TACOS) Calories: 298, Protein: 26 g, Total Fat: 11 g, Saturated Fat: 2 g, Cholesterol: 63 mg, Sodium: 339 mg, Carbohydrate: 26 g, Fiber: 4 g

Seafood Stew with White Beans and Cilantro

MAKES 6 servings
SERVING SIZE 2 cups
PREP TIME (START TO FINISH) 35 minutes

6 green onions
Oil spray
2 small red and/or green sweet peppers,
cut into thin bite-size strips
4 cloves garlic, minced, or 2 teaspoons
jarred minced garlic
1½ teaspoons ground cumin
5 cups purchased lower-sodium or
homemade seafood stock
2 15-ounce cans no-salt-added cannellini
beans, rinsed and drained

1 14.5-ounce can no-salt-added diced
tomatoes
¼ teaspoon crushed red pepper (optional)
12 ounces fresh or frozen peeled and
deveined shrimp, thawed if frozen
12 ounces fresh or frozen skinless cod,
thawed if frozen
⅓ cup chopped fresh cilantro
Kosher salt and freshly ground black
pepper (optional)

1 Thinly slice green onions, keeping the green tops separate from the white bottoms. Coat a 5- to 6-quart pot with oil spray. Heat the pot over medium heat. Add white parts of green onions and the sweet peppers. Cook for 3 to 5 minutes or until vegetables are almost tender. Add garlic and cumin. Cook and stir for 30 seconds. Add seafood stock, cannellini beans, diced tomatoes, and, if desired, the crushed red pepper. Bring to boiling. Reduce heat and simmer, covered, for 10 to 15 minutes to blend flavors.

2 Meanwhile, rinse shrimp and cod with cold water and pat dry with paper towels. Cut the cod into bite-size pieces.

3 Add the shrimp and cod to the stew. Cook, uncovered, for 2 to 3 minutes or until shrimp are opaque and cod is just cooked through and tender. Remove from the heat and stir in the sliced green onion tops and the cilantro. Season to taste with kosher salt and black pepper (skip the salt if you have high blood pressure).

NUTRITION INFORMATION Calories: 267, Protein: 31 g, Total Fat: 3 g, Saturated Fat: 0 g, Cholesterol: 111 mg, Sodium: 591 mg, Carbohydrate: 27 g, Fiber: 8 g

Honey-Lime Scallops with Wilted Spinach

MAKES 4 servings
SERVING SIZE about 1 cup wilted spinach mixture with 3 scallops and ¼ of the avocado
PREP TIME (START TO FINISH) 25 minutes

1 lime
2 medium shallots, thinly sliced
2 teaspoons olive oil
12 fresh or frozen sea scallops, thawed if frozen (about 1¼ pounds total)
½ teaspoon kosher salt
⅛ teaspoon freshly ground black pepper

Oil spray
1 tablespoon honey
8 cups fresh baby spinach (about 8 ounces)
1 medium avocado, halved, seeded, peeled, and thinly sliced

1 Finely shred enough of the lime peel to make 2 teaspoons zest. Cut the lime in half and juice enough to make 2 tablespoons. Set juice and zest aside.

2 In a large nonstick skillet cook the shallots in the olive oil over medium heat for 3 to 5 minutes or until shallots are just tender, stirring occasionally.

3 Meanwhile, rinse the scallops with cold water and pat dry with paper towels. Sprinkle the scallops evenly with ¼ teaspoon of the salt and the pepper. Lightly coat scallops on both sides with oil spray. Coat an indoor grill pan or another large nonstick skillet with oil spray. Heat the pan over medium-high heat. Add scallops to grill pan or skillet. Cook for 3 to 5 minutes or until scallops are opaque and cooked through, turning once halfway through cook time.

4 Add the lime juice, honey, and remaining ¼ teaspoon salt to the shallots in the skillet. Just before serving, add the spinach in two batches to the shallot mixture. Cook, tossing gently with tongs, for 30 to 60 seconds or until spinach is just wilted. Immediately divide spinach mixture among four serving plates. Top each serving with 3 of the scallops. Top each serving with one-fourth of the avocado slices and sprinkle with reserved lime zest.

NUTRITION INFORMATION Calories: 262, Protein: 28 g, Total Fat: 10 g, Saturated Fat: 1 g, Cholesterol: 49 mg, Sodium: 536 mg, Carbohydrate: 17 g, Fiber: 4 g

Veggie Bean Burger

MAKES 6 servings

SERVING SIZE 1 burger with 1 sandwich thin, ¼ cup spinach, 1 slice red onion, and 1 slice tomato (plus optional cheese and Roasted Pepper Ketchup if desired)

PREP TIME (START TO FINISH) 30 minutes

Oil spray

1 cup chopped fresh button or cremini mushrooms

2 stalks celery, chopped

¾ cup chopped onion

2 cloves garlic, minced, or 1 teaspoon jarred minced garlic

2 egg whites

2 teaspoons chopped fresh thyme or 1 teaspoon dried thyme

½ teaspoon kosher salt

¼ teaspoon freshly ground black pepper

2 15-ounce cans no-salt-added red beans, rinsed and drained

½ cup dry whole wheat bread crumbs

6 slices of your favorite reduced-fat cheese (such as provolone, mozzarella, cheddar, or Swiss) (about 4½ ounces total) (optional)

6 whole grain sandwich thins, split and lightly toasted

1½ cups fresh baby spinach leaves

6 thin slices red onion

6 thin slices fresh tomato

6 tablespoons Roasted Pepper Ketchup (optional) (see recipe, page 263)

1 Coat a large nonstick skillet with oil spray. Heat the skillet over medium heat. Add mushrooms, celery, and onion. Cook for 6 to 8 minutes or until vegetables are tender, stirring occasionally. Add garlic and cook and stir for about 1 minute. Remove from the heat.

2 Meanwhile, in a large bowl beat egg whites. Stir in thyme, salt, and pepper. Add red beans. Use a potato masher to mash beans. Stir in mushroom mixture and bread crumbs and mix well. Divide mixture into 6 equal portions. Shape each portion into a 4-inch-diameter patty about ½ inch thick.

3 Lightly coat an indoor grill pan or griddle with oil spray. Heat the pan over medium heat. Add bean patties to the hot pan. Cook for 6 to 8 minutes or until the internal temperature of the patties registers 160°F on an instant-read thermometer,* turning once halfway through cook time. If desired, add a slice of cheese to each burger for the last minute of cooking.

4 To serve, place each bun bottom on a serving plate. Top with spinach and a burger. Top each burger with an onion slice and tomato slice. Spoon 1 tablespoon Roasted Pepper Ketchup onto burgers, if desired, and top with bun tops.

*TIP To test doneness with the thermometer, stick the thermometer horizontally into the side of the patties so the reading is more accurate.

NUTRITION INFORMATION (WITHOUT CHEESE OR ROASTED PEPPER KETCHUP) Calories: 288, Protein: 18 g, Total Fat: 2 g, Saturated Fat: 0 g, Cholesterol: 0 mg, Sodium: 538 mg, Carbohydrate: 52 g, Fiber: 18 g

Roasted Pepper Ketchup

MAKES 17 servings
SERVING SIZE 1 tablespoon
PREP TIME 15 minutes | BAKE TIME 25 minutes

1 small head garlic
½ teaspoon olive oil
1 cup jarred roasted red sweet peppers, drained and dried with paper towels

½ of a 6-ounce can no-salt-added tomato paste (⅓ cup)
1 teaspoon white sugar
Dash kosher salt
Dash freshly ground black pepper

1 Preheat the oven to 425°F. Cut about ½ inch off the top of the garlic head. Remove a few layers of the outer papery skins from the garlic cloves, leaving the cloves intact and covered with several layers of skin. Place the garlic head in a small custard cup and drizzle the top with the olive oil. Cover with foil and roast for 20 to 30 minutes or until garlic cloves are soft. Let stand on a wire rack until cool enough to handle.

2 When the garlic is cool enough to handle, squeeze the garlic cloves from the skins and into a blender or food processor. Add roasted peppers and tomato paste. Cover and blend or process until smooth. For the blender, it works best to pulse the mixture until smooth, scraping down the sides of the container often.

3 Transfer pepper mixture to a bowl and stir in sugar, salt, and black pepper. Store the ketchup in an airtight container in the refrigerator for up to 1 week (up to 3 days for Herbed Pepper Ketchup).

NUTRITION INFORMATION Calories: 12, Protein: 0 g, Total Fat: 0 g, Cholesterol: 0 mg, Sodium: 10 mg, Carbohydrate: 2 g, Fiber: 1 g

Chipotle-Pepper Ketchup Prepare Roasted Pepper Ketchup as directed and stir in 1 teaspoon finely chopped canned chipotle pepper in adobo sauce in Step 3.

NUTRITION INFORMATION Calories: 12, Protein: 0 g, Total Fat: 0 g, Cholesterol: 0 mg, Sodium: 11 mg, Carbohydrate: 2 g, Fiber: 1 g

Balsamic-Roasted Pepper Ketchup Prepare Roasted Pepper Ketchup as directed and stir in 1 tablespoon balsamic vinegar in Step 3.

NUTRITION INFORMATION Calories: 13, Protein: 0 g, Total Fat: 0 g, Cholesterol: 0 mg, Sodium: 10 mg, Carbohydrate: 3 g, Fiber: 1 g

Herbed Pepper Ketchup Prepare Roasted Pepper Ketchup as directed and stir in 2 tablespoons finely chopped assorted fresh herbs (such as rosemary, oregano, basil, and/or thyme) in Step 3.

NUTRITION INFORMATION Calories: 13, Protein: 0 g, Total Fat: 0 g, Cholesterol: 0 mg, Sodium: 10 mg, Carbohydrate: 3 g, Fiber: 1 g

Vegetable Wraps with Edamame Hummus

MAKES 4 servings
SERVING SIZE 1 wrap
PREP TIME 25 minutes | **BAKE TIME** 25 minutes

1 head garlic	⅛ teaspoon freshly ground black pepper
½ teaspoon olive oil	4 9- to 10-inch whole grain wraps or
1 cup fresh spinach leaves	tortillas
1 cup frozen shelled edamame, thawed	1½ cups fresh arugula (or spinach) leaves
2 tablespoons water	½ of a medium cucumber, thinly sliced
2 tablespoons tahini (sesame seed paste)	½ of a medium red onion, very thinly sliced
2 tablespoons rice vinegar	¾ cup jarred roasted red peppers, drained
¼ teaspoon kosher salt	and cut into thin strips

1 Preheat the oven to 425°F. Cut about ½ inch off the top of the garlic head. Remove a few layers of the outer papery skins from the garlic cloves, leaving the cloves intact and covered with several layers of skin. Place the garlic head in a small custard cup and drizzle the top with the olive oil. Cover with foil and roast for 20 to 30 minutes or until garlic cloves are soft. Let stand on a wire rack until cool enough to handle.

2 Meanwhile, place spinach in a food processor. Cover and pulse until spinach is chopped. Transfer spinach to a medium bowl. Add the edamame, water, tahini, vinegar, salt, and black pepper to the food processor. Cover and process until smooth. When the garlic is cool enough to handle, squeeze the garlic cloves from the skins and into the edamame mixture in the food processor. Cover and process until well combined. Add the edamame mixture to the spinach in the bowl and stir until well combined.

3 To serve, spread the edamame hummus evenly over the lower half of the wraps. Top with the arugula, cucumber slices, red onion slices, and red pepper strips, keeping the vegetables in the lower third of the wraps. Roll up the wraps and cut in half to serve.

TIP Wraps may be made ahead. Prepare the wraps as directed and wrap in plastic wrap or place in an airtight container. Refrigerate up to 5 hours. Edamame hummus may be made ahead and stored in an airtight container in the refrigerator up to 24 hours. Feel free to swap your favorite vegetables for the red onion, cucumber, and roasted peppers.

NUTRITION INFORMATION Calories: 346, Protein: 13 g, Total Fat: 13 g, Saturated Fat: 3 g, Cholesterol: 0 mg, Sodium: 580 mg, Carbohydrate: 47 g, Fiber: 11 g

Barley and Bean Soup with Squash

MAKES 4 servings

SERVING SIZE about 2 cups

PREP TIME 5 minutes | COOK TIME about 15 minutes

Oil spray

3 medium leeks, trimmed and thinly sliced, or 1 medium onion, chopped

3 cups lower-sodium vegetable broth

2 cups ½-inch cubes peeled butternut squash

1 15-ounce can no-salt-added cannellini beans, rinsed and drained

½ cup quick-cooking barley

1½ tablespoons chopped fresh sage or 1½ teaspoons dried sage

1 medium zucchini, trimmed, halved lengthwise, and thinly sliced crosswise

4 ounces reduced-fat cream cheese, cut into cubes

2 cups nonfat milk

Kosher salt and freshly ground black pepper (optional)

¼ cup slivered almonds, toasted

1 Coat a large saucepan with oil spray. Heat the pan over medium heat. Add leeks. Cook for 5 minutes, stirring occasionally. Add vegetable broth, squash, beans, barley, and dried sage (if using). Bring to boiling. Reduce heat and simmer, covered, for 6 minutes.

2 Add zucchini to the soup. Return to simmering. Cook, covered, for 8 to 10 minutes more or until squash, barley and zucchini are tender. Reduce heat to low. Add cream cheese and stir until cheese is melted and incorporated into the soup. Stir in milk and fresh sage (if using). Heat through over low heat. Season to taste with kosher salt and black pepper (skip the salt if you have high blood pressure).

3 Ladle soup into four serving bowls. Sprinkle each serving with 1 tablespoon slivered almonds.

NUTRITION INFORMATION Calories: 418, Protein: 18 g, Total Fat: 13 g, Saturated Fat: 4 g, Cholesterol: 23 mg, Sodium: 613 mg, Carbohydrate: 63 g, Fiber: 11 g

Edamame-Wasabi Spring Rolls with Lox

MAKES 4 servings
SERVING SIZE 4 spring rolls
PREP TIME (START TO FINISH) 45 minutes

¾ cup frozen shelled edamame, thawed
⅓ cup water
1½ teaspoons wasabi
1½ teaspoons finely chopped, peeled fresh ginger
1 clove garlic, minced, or ½ teaspoon jarred minced garlic
⅛ teaspoon kosher salt

2 medium yellow and/or red sweet peppers
1 medium cucumber
1 3-ounce package cold-smoked salmon (lox)
16 8-inch rice papers
48 fresh mint leaves or 32 fresh chives

1 In a food processor combine edamame, water, wasabi, ginger, garlic, and salt. Cover and process until smooth. Spoon the edamame mixture into a small zip-top plastic bag and seal the bag. Cut a small amount off one of the corners so there is about a ½-inch-diameter hole in the corner.

2 Cut each pepper lengthwise into quarters and remove the stems and seeds. Cut each pepper quarter into 8 strips, for a total of 64 strips. Trim the ends off the cucumber and discard. Cut the cucumber lengthwise in half. Using a small spoon, scrape out the seeds and discard. Cut each half crosswise in half. Cut each portion of the cucumber into 16 long strips, for a total of 64 strips. Cut the salmon evenly into 16 long strips.

3 Fill a large skillet about half full with water. Bring the water just to boiling and remove from the heat. Dip 1 rice paper in the skillet of hot water, carefully pushing it into the water to cover completely. Let the paper sit in the water for about 10 seconds or until just softened. Use tongs to carefully remove the paper from the water and quickly lay the paper completely flat on a large plate.

4 Pipe a thin line of the edamame mixture across the lower third of the rice paper, using about 2 teaspoons of the edamame mixture per rice paper. Arrange 4 strips of sweet pepper, 4 strips of cucumber, and 1 strip of salmon atop the edamame mixture.

continued on page 269

continued from page 267

5 Fold the bottom of the rice paper up over the filling; fold in the sides of the rice paper. Roll one turn so the filling is completely enclosed but so there is about 2 or 3 inches of paper left to roll up. Place 3 fresh mint leaves or 2 fresh chives on the paper, right above where the roll stops. Finish rolling up the spring roll, enclosing the mint or chives in the roll. Place the finished roll on a tray that is lined with damp paper towels. Cover the roll with a damp paper towel. Repeat with the remaining rice papers, edamame mixture, vegetables, salmon, and herbs to make 16 total spring rolls. If the dipping water cools off, reheat just to boiling and remove from the heat.

6 To serve, cut spring rolls in half.

TIP Keeping the finished spring rolls covered with damp paper towels will keep them from drying out. Be patient with the rice papers. Once you make a few spring rolls, you'll get the hang of using the paper and the rolling will go much quicker.

MAKE AHEAD Prepare as directed. Line a large shallow airtight container with damp paper towels. Arrange one layer of finished spring rolls in the container, making sure there is space between the rolls (if the rolls touch, they will stick together and could cause the rice papers to tear). Cover the spring rolls with a layer of damp paper towels, pushing the towels down along the sides of the rolls a little. Make a second or third layer as needed, placing damp paper towels between each layer. Cover the container and refrigerate the spring rolls for up to 48 hours.

NUTRITION INFORMATION Calories: 264, Protein: 11 g, Total Fat: 3 g, Saturated Fat: 0 g, Cholesterol: 5 mg, Sodium: 546 mg, Carbohydrate: 50 g, Fiber: 4 g

Greek-Style Eggplant Lasagna

MAKES 8 servings
SERVING SIZE ⅛ of the pan of lasagna
PREP TIME 35 minutes | **BAKE TIME** 55 minutes | **STAND TIME** 15 minutes

Oil spray
1 medium sweet onion, chopped
4 cloves garlic, minced, or 2 teaspoons jarred minced garlic
1 tablespoon chopped fresh thyme or 1 teaspoon dried thyme
¾ teaspoon kosher salt
¼ teaspoon freshly ground black pepper
3 14.5-ounce cans no-salt-added diced tomatoes with basil, garlic, and oregano

1 6-ounce can no-salt-added tomato paste
9 whole wheat lasagna noodles
2 small eggplants (about 12 ounces each), trimmed and cut crosswise into ¼-inch-thick slices
2 egg whites
1 15-ounce container low-fat or part-skim ricotta cheese
⅔ cup finely shredded Parmesan cheese
4 ounces feta cheese, crumbled

1 Preheat oven to 375°F. Coat a large nonstick skillet with oil spray. Heat skillet over medium heat. Add onion. Cook for 6 to 8 minutes or until tender, stirring occasionally. Add garlic, thyme, ½ teaspoon of the salt, and the pepper. Cook and stir for 30 seconds. Transfer onion mixture to a blender. Add the undrained tomatoes and tomato paste. Cover and blend until smooth.

2 In a large pot cook the lasagna noodles 1 minute less than the time given on the package (it should be about 9 minutes). While the lasagna is cooking, add the eggplant slices, in three batches, to the boiling water and cook for 3 minutes per batch (the eggplant will float on top of the lasagna noodles). Remove the eggplant slices from the water and drain in a large colander. Drain the lasagna when it is done cooking.

3 In a medium bowl beat egg whites lightly with a fork. Stir in the remaining ¼ teaspoon salt, the ricotta cheese, Parmesan cheese, and half of the crumbled feta cheese.

4 Spread about ½ cup of the tomato sauce in the bottom of a 3-quart rectangular glass baking dish. Top with 3 of the noodles. Top with one-third of the ricotta mixture and spread to an even layer. Top with one-third of the eggplant slices. Pour one-third of the remaining tomato sauce over the eggplant. Repeat layers twice, starting with lasagna noodles and ending with the tomato sauce.

5 Bake, uncovered, for 55 to 65 minutes or until lasagna is heated through (an instant-read thermometer should read 160°F in the center of the lasagna). Let stand for 15 to 20 minutes before serving. Cut lasagna into 8 servings and place one serving on each of eight dinner plates. Sprinkle with remaining crumbled feta cheese before serving.

NUTRITION INFORMATION Calories: 325, Protein: 16 g, Total Fat: 9 g, Saturated Fat: 4.5 g, Cholesterol: 30 mg, Sodium: 554 mg, Carbohydrate: 45 g, Fiber: 9 g

Sesame Tofu with Cabbage

MAKES 4 servings
SERVING SIZE 1¼ cups cabbage mixture, about ¾ cup tofu mixture, and ¾ teaspoon sesame seeds
PREP TIME (START TO FINISH) 35 minutes

⅓ cup rice vinegar
1 tablespoon toasted sesame oil
1 tablespoon reduced-sodium soy sauce
3 cloves garlic, minced, or 1½ teaspoons jarred minced garlic
1 teaspoon cornstarch
¾ teaspoon kosher salt
¼ teaspoon crushed red pepper
1 18-ounce package firm or extra-firm water-packed tofu (not silken), drained and patted dry with paper towels

2 teaspoons sesame seeds
Oil spray
1 orange sweet pepper, cut into thin strips
½ of a medium red onion, thinly sliced
6 cups thinly sliced, trimmed napa cabbage (about 12 ounces)

1 In a large bowl whisk together vinegar, sesame oil, soy sauce, garlic, cornstarch, ¼ teaspoon of the salt, and the crushed red pepper. Cut the tofu into 1-inch cubes and add to the vinegar mixture. Stir gently to coat the tofu. Let stand at room temperature for 15 minutes, stirring occasionally.

2 Meanwhile, spread sesame seeds in an even layer in a large dry nonstick skillet. Heat over medium heat for 2 to 3 minutes or until sesame seeds are lightly toasted, stirring occasionally. Transfer seeds to a small bowl and set aside.

3 Lightly coat the same skillet with oil spray. Heat the skillet over medium heat. Add sweet pepper and onion. Cook for 5 minutes, stirring occasionally. Transfer to a medium bowl and set aside. Add the tofu cubes and any liquid remaining in the bowl to the same skillet. Cook for 4 to 6 minutes or until tofu is heated through and liquid is thickened, gently stirring constantly. Remove tofu mixture from the skillet and keep warm.

4 Add the sweet pepper and red onion back to the skillet along with the remaining ½ teaspoon salt and the cabbage. Cook for 1 to 2 minutes or until cabbage is just wilted, tossing with tongs to wilt cabbage evenly.

5 Divide cabbage mixture evenly among four serving plates. Top evenly with tofu mixture and sprinkle with toasted sesame seeds.

NUTRITION INFORMATION Calories: 224, Protein: 14 g, Total Fat: 11 g, Saturated Fat: 1 g, Cholesterol: 0 mg, Sodium: 520 mg, Carbohydrate: 14 g, Fiber: 3 g

Garlic-Roasted Vegetables with Red Lentils

MAKES 4 servings
SERVING SIZE about ¾ cup lentils, about 1¼ cups vegetable mixture,
  1 tablespoon cilantro, and 1 tablespoon pumpkin seeds
PREP TIME 25 minutes | COOK TIME 10 minutes | BAKE TIME 25 minutes

4 cups fresh cauliflower florets
   (1 small head)
2 small zucchini, trimmed, halved
   lengthwise, and cut crosswise into
   1-inch thick slices
4 cloves garlic, thinly sliced
1 tablespoon olive oil
½ teaspoon kosher salt

¼ teaspoon freshly ground black pepper
2 cups lower-sodium vegetable broth
1½ cups dry red lentils, rinsed and drained
1 teaspoon ground cumin
¼ cup chopped fresh cilantro
¼ cup roasted unsalted pumpkin seeds
   (pepitas)
   Juice of ½ lemon (optional)

1 Preheat oven to 425°F. In a 3-quart rectangular glass baking dish combine cauliflower, zucchini, and garlic. Drizzle with olive oil and sprinkle with salt and pepper. Toss to coat. Roast for 25 to 30 minutes or until vegetables are just tender and lightly browned, stirring once or twice.

2 Meanwhile, in a large saucepan combine vegetable broth, lentils, and cumin. Bring to boiling. Reduce heat and simmer, covered, for 10 minutes, stirring once or twice. Remove from the heat and let stand, covered, for 5 minutes.

3 Divide lentils among four serving plates. Top evenly with cauliflower and zucchini mixture. Sprinkle with cilantro and pumpkin seeds. If desired, drizzle with lemon juice.

NUTRITION INFORMATION Calories: 386, Protein: 25 g, Total Fat: 10 g, Saturated Fat: 2 g, Cholesterol: 0 mg, Sodium: 585 mg, Carbohydrate: 52 g, Fiber: 14 g

Cream Puffs with Ricotta Cream and Fruit

MAKES 6 servings
SERVING SIZE 1 cream puff with ¼ cup ricotta cream and ⅓ cup fruit
PREP TIME 25 minutes | **BAKE TIME** 25 minutes

3 tablespoons honey
1 teaspoon unflavored gelatin
½ cup low-fat or part-skim ricotta cheese
1 cup nonfat plain Greek yogurt (be sure to use a thicker brand such as Fage or Chobani)
½ cup water
2 tablespoons canola oil
2 tablespoons butter

⅛ teaspoon kosher salt
⅓ cup whole wheat pastry flour
2 tablespoons all-purpose flour
2 egg whites
1 whole egg
2 cups assorted cut-up fresh fruit (such as kiwi, mango, raspberries, strawberries, and/or blueberries)

1 For cream filling, in a small saucepan combine honey and gelatin. Cook, stirring constantly, over medium-low heat for 2 to 3 minutes or until mixture is just bubbling on the edges. Remove from the heat and stir in ricotta cheese until smooth. Whisk in yogurt until smooth. Transfer ricotta cream to a medium bowl. Cover and chill for at least 2 hours or up to 24 hours.

2 Preheat oven to 400°F. Line a baking sheet with parchment paper and set aside. In a small saucepan combine water, oil, butter, and salt. Bring just to boiling over medium heat. Add pastry flour and all-purpose flour, stirring constantly. Continue to cook and stir until mixture is well combined. Remove from the heat and let cool for 10 minutes. Add egg whites and stir until well combined. Add the whole egg and stir until well combined.

3 Drop the dough into 6 equal mounds on the prepared baking sheet. Bake for 25 to 30 minutes or until cream puffs are golden brown. Cool on a wire rack.

4 To serve, cut the tops off the cream puffs and set aside. Set 1 cream puff bottom on each of six dessert plates. Spoon cream filling evenly onto the bottoms of the cream puffs. Top with fruit and replace cream puff tops.

NUTRITION INFORMATION Calories: 228, Protein: 10 g, Total Fat: 11 g, Saturated Fat: 4 g, Cholesterol: 52 mg, Sodium: 164 mg, Carbohydrate: 26 g, Fiber: 3 g, Total Sugar: 16 g

Chocolate-Peanut Butter Bread Pudding

MAKES 8 servings
SERVING SIZE ⅛ of the pudding with 1½ tablespoons sauce
PREP TIME 25 minutes | **BAKE TIME** 25 minutes | **COOL** 15 minutes

- 6 cups light oatmeal bread cubes or light whole wheat bread cubes (about 8½ ounces or 12 slices)
- 3 ounces dark chocolate, chopped
- 3 egg whites
- 1 whole egg
- ¼ cup white sugar
- 1⅓ cups nonfat milk or unflavored soy milk
- 1 teaspoon vanilla
- ½ cup nonfat milk or unflavored soy milk
- ¼ cup natural creamy peanut butter
- 2 tablespoons packed brown sugar

1 Preheat the oven to 350°F. Lightly grease a 2-quart square glass baking dish. Arrange bread cubes in an even layer in the dish. Sprinkle evenly with chocolate.

2 In a medium bowl whisk together egg whites, whole egg, and sugar. Add 1⅓ cups milk and the vanilla and whisk until combined. Slowly and evenly pour the milk mixture over the bread and chocolate in the dish.

3 Bake for 25 to 30 minutes or until a knife inserted near the center comes out clean. Cool on a wire rack for 15 to 20 minutes before serving.

4 Meanwhile, in a small saucepan combine ½ cup milk, the peanut butter, and brown sugar. Cook, whisking constantly, over medium-low heat for 5 minutes or until mixture is well combined and just bubbly. Remove from the heat and cool for 5 to 10 minutes before serving. The sauce will thicken slightly as it cools.

5 Cut pudding into 8 rectangles and divide among eight serving plates. Drizzle about 1½ tablespoons of the sauce over each serving. Serve warm.

NUTRITION INFORMATION Calories: 245, Protein: 10 g, Total Fat: 9 g, Saturated Fat: 3 g, Cholesterol: 29 mg, Sodium: 190 mg, Carbohydrate: 34 g, Fiber: 3 g, Total Sugar: 19 g

Decadent Chocolate Mousse with Berries

MAKES 6 servings
SERVING SIZE ½ cup mousse with ¼ cup berries
PREP TIME 30 minutes | CHILL TIME 2 hours

½ cup sugar
⅓ cup unsweetened cocoa powder
3 tablespoons cornstarch
1 teaspoon instant espresso powder
⅛ teaspoon kosher salt
2¼ cups nonfat milk or original/plain
    soy milk
1 egg
1 ounce dark chocolate, finely chopped

1 teaspoon butter
1 teaspoon vanilla
⅓ cup whipping cream
1½ cups assorted fresh berries (such as
    raspberries, blackberries, cherries,
    and/or sliced strawberries)
½ ounce dark chocolate, chopped or made
    into curls

1 In a medium saucepan combine sugar, cocoa powder, cornstarch, espresso powder, and salt. Gradually whisk in milk. Cook and stir over medium heat for 9 to 11 minutes or until large bubbles are just starting to break the surface of the pudding (pudding will be thick, so to check for bubbles stop stirring for 3 to 4 seconds). Reduce the heat to low and cook and stir for 2 minutes more. Remove from the heat.

2 In a medium bowl lightly beat the egg. Gradually whisk about ½ cup of the hot milk mixture into the egg. Add all the egg mixture along with the 1 ounce chopped chocolate into the saucepan with the rest of the pudding. Cook and stir over medium-low heat for 30 seconds to 1½ minutes or until large bubbles are just starting to break the surface of the pudding (again, pudding will be thick so stop stirring for a few seconds to check for bubbles). Cook and stir over medium-low heat for 2 minutes more. Remove from the heat and stir in the butter and vanilla.

3 Place the saucepan of pudding in a large bowl half-filled with ice water. Stir the pudding for 1 to 2 minutes to cool it quickly. Transfer the pudding to a large bowl. Cover the surface of the pudding with plastic wrap and refrigerate for 2 to 3 hours or until well chilled.

4 Place whipping cream in a medium chilled bowl. Whisk or beat with a rotary beater until thick, soft peaks form. Gently fold half of the whipped cream into the chilled pudding. Gently fold in the remaining whipped cream. Divide mousse among six dessert dishes. Top with berries and garnish with chocolate.

Fiery Chocolate Mousse with Berries Prepare as directed above except add ¼ teaspoon cayenne pepper to the pudding in Step 1 with the salt.

NUTRITION INFORMATION (FOR BOTH MOUSSE RECIPES) Calories: 240, Protein: 6 g, Total Fat: 10 g, Saturated Fat: 5 g, Cholesterol: 58 mg, Sodium: 103 mg, Carbohydrate: 36 g, Fiber: 4 g, Total Sugar: 26 g

Lime-Ginger Baby Cakes with Creamy Coconut Frosting

MAKES 12 servings
SERVING SIZE 1 cupcake
PREP TIME 35 minutes | **BAKE TIME** 14 minutes

¾ cup whole wheat pastry flour or brown rice flour
¼ cup all-purpose flour
1 teaspoon baking powder
¼ teaspoon kosher salt
2 egg whites
1 whole egg
¾ cup white sugar
½ cup nonfat milk or original/plain soy milk

2 tablespoons canola oil
2 teaspoons finely shredded lime zest
1 teaspoon grated peeled fresh ginger or ½ teaspoon ground ginger
2 ounces reduced-fat cream cheese, softened
1 tablespoon powdered sugar
1 6-ounce carton nonfat vanilla yogurt
¼ cup shredded coconut, lightly toasted

1 Preheat oven to 375°F. Place a cupcake liner in each of 12 standard-size muffin cups. In a small bowl combine pastry flour, all-purpose flour, baking powder, and salt. In a large bowl combine egg whites and whole egg. Beat with an electric mixer on high for 5 minutes. Add sugar and beat on high for 3 minutes.

2 Add the flour mixture to the egg mixture. Beat just until combined. In a small bowl combine milk, oil, lime zest, and ginger. Add all at once to the egg mixture. Stir just until combined. Spoon batter evenly into the prepared cupcake liners.

3 Bake for 14 to 18 minutes or until a toothpick inserted in the centers comes out clean. Let cupcakes cool in the pan on a wire rack for 5 minutes. Remove cupcakes from the pan and cool completely.

4 In a medium bowl beat cream cheese and powdered sugar with an electric mixer on medium until smooth. Gradually beat in yogurt until mixture is smooth. Spoon yogurt mixture evenly on top of cooled cupcakes and sprinkle with coconut.

TIP To pipe frosting on cupcakes, prepare the frosting as directed and then chill the frosting for 2 hours to make it firmer. Transfer frosting to a piping bag fitted with an open star tip or a large round tip. Pipe frosting onto cupcakes and sprinkle with coconut as directed.

NUTRITION INFORMATION (BASIC) Calories: 149, Protein: 4 g, Total Fat: 4 g, Saturated Fat: 1 g, Cholesterol: 21 mg, Sodium: 106 mg, Carbohydrate: 24 g, Fiber: 1 g, Total Sugar: 16 g

Gluten-Free Lime-Ginger Baby Cakes Prepare as directed above except, substitute 1 cup brown rice flour for the whole wheat pastry flour and the all-purpose flour.

NUTRITION INFORMATION (GLUTEN-FREE) Calories: 160, Protein: 3 g, Total Fat: 5 g, Saturated Fat: 1 g, Cholesterol: 21 mg, Sodium: 107 mg, Carbohydrate: 26 g, Fiber: 1 g, Total Sugar: 16 g

Apple Dumplings with Cinnamon Sauce

MAKES 4 servings
SERVING SIZE 1 apple dumpling with 2 tablespoons cinnamon sauce
PREP TIME 35 minutes | BAKE TIME 20 minutes | COOL TIME 20 minutes

Apple Dumplings

- 6 sheets thawed phyllo dough (14×9-inch)
- 3 tablespoons light, trans fat-free soft tub buttery spread, melted
- 1 teaspoon granulated sugar
- ⅛ teaspoon ground cinnamon
- 4 small cooking apples (such as Jonathan, Rome, Cortland, or Braeburn) (about 1¼ pounds total), cored

Cinnamon Sauce

- 3 tablespoons packed brown sugar
- 2 teaspoons cornstarch
- ⅛ teaspoon kosher salt
- ⅛ teaspoon ground cinnamon
- ½ cup nonfat evaporated milk
- 1 teaspoon light, trans fat-free soft tub buttery spread
- ½ teaspoon vanilla extract

1 Preheat oven to 375°F. Line a baking sheet with parchment paper; set aside. Unroll phyllo. Cover top of phyllo with plastic wrap so it doesn't dry out while you are working with it.

2 Lay 1 sheet of phyllo dough on a clean, flat surface. Brush top of the sheet very lightly with some of the melted butter spread. Top with a second sheet of phyllo. Brush top of the second sheet very lightly with melted butter spread. Top with a third sheet of phyllo and brush very lightly with melted butter spread. Cut the stack of 3 phyllo sheets in half crosswise.

3 In a small bowl combine sugar and ⅛ teaspoon of the cinnamon. Sprinkle ¼ teaspoon of the sugar mixture inside one of the apples and place upright in center of one half of phyllo stack. Fold phyllo up and around apple to enclose it. Lightly brush outside of phyllo-wrapped apple with melted butter spread. Place on baking sheet. Repeat with remaining half of phyllo stack.

4 Repeat with remaining phyllo, melted butter spread, cinnamon-sugar mixture, and apples.

5 Bake apples for 20 to 30 minutes or until apples are just tender and phyllo is golden brown. If necessary, cover tops of apples loosely with foil for the last 5 to 10 minutes of baking time to prevent phyllo from overbrowning. Cool apples on pan on a wire rack 20 minutes before serving.

6 Prepare Cinnamon Sauce: In a small saucepan combine brown sugar, cornstarch, salt, and ⅛ teaspoon cinnamon. Add evaporated milk. Cook and stir over medium heat until sauce is thickened and bubbly. Reduce heat and cook and stir for 1 minute more. Remove from heat; stir in 1 teaspoon butter spread and vanilla extract. If necessary, add more evaporated milk to thin sauce.

7 Place one apple dumpling on each of four dessert plates. Spoon warm sauce over dumplings.

NUTRITION INFORMATION Calories: 243, Protein: 4 g, Total Fat: 5 g, Saturated Fat: 2 g, Cholesterol: 8 mg, Sodium: 231 mg, Carbohydrate: 45 g, Fiber: 4 g, Total Sugar: 30 g

Index